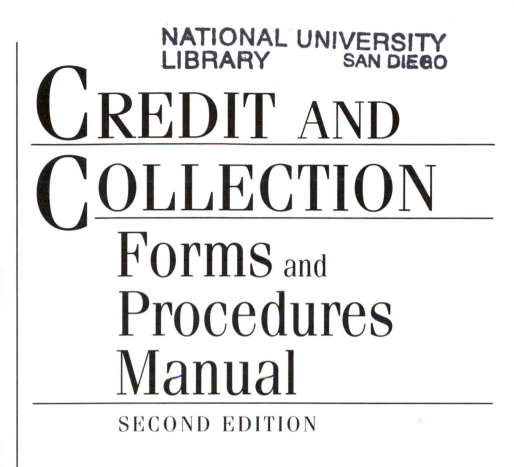

CREDIT AND COLLECTION

Forms and Procedures Manual

SECOND EDITION

JACK HORN   MICHAEL DENNIS

PRENTICE HALL

Library of Congress Cataloging-in-Publication Data

Horn, Jack.
    Credit & collection forms and procedures manual / Jack Horn,
Michael Dennis.—2nd ed.
      p. cm.
    Rev. ed. of: Handbook of credit and collection management forms
and procedures. 1980.
    Includes index.
    ISBN 0-13-080811-3 (case)
    1. Credit—Management—Handbooks, manuals, etc.   2. Collecting of
accounts—Handbooks, manuals, etc.   I. Dennis, Michael, 1957– .
II. Horn, Jack.   Handbook of credit and collection management forms
and procedures.   III. Title.
HG3751.H75   1998   98-23582
658.8′8—dc21   CIP

Acquisitions Editor: Luis Gonzalez
Production Editor: Fred Dahl
Formatting/interior Design: Inkwell Publishing Services

© *1999 by Prentice Hall*

Printed in the United States of America

10 9 8 7 6 5 4 3 2

ISBN 0-13-080811-3

ATTENTION: CORPORATIONS AND SCHOOLS

Prentice Hall books are available at quantity discounts with bulk purchase for educational,
business, or sales promotional use. For information, please write to: Prentice Hall Special
Sales, 240 Frisch Court, Paramus, New Jersey 07652. Please supply: title of book, ISBN
number, quantity, how the book will be used, date needed.

PRENTICE HALL
Paramus, NJ 07652

On the World Wide Web at http://www.phdirect.com

Prentice-Hall International (UK) Limited, *London*
Prentice-Hall of Australia Pty. Limited, *Sydney*
Prentice-Hall Canada Inc., *Toronto*
Prentice-Hall Hispanoamericana, S.A., *Mexico*
Prentice-Hall of India Private Limited, *New Delhi*
Prentice-Hall of Japan, Inc., *Tokyo*
Pearson Education Asia Pte. Ltd., *Singapore*
Editora Prentice-Hall do Brasil, Ltda., *Rio de Janeiro*

ISBN 0-13-080811-3

90000

9 780130 808110

This book is dedicated to Myrtle Coley Wallace

Introduction

Many have said: "Credit is man's faith in his or her fellow man." This is not strictly correct. A better definition of credit (or terms of sale) is: "Credit is one person's estimate of another person's ability and willingness to pay."

Gauging an Intangible

Credit is an intangible. Credit professionals are asked to judge an applicant or a customer's ability to pay by evaluating a series of intangible factors including the character and capacity of the debtor to pay. It is simply not enough to rate applicants as either good or bad credit risks. One must quantify the degree of goodness or badness, and establish both a credit limit and credit term accordingly.

Two experienced credit professionals examining the same set of facts could arrive at different opinions about the creditworthiness of a particular business. Why? Because each of them has a different set of experiences; each works for a different company with different credit policies and profit margins; each operates in different competitive environment; as a result each has different tolerances for credit risk and for bad debt losses.

New Tools and Tough Decisions

Credit professionals have more information available than ever before to make credit decisions. Yet serious mistakes continue to be made. Even the most experienced and conservative credit professionals experience bad debt losses. Why? Because even with mountains of information the credit professional still has to make a decision about what someone else will do at some point in the future. Adding to the complexity of the credit decision-making process is this one simple fact: It has never been easier for a company to file for bankruptcy protection.

Profit Versus Loss

The credit professional has to walk a thin line between increased business and increased bad debt losses. If the credit manager allows sales to grow too quickly, the risk is higher bad debt losses. On the other hand, in an effort to reduce bad debt losses, credit managers can inadvertently turn away potentially good customers.

Few managers in the company realize the impact the credit manager can have over sales levels and profits. The credit manager has the ability to drive both new accounts and active customers into the waiting hands of competitors. Credit policies can help—or choke—the company's cash flow.

Opposition surrounds the credit manager. First, there are the customers who sometimes view their supplier's credit manager as an enemy. Second, there are the other managers in the company—some of whom receive recognition and rewards by increasing sales and market share. Obviously, the credit department has no objection to increased sales—provided those sales can be made without an unnecessary amount of credit risk.

Finally, there is the sales department. A salesperson should not be thought of as an opponent of the credit manager. Instead, the sales rep is the other side of the scales. Let's face it—given a choice, credit professionals would opt to sell only to accounts they could count on to pay on time and at the same time represented little or no credit risk. On the other hand, because they are typically paid on commission, most salespeople are eager to make a sale and optimistic about the debtor's ability and willingness to pay. Between the two extremes of selling to everyone and selling only to low-risk accounts is the right balance between risk and reward.

The credit manager is on the horns of a dilemma. The credit manager is often held accountable for all of the bad debt losses the company incurs. At the same time, the credit manager is often characterized and criticized by sales and senior management as being "too conservative."

A Case in Point

At one of the divisions of a large paper products manufacturer, the credit manager was fired after 20 years of service. Twenty years as a loyal and faithful employee. Why? In the year prior to his termination, the bad debt expense was $57. Yes, the credit manager had kept bad debt experience down to a minimal amount. But, to do that, how much profitable business had been turned away!

Learn, Learn, Learn

Being a credit professional is not boring. There are always new techniques to learn, new laws taking effect, and changing dynamics in the marketplace, including changes in the credit policies of competitors. Credit professionals must constantly strive to learn and to adapt.

As a member of the company management team, the credit manager has an obligation to the company and the management team to make certain that the credit policies, processes, procedures, forms, and staff are as good as they can be. One method to improve the credit department's overall effectiveness and efficiency is to learn from others. That is the purpose of this book—to supply the reader with tested methods and procedures that have worked well for other credit professionals. This book is intended as a reference to be kept on the desk to provide quick answers to problems credit managers encounter every day.

Changing Times

Over the years, people who have been in charge of the credit function have been just as innovative as others on the management team. They have adapted credit systems to computers and other current business tools and techniques. From the professional credit organizations, industry associations and elsewhere they have learned, and subsequently tested, new methods and ways to constantly improve their organization's profitability.

More Help

This reference book explains and illustrates many methods to manage credit risk and to collect delinquent accounts. The ideas and innovations presented here are working successfully elsewhere.

Jack Horn
Michael Dennis

A Vote of Thanks

John Drexler of the Standard Register Company was able to provide some uniquely designed forms. Organizations that were more than helpful included Dun and Bradstreet and the National Association of Credit Management. The NACM is a professional organization of credit and collection personnel.

Many individuals gave invaluable assistance in one way or another or provided encouragement for this work. They include Marc Rich, Pinky Green, Alex Hackel, Anne Snipper, Al Geller, Henry Cohen, Thelma Biviano, Hilda and Oscar Weisberg, Fred Mesa, and many others.

A special thanks goes to my wife, Jean Horn, who made this book possible.

Jack Horn

I would like to thank Steven Kozack, Troy Anglin, and Dorothy Siegel for their contributions. I would like to thank my wife and family for their love and support.

Michael Dennis

Contents

Chapter 3

Solving New Account Problems   *89*

Chapter 4

Resolving Special Situations 123

Chapter 5

Collection Letters That Collect   *179*

Chapter 6

Other Effective Credit Letters   *305*

	TEXT	ILLUSTRATION
Refusal to Increase Credit Line	318	319
Section Title???	320	321
Moratorium Denied, Partial Payment Requested	322	323
Moratorium on Payment Denied, Partial Payment Requested	324	325
Delinquent Account—Installment Payment Plan Approved	326	327
Long Installment Plan Rejected	328	329
Letter to Attorney Turning Over an Account	330	331
Letter Rejecting a Settlement Offer	332	333
Follow-Up Letter to an Attorney	334	335
Counterclaim Denied—Attorney Letter	336	337
Information Letter to a Credit Guarantor	338	339
NSF Check Put in for Second Presentment	340	341
NSF Check Put in for Bank Collection	342	343
NSF Check Handling	344	345
How to Handle Two NSF Checks	346	347
Request for a Replacement Check	348	349
Alternative Request for Replacement Check	350	351
Letter Addressing a Series of Lost Checks	352	353
Customer Inquiry—Proof of Delivery	354	355
Restrictive Endorsements	356	357
Customer Makes Frequent Request for Proof of Delivery	358	359
Skipped Invoice—Old Invoice Overlooked	360	361
Letter Appealing to Mutual Interest in Releasing an Order	362	363
Clearing On-Account Payments	364	365
Old Credit Balance—Suggest Ordering	366	367
Approving a Request for a Monthly Statement	368	369
Denying Request for End-of-Month Terms	370	371
Customer Seeks to Reinterpret the Cash Discount Terms	372	373
Letter Recommending Discounting to Slow Paying Account	374	375
Unearned Discounts Disallowed	376	377
Unjustified Discount Allowed	378	379
Unearned Cash Discount—Disputed Invoice	380	381
Second Letter Regarding Unearned Cash Discounts Taken	382	383
Accepting an Unearned Cash Discount	384	385
Requesting an Explanation for a Decision Not to Discount	386	387
Extended Terms Rescinded	388	389
Order Received Prior to Receipt of Credit Application	390	391
Unacceptable Purchase Order Terms	392	393
New Order Approved for Marginal Account	394	395
Written Warning to an Irregular Paying Account	396	397

Chapter 7

Managing Slow Paying Accounts 443

Chapter 8

Legal Matters and Bankruptcy 483

Credit & Collection Forms and Procedures Manual

Second Edition

Chapter 1

Successful Credit Management

The Eternal Triangle

In many organizations, the customer and the salesperson are often at odds with the credit department. The customer apparently wants unlimited credit and extended dating. The salesperson looks for ways to justify offering the extended dating and argues in favor of increasing the credit limit—often without understanding the factors the credit manager takes into consideration when establishing a line of credit.

Even when it seems the salespeople realize that a sale made regardless of the amount of risk involved may result in a bad debt loss, they tend to favor the sale. Why? Making sales is what companies reward them to do. Even if there is only a 50/50 chance the customer will pay, salespeople are not paid a commission if the sale is not made. Therefore, they have a vested interest in pushing the credit department as hard as possible to ship the order. This does not mean salespersons are ignorant or self-absorbed. On the contrary, they are acting in their best interest and as advocates for customers. This is exactly what the company asks them to do and exactly what it rewards them to do.

Without the customer there would be no sales. Without sales there would be no company and no jobs. The key is to look for ways to meet the customer's requirements, not for reasons not to make the sale. If you look for a reason not to ship, you are almost certain to find one.

Who Is Expendable?

No company wants to lose customers. It is far easier to find a way to keep an existing customer than it is to try to find a new one. Good salespeople are hard to find, and the results of their efforts are immediate and tangible. That puts the credit manager in a dangerous and vulnerable position.

How is the credit department evaluated? Often, it is evaluated in irrelevant ways because the criteria do not and cannot measure the effectiveness and efficiency of the credit department. For example, one popular method of evaluating the credit department is to measure bad debt losses. Fewer losses are seen as good; more losses are consider bad. In reality, bad debt losses are a cost of doing business on open account terms. Every sale on open terms represents a degree of risk. Like playing Russian roulette, every once in a while the player runs into some bad luck. This is not intended to trivialize bad debt losses. No credit manager wants them. The question is not how the bad debt happened. The real question is, at the time the credit decision was made, was the decision reasonable and appropriate?

Another example of the wrong way to measure the credit department is to evaluate changes in days sales outstanding—DSO. This is a popular method of measuring the credit department's collection efforts. In reality, the DSO calculation suffers from a variety of weaknesses including its sensitivity (1) to changes in sales volume (since sales volume is largely beyond the control of the credit manager) and (2) to distortions based on timing issues. For example, most credit professionals know that, if the end of the month falls on a certain day of the week, DSO will be better than if the end of the month occurs on a Saturday or a Sunday.

If a company has a very low ratio of bad debt losses to sales, someone in top management should ask, "How much business was turned away in order to achieve a low bad debt to sales ratio?"

A credit manager's mistakes are easy to see after the fact. Everyone has 20/20 hindsight. However, his/her success is far more difficult to measure.

A Tightrope

Few people in management have to walk the line the credit manager walks. On one side is the waiting chasm of bad debts and a high percentage of past due balances. On the other side are the sales that should not have been rejected—sales that went to a competitor who got paid reasonably well. Even if the credit professional is able to maintain the balancing act for a long time, sooner or later the balance swings one way or the other. No matter which way it falls, the credit manager will not escape criticism.

Use the Professional Approach

The credit function is one that involves a great deal of judgment. Training, experience, maturity and continuing education help improve credit professionals' decision-making ability. However, credit managers must constantly strive to upgrade their skills in this area.

If credit managers want to be treated as professionals, they must look and act that way. One thing to avoid is a snap decision. Decisions can be made quickly once the necessary information has been gathered. If challenged, credit managers must be able to explain their credit decisions in a manner that indicates confidence.

Typical Duties of the Corporate Credit Manager

In most small companies, the corporate credit manager wears several hats. Frequently, that person is also the Controller or the Chief Financial Officer. In larger companies, the credit manager function is a full-time job. Yet even in larger companies, the credit manager can expect to oversee collections and, in many instances, the cash application function.

A typical credit manager has a background or education in finance, accounting, bankruptcy law and commercial law. In addition, this individual must have the interpersonal skills to deal effectively with an assertive sales department and an occasionally belligerent customer base.

Typical Duties of a Corporate Credit Manager

1. Subject to review by the Controller, CFO or Treasurer, this position establishes corporate-wide credit policies and procedures.
2. Interprets approved policies and procedures to the credit department staff.
3. Reviews sales agreements, rental-purchase plans, agency licenses, financing agreements or arrangements, installment agreements, etc.
4. Establishes standards for credit granting; development of criteria for establishing open account credit limits, determining how and when credit terms will be extended, etc.
5. In a decentralized credit environment, reviews the efforts of the divisional or branch credit operations.
6. Participates in the training and orientation of credit personnel.
7. Selects forms and procedures for use in the credit department.
8. Develops a corporate credit manual; maintains credit manual updating procedures.
9. Personally handles or review collection activities with larger problem accounts.
10. Maintains liaison with corporate counsel, outside attorneys, accountants, trade organizations, credit groups, financial institutions, etc.
11. Represents the corporation in creditor committees in bankruptcy cases.
12. Recommends changes in software that will benefit the credit department.
13. Participates in certain sales and other management meetings.
14. Periodically reviews the performance of credit personnel. Makes recommendations with regard to promotions and salary increases.
15. Investigates new techniques and equipment for improved credit department performance.

Typical Corporate Credit Policies

All companies are different, and credit policies are subject to interpretation. At the same time, every company needs formal, written credit policies. Companies that fail to commit their credit policies to writing tend to be less well managed than companies that do. Why? If the credit department fails to have a master strategy, chances are that the strategy will be constantly changing and subject to individual interpretation.

In addition, credit managers who operate without a written credit policy will undoubtedly have more authority and control over sales and management than senior management may have intended them to have. If no credit policy exists, the credit manager should draft a policy for senior management to review and approve. If the existing policy is outdated, it is in the credit manager's best interest to make certain that the guidelines it contains are consistent with how the credit department operates currently.

Typical Corporate Credit Policies

1. The credit department shall be under the control of the Treasurer (or alternatively the CFO, or the Controller).

2. All extension of credit shall be approved, directly or indirectly, by the credit manager.

3. The credit department will maintain as broad a base of customer potential as possible while assuring a desirable turnover of receivables with a minimum of bad debt losses.

4. In conformity with our corporate ethics, the credit department will take such measures as are necessary to collect delinquent accounts to protect its legal right to payment, participate in creditor committees, and process our claims in bankruptcy or legal proceedings.

5. When litigation or other legal action is necessary, the credit manager will seek the assistance and advice of legal counsel.

6. A copy of all credit department correspondence to customers shall be routed to the appropriate sales executive.

7. Credit department files are confidential. Confidential information is not to be shared with third parties or with the sales department.

8. The credit department shall develop standards of credit granting without any discrimination as to types of customers.

9. After consulting with competent legal counsel, the credit manager will determine when and how to obtain security in order to become a secured creditor.

Developing a Credit Manual

Corporations without a credit manual tend to have more bad debt losses, more delinquent accounts, and more unnecessary red tape.

Often, problems in the credit department can be traced to the fact that the individual hired into the credit manager's position does not have the skills necessary to do the job. If nothing else, an up-to-date credit manual assists an inexperienced (and possibly underqualified) credit manager in getting over the rough spots.

Once written, a draft of the manual should be circulated to obtain comments and suggestions. It is best to keep the manual in a loose-leaf form (rather than in bound form) so that changes can be made more easily.

Topics to Be Included in the Credit Manual

1. *Introduction.* Background of company. Corporate organization chart. Corporate policies with regard to credit granting, etc.

2. *Organization.* Titles and location of key credit personnel. Organizational chart. Job descriptions. Definitions of territorial, product or other delegations of responsibility. Limits on regular or special authority.

3. *Terms.* Descriptions of various regular terms by product or service. Procedures for granting extended dating. How and when cash discounts will be offered. How and when interest will be charged on past due balances. Conditions under which COD terms will be required, and when cash in advance is appropriate.

4. *Investigations.* Use of Dun & Bradstreet and other agencies. Bank relationships. Use of trade and other references. Financial statement analysis. Score sheets. Customer insurance. Salespeople's reports. Follow-up files.

5. *Open credit.* Customer payment histories. Determining credit limits. Extending credit limits. Handling of guarantees. Routing of orders. Partial shipments. Customer applications. New customer correspondence.

6. *Secured credit.* Consignment transactions. Purchase money security interests. UCC-1 financing statements. Documentary and standby letters of credit. Trust deeds. Chattel mortgages.

7. *Order processing.* Pricing. Pending files. Back orders. Release procedure. Coordination with shipping department. Remote warehouse shipping.

8. *Credit control.* Managing any decentralized credit functions. Determining under what conditions orders will and will not bypass credit approval. Methods to measure credit department effectiveness.

9. *Collateral handling.* Documents required for various types of secured credit. Desirable records. Evaluating collateral. Collateral substitution. Insurance. Coordination with corporate counsel.

10. *Forms.* Standard forms. Standard agreements. Internal documentation. Monthly report formats. Records retention policies. Data input requirements.

11. *Collections.* Correspondence techniques. Telephone procedures. Remittance deductions and unearned discounts. Approval procedure for write-offs. Use of liens. Turning accounts over to attorneys or collection agencies. Bankruptcies and creditor committees. Foreclosures on collateral.

12. *Accounting.* Internal and external audit requirements.

13. *Management.* File systems. Follow-up procedures. Work flow. Department reports. Correspondence.

Credit Department Workload

Any extended breakdown of the daily routine of the credit department will have an adverse effect on the company. For example, a failure to call delinquent customers will result in cash flow problems. A failure to regularly update credit files and monitor customers' credit limits will result in more bad debt losses. The loss of a single document such as a personal guaranty due to a sloppy filing system can result in an expensive and unnecessary loss to the company.

A company can no more afford to do away with or outsource the credit function than it can do without the order entry or marketing department.

Typical Daily Duties of the Credit Department

1. *Credit limits.* Developing and revising credit limits offered to various customers.
2. *Checking orders.* Reviewing orders placed onto credit hold by the system to determine which of them can be released.
3. *New accounts.* Setting up files, initiating investigations, and following processing and approval procedures.
4. *Credit information.* Maintaining an orderly filing system.
5. *Updating files.* Requesting updated information. Processing the responses received.
6. *Credit inquiries.* Responding to inquiries from credit agencies, trade creditors and banks.
7. *Unauthorized cash discounts.* Collecting unearned cash discounts.
8. *Collections.* Identifying past due accounts, calling for payment commitment and appropriate follow up.
9. *Customer service.* Handling of customer correspondence explaining credit policies.
10. *Marginal accounts.* Flagging and then carefully monitoring marginal accounts.
11. *Credit remittances.* Approving payments to customers for credit balances.
12. *Statements.* Generating and mailing monthly statements along with dunning notices.
13. *Agings.* Reviewing A/R agings for problem accounts and monitoring collection efforts.

Minimizing Lost Business

One of the most frequent criteria used in verifying the success of the credit function is the use of the ratio of bad debts to total sales. However, that ratio is only one side of the coin.

It is possible to have a very favorable bad debt-to-sales ratio by refusing credit to all marginal credit risk accounts. Not only is the truly bad risk avoided, but also those who might become a bad risk. However, the marginal risk may be a good customer—if not to the supplier who has refused credit, then to the supplier who was flexible enough to accept some risk.

Policy Verification

There will always be a certain number of accounts for which the wrong credit decision was made. Some of those wrong decisions will result in bad debt losses. Others will result in lost opportunities for profitable sales. Credit professionals need to avoid the mistakes that occur due to inaccurate or incomplete information.

List of Credit-Related Reasons for Lost Business

1. Incorrect identification of the account.
2. Use of a credit limit which a competitor exceeded.
3. Unusual delay in credit approval causing an order cancellation.
4. Poor liaison with sales personnel.
5. Customer resentment over certain credit information gathering procedures.
6. Unacceptable credit conditions imposed.
7. Decisions made at too low a level of authority.
8. A competitor offered special terms to gain the account.
9. A lack of urgency in correspondence with the account.
10. Failure to seek acceptable alternatives to the use of open account shipments.
11. Preconceived ideas about certain types of customers, resulting in inaccurate evaluation of the applicant.
12. Lack of awareness of industry trends.
13. Minimal effort to modify outdated or arbitrary standards. (Thinking in a rut.)
14. A failure to recognize the cyclical or seasonal nature of certain industries' debtor companies.
15. Inability to distinguish between temporary and more permanent types of financial problems.
16. A failure to maintain current credit files that results in the wrong decision— a decision not to ship the order.

Controlling Overextensions of Credit

Why do two companies of similar size in the same industry have widely differing bad debt-to-sales ratios? The reasons could include the following:

1. The amount of risk each company is prepared to take to obtain new business.
2. The use of COD terms and other techniques for reducing credit risk, as an alternative to open account credit terms.
3. Different capital structures and bank borrowing capacity, which require the supplier to offer different credit decisions and establish different credit limits.
4. Any deficiencies in the credit review, approval or delinquent account follow-up and collection process.

Experienced credit professionals who wish to improve their performance make a deliberate effort to learn from their own mistakes. Improvement rarely occurs at a constant rate, but credit professionals must try to constantly improve their performance and effectiveness, even if some improvements involve only minor changes.

Most of the items listed on the opposite page are within credit managers' control. Others (such as the budget for the credit department) may be beyond credit managers' control, but certainly not outside their area of influence.

In-House Causes for Overextending Open Account Credit Terms

1. Mistakes made by inexperienced credit personnel.
2. Inadequate or outdated credit references.
3. Accounts receivable that are not updated daily with invoices billed and/or payments received.
4. Out-of-date financial information from the debtor company.
5. Pending orders released without going through a credit review and approval cycle.
6. Unnecessary delays in following up on past-due balances.
7. Failure to personally visit customers even when doing so would improve the business relationship.
8. Disorganized customer credit files including misfiled documents.
9. Poor telephone collection techniques.
10. Misapplication of invoices, credits or payments, making it difficult to know the exact amount due.
11. A failure to systematically and periodically review customer credit files.
12. A reluctance to require additional assurances of payments (such as a personal guaranty) from marginal accounts.
13. An unwillingness to require substandard credit risks to buy on COD terms.
14. A small budget for the credit function.
15. Poor internal accounting techniques at the creditor company, resulting in misapplications and inadequate bad debt reserves.
16. An inability to review and change the credit limit or the credit terms as soon as conditions change.
17. An unrealistically pessimistic review of credit risks that results in the creditor company being overreserved. As a result, the creditor may be able to accept additional risk that the creditor would not otherwise do.

Tackling the Causes of Overdue Payments

An experienced credit professional knows that it is not always the customer's fault that invoices are being paid late. Late shipments, mis-shipments, lost invoices, and defects are only some of the reasons customers may feel justified in delaying payment.

Of course, sometimes customers use these situations as excuses to delay payment. The trick is to know the difference between a legitimate reason for delayed payment and an excuse to conceal serious cash flow problems.

It is important for the credit department to document the number and the frequency of problems such as mis-shipments and pricing errors. When the number of instances of the seller making mistakes grows, the credit manager has an obligation to their employer and to its customers to bring the problem(s) to the attention of senior management.

In-House Causes for Delayed Payments

1. Misapplied payments result in monthly statements with serious errors.
2. The quantity shipped does not agree with the quantity ordered.
3. Pricing variances between the purchase order and the invoice.
4. Items are substituted without the approval of the customer.
5. Orders are short-shipped without the approval of the customer.
6. Orders were shipped to the wrong ship-to location.
7. Customers were charged sales tax on an order when the account and the order were to be tax-exempt.
8. The creditor company has delayed issuing a credit memo.
9. The salesperson delayed processing the paperwork necessary to generate a credit memo.
10. Misapplication of cash receipts from a lockbox.
11. Failure to comply with the customer's shipping instructions.
12. The creditor delayed mailing invoices, credit memos or monthly statements.

Categorizing Accounts

Accounts can be classified according to their size, their type of business, their geographic location, or their payment habits and overall risk characteristics. The classification of accounts based on their payment habits can have several benefits, including:

1. Less experienced credit personnel can handle accounts that are considered low risk.
2. Customers coded as high risk can be monitored more carefully and more frequently than other accounts by the more senior credit professionals.
3. Debtor companies coded as high risk could receive more frequent computer-generated dunning notices.
4. All orders for an account coded as being very high risk can be reviewed by the credit manager before release.

Decisions, Decisions, Decisions

For several reasons, the toughest category to manage is possibly the below average accounts, for these reasons: The account is not good enough not to worry about, but not bad enough to either cut off or review every order. The below average account sometimes pays right on time, and other times can be as much as 30 days past due on certain invoices. That is one of the characteristics of a below average account: The customers tend to alternate between paying right on time and being seriously past due.

Describing Each Type of Account

1. *Solid account.* The solid account has almost unquestionable creditworthiness. The account pays promptly, and asks your sales department for a cash discount for prompt payment.

2. *Good account.* This customer is fundamentally similar to a solid account, but there is some history of sporadic slowness. The account may be affected by cyclical or seasonal business fluctuations.

3. *Average account.* At times, this customer has cash flow problems and delays payment. This customer has limited access to bank financing. It relies on creditors—apparently on a rotating basis—to supply the company with the working capital it needs.

4. *Marginal account.* This customer has a poor payment history with your company and other creditors. Payment delays may be in the range of 60 days or more.

5. *Risk account.* The records indicate this customer pays any creditor that offers them open account terms slowly. Many suppliers are selling on terms such as COD, cash in advance or on flooring.

6. *Unacceptable account.* The credit history includes the applicant's being placed for collection and being sued by trade creditors.

7. *Low profit margin account.* This customer buys in small quantities, making the cost per transaction high.

8. *Institutional account.* This classification includes governmental agencies and institutions including colleges, hospitals and nonprofit organizations. Bureaucracy and paperwork are hallmarks of collection effort here.

9. *Foreign account.* Sales to such accounts typically require the use of letters of credit, export loans and special guarantees. Open account credit is difficult to manage effectively. Certain foreign courts are adverse to accepted collection procedures.

The Computer System—The Credit Department's Friend

No one would want to manage the credit function in anything but an extremely small business without a computer to assist the credit department to function effectively. Most credit software performs a number of basic functions. The key is to work with the MIS (management information systems) department to improve on the basic package to make it more user-friendly and more helpful to credit department personnel.

Suggestion: In addition to mastering the information on the mainframe, everyone in the credit department should be familiar with (and be using when appropriate) such software applications as word processing programs, electronic mail and spreadsheets. If any employee's skills are deficient, a large number of how-to books on the market teach readers how to use these software applications.

Typical Functions of a Credit Software

1. Statements are printed automatically at least once a month, as well as selectively or individually on demand.
2. Special reports are available through a customized report menu.
3. The cash application function dovetails into the accounts receivable database in real time, so that collections and the credit manager have up-to-the-minute information.
4. A variety of special terms of sale can be selected.
5. Messages, such as "PAST DUE, PLEASE SEND PAYMENT" can be added to every statement or dunning notice generated.
6. The system allows the credit department to reprint credits, invoices and statements on demand.
7. The summary accounts receivable aging report lists aging by due date rather than by invoice date.
8. The system allows for on-line credit—and collection notes.
9. Changes to the customer master are password authorized, but easy to complete.
10. The system can interface with a software program to create dunning notices and letters.

Automated Credit Information Systems

No two computerized credit software programs are identical. Even canned software programs will be modified by the credit department to make it more user-friendly.

Some companies developed their credit-related software programs in house. These programs tend to be less sophisticated than the software programs available commercially. Why? Because the marketplace demands that software companies compete with each other for the customer's business, each software company must constantly improve its product to keep up with the competition. Software developed in house is not subject to competition and therefore less likely to be regularly modified and improved.

There are dozens of software programs that can help credit professionals manage their accounts receivable portfolio and credit risk. Some programs are part of a "global" accounting software package. Some are stand-alone programs into which the creditor must contantly download information from the company's accounts receivable records. Other so-called "bolt-on" software packages can be added to and made a part of the company's main operating systems. Bolt-on programs are convenient because they do not require the credit department or the MIS department to download information.

The "best" software program is the one that meets your needs. As a general rule, credit professionals prefer not to work with software developed in-house because it tends not to have the most up-to-date features. The features credit professionals care most about:

- make it easy to manage credit risk by flagging high risk accounts for special attention,
- help identify delinquent accounts quickly,
- offer on-line notes capability,
- generate reports that allow the credit manager to measure the effectiveness of each person in the credit department and to measure the effectiveness of the credit department as a whole.

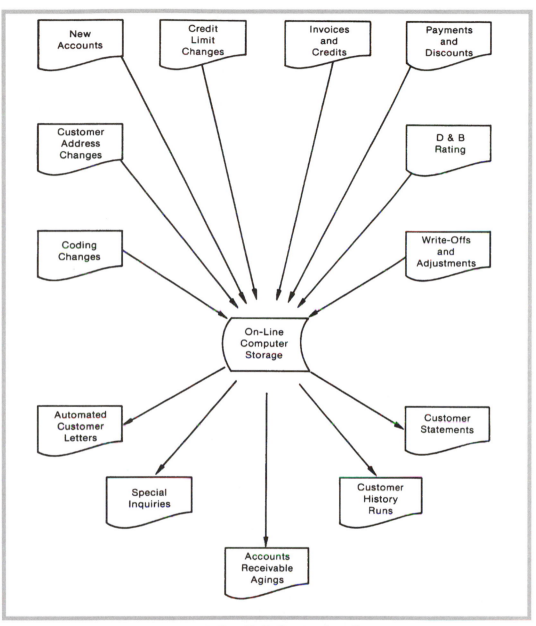

Automated Credit Information System

Computerized Credit Decisions

Computers can never replace credit managers. However, a good software package can give the credit department valuable and timely information, making the entire department more effective and efficient.

The credit professional will always be a part of the credit decision-making process. Computers can review orders quickly, and refer only those that fall outside the criteria established by the credit department to credit for approval. Other orders are released automatically by the system. The key is to make certain the computer has been given enough instructions so that it forwards pending orders requiring individual attention to the credit department for review and approval.

When a mistake is made, it is normally due to operator error. Computers have almost unfailing memory. Orders that get released in error occur as a result of operator error. Typically the error is one that allows orders to be released without credit approval.

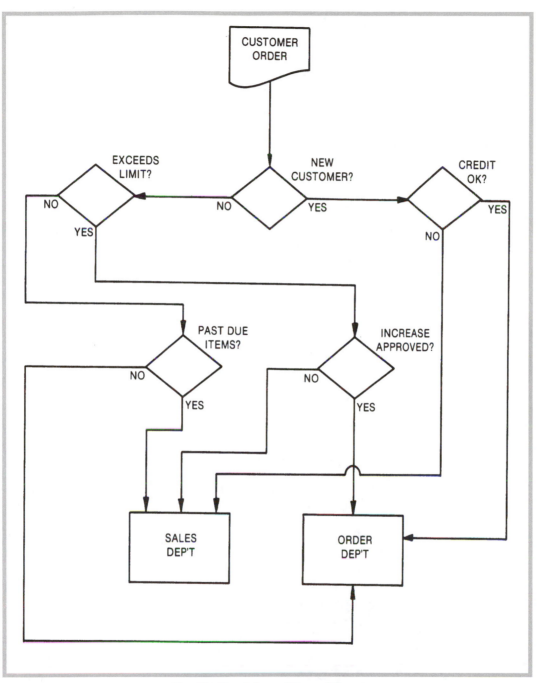

Credit Decisions Flow Chart

Order Processing Computerized Credit Decisions

In almost every credit operation of any size, it is now economically feasible to automate the order release process, a least to the extent that only problem orders require human intervention to be released.

Order Processing

In some companies, every order is reviewed and approved by the credit department manually and then forwarded for completion. However, adding a credit decision matrix to the end of the order entry software can result in significant timesavings if the system routes to credit only orders that meet certain criteria. The matrix typically reviews orders and asks these questions:

1. Is the account over its credit limit?
2. Is the account past due?
3. Would this order put the account over the credit limit?
4. Irrespective of the answers to questions 1 to 3, has anyone designated this as an account for which all orders must be approved by the credit department?

The advantages of using a credit decision-making matrix include:

1. The computer is unfailingly accurate, referring or releasing orders based on the instructions programmed.
2. The fewer people who handle an order, the lower the chance it will get lost.
3. The computer is always working with the most up-to-date information, not on data from older reports.
4. By relieving credit department personnel of such mundane chores as reviewing every order received, the software benefits the company since the credit department staff can concentrate their time on risk management and collections.

Computerized Credit Decision Table

In almost every credit operation of any size, it is now economically feasible to automate the order release process, at least to the extent that only problem orders require human intervention to be released.

		POSSIBILITIES							
		1	2	3	4	5	6	7	8
DECISIONS	1. Is the dollar value of the order over the credit limit?	NO	YES	YES	YES	YES	NO	NO	NO
	2. Is the customer's credit history a defined problem?	NO	NO	YES	YES	NO	YES	YES	NO
	3. Are any of the open items (debits) over 90 days old?	NO	NO	NO	YES	YES	NO	YES	YES
COMPUTER ACTION	1. Process the new order.	YES	YES				YES		YES
	2. Process for order refusal.				YES			YES	
	3. Enter on listing for review by the Credit Officer.			YES		YES			

Computerized Credit Decision Table

Chapter 2

Processing New Accounts

The secret to properly evaluating a new account is adequate information. Frequently, a faulty credit decision can be traced back to incomplete data.

Gathering Information

Gathering information costs money. Credit professionals certainly need to be aware of when they are approaching the point of diminishing returns. As a general rule, gathering too little information about an applicant can be far more expensive than getting too much data.

One of the best sources of information is the applicant company itself. One of the most important pieces information an applicant can provide is a set of financial statements. If the statements are not audited, they can contain inaccurate or questionable information—but some financial information is better than none.

Much of the information contained in a credit report was probably supplied by the applicant company itself. The fact that the credit reporting agencies does not take full responsibility for the accuracy of the report may be proof enough that the information is suspect.

Another source of information is the applicant's bank. The applicant should be willing to provide you with the name and telephone number of the bank officer handling the account. The bank should be able to provide general but useful information about the applicant.

Note: Do not expect a banker to provide derogatory information. Bankers tend to be conservative, and are not likely to provide a trade creditor with any information that might be defamatory.

Evaluation

A credit limit is determined after evaluating a number of factors. To save time, some companies will authorize a credit limit of 10% of a company's tangible net worth (where tangible net worth is calculated as stated net worth minus intangible assets such as trademarks and patents).

Other creditors use a series of financial ratios to evaluate an applicant for open account terms. The financial ratios of an applicant are normally compared to so-called industry norms. On the surface, this approach seems entirely reasonable. However, below the surface lies this key issue: Industry norms are developed using data gathered from companies that share financial information. Usually, only public companies and, to a lesser extent, privately held companies in good financial condition share financial information. As a result, industry norms might be more representative of the best companies in the industry, rather than true industry averages.

Some of the biggest mistakes in granting credit occur as a result of snap judgments. Speedy credit decisions are desirable, but not at the cost of accuracy.

Reputation

A few months of slow sales, a fire or flood, a strike, or a couple of poor business decisions could turn a good account into a credit risk very rapidly. The moral of the story is this: The past is not necessarily a perfect predictor of the future. Even with current data, mistakes happen daily. The older the data, the more tangible the risk to the creditor.

The singular value of a good credit reputation is this: Companies with a good reputation will strive to keep it. Companies with a spotty past or with a poor reputation will have little to gain and little to lose since credit reputations are created over time.

Credit Salesmanship

In contacts with potential customers, the credit professional should always leave the applicant with the impression that they want to help and want to release the order(s) pending and authorize the credit limit requested. Often, this can be accomplished if the debtor cooperates by providing requested information. All contacts with applicants (as well as with active customers and delinquent accounts) should be made courteously and professionally.

Improving Credit Investigation Techniques

A credit investigation might reveal nothing about a new, start-up business. Normally, unless the business is brand new, there is information somewhere. Credit bureaus might not yet have a report available, there might not yet be a trade clearance report on the company, but the company had to be buying goods and services from someone and banking somewhere.

With a new customer, the best source of information might be the customer itself. It is not unreasonable to request bank reference along with an opening balance sheet before considering a request for open account terms.

What If I Make the Wrong Decision?

Wrong decisions go in both directions. Credit professionals can offer open account terms only to regret their actions later. On the other hand, credit managers tend to be conservative. Occasionally, an account that has been refused credit goes to a competitor and manages to pay well. When that happens, occasionally the salesperson will second-guess your credit decision. Of course, the same salesperson would never say a word if the applicant went to another company and turned out to be a no-pay.

The best that credit managers can hope for is to say they did everything possible—within reason—to secure sufficient positive information to release the order on open account terms.

Typical Information Gathering for Credit Investigation

Before granting the credit limit requested, credit professionals typically need:

1. An estimate of sales volume and credit limit requirements from the sales department.
2. A copy of the applicant's Dun & Bradstreet report.
3. Copies of any industry trade clearance reports.
4. If available, a copy of the applicant's financial statements.
5. A bank reference and, if possible, a conversation with the bank officer handling the applicant's account.
6. For publicly traded companies a review of the customer's 10Q or 10K SEC filing statements.
7. Occasionally, a visit to the customer's place of business.
8. If possible, background information about key personnel, which provides information about the company's ability to manage the business properly.
9. The ability to liaise with other credit professionals to learn first-hand about their experience with the debtor company.
10. At least three trade references.

Answering New Account Requests

Comments

1. *Any response from the credit department must be sent promptly. If there is an unusually long delay and the customer gets tired of waiting, the credit department will be accused of incompetence or complacency.*

2. *If additional data is required, creditors should be as specific as possible about the information they need.*

3. *Credit professionals should be certain their request for information is reasonable and customary. For example, requesting a personal financial statement from the president of a corporation is not reasonable unless the president of the corporation is offering his or her personal guaranty. Requesting an unusual amount of information might indicate that the creditor is just nosy or too conservative in granting credit.*

4. *A letter from the credit department should indicate a sense of urgency. Otherwise, the request can be ignored or forgotten.*

5. *A copy should be sent to the appropriate salesperson, who might want to try to expedite a response from the customer.*

[date]
[customer name]
[address]

Attention: Thomas Jones
          [title]

Dear Mr. Jones:

Thank you for your inquiry about opening an account with us. To process your request, we need some additional information. Please send a copy of your company's financial statements to my attention at the address shown on the letterhead. Specifically, please send a copy of your company's fiscal year-end Balance Sheet and Income Statement, along with a copy of the most currently available interim Income Statement and Balance Sheet—even if these interim statements are unaudited.

Your prompt reply will enable us to process your request promptly.

Thank you.

Sincerely,

Lynn Warren
Credit Manager
[creditor company name]

cc: sales representative
    credit file

Letter Answering New Account Requests

Combined Credit Application and Guaranty

Comments

1. *This is a short and simple credit application.*

2. *The personal guaranty is similarly uncomplicated.*

3. *Creditors should understand that a personal guaranty does not guarantee payment. If the company defaults, the creditor seeks payment from the guarantor, and the guarantor refuses to pay, then the creditor must sue the guarantor like any other debtor who refuses to pay a debt owed.*

4. *A cover letter could indicate that any information the applicant shared would be kept confidential.*

5. *A wise person once said that the only type of person who would willingly sign a personal guaranty is (1) a person with nothing to fear or (2) a person with nothing to lose.*

Date _____ 19 _____

Maximum credit applied for:

$ _____

ONE ALLEN CENTER
HOUSTON, TX 77002
713 - 658-9711

CREDIT APPLICATION
(Please type or print)

NAME OF FIRM _____

Street and/or Building _____ Phone No. _____

Mailing Address _____

City _____ State _____ Zip Code _____

Kind of Business _____

Name of Officers or Owners of Firm _____

_____

Years Established _____ Is business incorporated? _____

Bank Affiliation _____ Bank Officer _____

Names of authorized buyers on this account
1. _____
2. _____
3. _____

Are Purchase Orders required to charge your account? _____

Business References:

1. _____   2. _____   3. _____
   _____   _____   _____
   _____   _____   _____

Note: If account is authorized to purchase printing on open account, be it understood that all purchases be due and payable by tenth of month following date of purchase. The undersigned official, to induce the granting of credit to the above-named firm, hereby personally guarantees the company's credit.

Signed By: _____
Individually and as an officer of the Firm.

FOR CREDIT DEPARTMENT USE ONLY:

Length of time sold: 1. _____ 2. _____ 3. _____
High Credit   _____   _____   _____
Terms   _____   _____   _____
Pays when due   _____   _____   _____
Other comments   _____   _____   _____

Credit Limit Authorized: $ _____

Authorized By: _____ Date: _____

Combined Credit Application and Guaranty

Obtaining Insurance Information

Comments

1. *While a potential customer or existing account might seem financially sound, a large uninsured loss could spell financial disaster for the company.*

2. *A complete insurance program on the part of the account is an additional indication that the account is well managed.*

3. *Comprehensive insurance coverage protects the applicant/debtor and its creditors.*

4. *The completed questionnaire could be forwarded to the company's insurance manager for suggestions or comments.*

5. *An additional step would be to ask the account to request the customer's insurance broker to forward a copy of the latest insurance policies schedule to the credit department.*

6. *Insurance policies schedules could be requested at least once a year.*

7. *When a creditor has a lien, it may ask to be added as a leinholder on the debtor's insurance policies. As such, the creditor would receive payments first on any insurance payment. An additional advantage is that the creditor is notified of any lapse in coverage.*

8. *Special Note: In most industries, it is very rare for a creditor to inquire about a customer or applicant's insurance coverage.*

INSURANCE INFORMATION QUESTIONNAIRE
(To be completed by customer)

1. Customer's Name _____

2. Account No. _____ Date of Request _____

3. Does your firm own and operate from more than one building? Yes _____ No _____
   If "Yes," how many buildings? _____
   What is the total replacement cost of all buildings? _____ (Estimate)
   How much insurance is carried? _____

4. In buildings occupied as a tenant, has landlord furnished "Waiver of Subrogation?"
   Yes _____ No _____

5. Are contents insured at all locations (owned or rented)?
   Yes _____ No _____
   If "Yes," what is the replacement cost of contents? $ _____
   How much insurance is carried? $ _____

6. Do you ever ship materials or merchandise which you own?
   Yes _____ No _____

7. Do you carry Floater Policy on shipments in and out?
   Yes _____ No _____

8. Do you carry Business Interruption Insurance?
   Yes _____ No _____

9. If there is a steam boiler on any of the premises, is it insured?
   Yes _____ No _____
   If "Yes," show limits carried _____

10. Does your firm carry General Liability Insurance?
    Yes _____ No _____
    If "Yes," show limits carried: *Limits*
    Comprehensive _____
    Elevators _____
    Independent Contractors _____
    Product Liability _____
    Libel, etc. _____
    Malpractice _____

11. Does your firm carry Automobile Liability Insurance?
    Yes _____ No _____
    If "Yes," show limits carried: *Limits*
    Comprehensive Liability _____
    Employers non-ownership _____
    Drive Other Car _____

12. Does your firm carry Fidelity-Forgery Coverage?
    Yes _____ No _____
    If "Yes," please indicate the amount of coverage. $ _____

13. Please check any of the additional insurance policies listed below which are carried by your firm:
    Credit Insurance _____   Key Man Life Insurance _____
    Accounts Receivable _____   Officers' & Directors' Liability _____
    Money and Securities _____   Blanket Contractual _____

Insurance Information Questionnaire

Simplified Credit Application

Comments

1. *Small businesses are sometimes intimidated when they receive multiple page credit applications. The size can cause the potential customer to decide not to pursue establishing an open account or go elsewhere.*

2. *One of the principles credit professionals follow is to extend credit when they have enough information to do so. Depending on the size of the credit line requested, it is sometimes not necessary to have perfect or complete information to make a decision.*

3. *The section requesting insurance coverage information is optional.*

4. *A cover letter should accompany the credit application. The application itself can be supplied to the sales department, whose staff can fax it to the applicant and back to the creditor, if necessary to save time.*

5. *The note at the bottom is an important element of this credit application. With small companies, creditors must often settle for internally prepared financial statements.*

CONFIDENTIAL CREDIT APPLICATION

Date _____

<table>
<tr><td></td><td>NAME OF FIRM
Requesting Statement</td></tr>
</table>

To: _____

We hereby apply for the extension of credit by your firm.
The following information is submitted as a basis for your consideration of our application.

Firm name _____

Type of business _____

Street _____ City _____ State _____ Zip _____

Established in 19 _____

Corporation ☐   Partnership ☐   Limited Partnership ☐   Proprietorship ☐

If incorporated, state in which incorporated: _____

Principal owners or stockholders:

NAME	ADDRESS	TITLE

Our tax returns have been cleared with the taxing authorities through 19_____.

We expect our monthly credit requirements from you to be about $_____.

We believe that our firm is financially able to meet any commitments we have made and we expect to pay our invoices according to your terms.

INSURANCE COVERAGE

Kind	Amount	Kind	Amount
Fire Insurance on:_____		Employee Fidelity Bonds ____	
Merchandise _____		Burglary Insurance _____	
Buildings _____		Forgery _____	
Furniture & Fixtures _____		Life Insurance for benefit	
Business Interruption _____		of business _____	
Liability Insurance on: _____		Accounts receivable _____	
Premises _____		Miscellaneous:	
Autos _____			
Products _____			
Contractual _____			

Name	Address

SUPPLIERS AND BANKS

Title _____   Signature _____

Simplified Credit Application

Commercial Credit Application (Front)

Comments

1. *See page 45 for the back of the form.*

2. *This form is more detailed than the form on the previous page.*

3. *The transmittal of the form should have an explanatory cover letter. Such letter could request the submission of the latest financial statement.*

4. *Invoicing terms could be inserted above the firm's signature by the credit department.*

5. *The form contains an authorization for a credit investigation, and therefore expressly waives rights to privacy.*

APPLICATION FOR CREDIT

Date _____ 19 _____

ISSUED TO _____ NAME OF FIRM

[PLEASE ANSWER ALL QUESTIONS. WHEN NO FIGURES ARE INSERTED, WRITE WORD "NONE"] Requesting Statement

FIRM NAME	TRADE STYLE	
STREET ADDRESS	PHONE	
CITY	STATE	ZIP CODE

FULL NAME OF OWNER OR OWNERS (OR AN AUTHORIZED OFFICER OF CORPORATION); LIST HOME ADDRESS & ZIP FOR PARTNERSHIP OR INDIVIDUAL

	INDIVIDUAL	PARTNERSHIP	CORPORATION	FED. TAX NO. (FOR CORPORATION)	MARITAL STATUS
PLEASE CHECK ONE					

ADDITIONAL INFORMATION REQUIRED FOR CONDITIONAL SALES CONTRACTS UNDER THE UNIFORM COMMERCIAL CODE

DEBTOR (INDIVIDUAL SIGNING CONTRACT) _____ TITLE: _____

DEBTOR'S SOCIAL SECURITY NO. (FOR PARTNERSHIP OR INDIVIDUAL) _____

TYPE OF BUSINESS	DATE STARTED
ESTIMATED ANNUAL SALES	
FORMER BUSINESS	LOCATION
OWN OR RENT BUILDING—IF RENT—FROM WHOM?	VALUE
REAL ESTATE MORTGAGE	

TRADE REFERENCES

NAME	ADDRESS

NAME OF BANK	
STREET ADDRESS	
CITY	STATE

APPLICANT'S SIGNATURE ATTESTS FINANCIAL RESPONSIILITY, ABILITY AND WILLINGNESS TO PAY OUR INVOICES IN ACCORDANCE WITH FOLLOWING TERMS:

THE ABOVE INFORMATION AS WELL AS THAT GIVEN ON THE REVERSE SIDE IS FOR THE PURPOSE OF OBTAINING CREDIT AND IS WARRANTED TO BE TRUE. I/WE HEREBY AUTHORIZE THE FIRM TO WHOM THIS APPLICATION IS MADE TO INVESTIGATE THE REFERENCES LISTED PERTAINING TO MY/OUR CREDIT AND FINANCIAL RESPONSIBILITY.

FIRM NAME _____

BY _____
  TITLE

BY _____
  TITLE

Commercial Application for Credit (Front)

Commercial Credit Application (Back)

Comments

1. *See page 43 for the front of the form.*

2. *The account classifications are not in the same order as a conventional financial statement. However, this order permits quicker comparisons, such as current assets to current liabilities.*

3. *Some applicants may resist supplying the information that is requested after the net worth section. It may be easier to request the financial statements.*

4. *Financial information without a particular date that such information relates to may be useless.*

5. *A cover letter containing helpful instructions would be useful.*

The following figures are present financial standing and business operation upon which you may rely for the purpose of establishing our credit:

CURRENT ASSETS:

Cash on hand and in banks .... $ _____

Accounts Receivable .... _____

Cost of merchandise on hand................ _____

Other current assets .... _____

TOTAL $ _____

CURRENT LIABILITIES:

Bank loans payable within a year .... _____

Tax obligations due .... _____

Accounts Payable .... _____

Other debts due within a year .... _____

TOTAL $ _____

FIXED ASSETS:

Business equipment .... _____

Land used in business .... _____

Buildings used in business .... _____

*Other assets .... _____

TOTAL $ _____

INDEBTEDNESS NOT DUE WITHIN A YEAR:

Chattel mortgages due on merchandise _____

Chattel mortgages due on other assets . _____

Real estate mortgages .... _____

*Other long term debt .... _____

TOTAL $ _____

NET WORTH .... _____ $ _____

Average monthly sales .... _____

% of sales made on credit .... _____

% of sales at retail .... _____

% of sales at wholesale .... _____

% of sales on time-payment plan .... _____

Peak season of year .... _____

Date of last inventory .... _____

Profit shown latest U.S. Income Tax Return _____

Our firm is financially able to meet any commitments we have made and we will pay our invoices according to your terms.

*PLEASE SPECIFY:

Date _____

Title _____ Signature _____

Commercial Credit Application (Back)

Dealer Type Credit Application

Comments

1. *A dealer is not simply a customer. A dealer is also a representative of your company.*

2. *Dealers must be qualified by the credit department and by the sales or marketing group.*

3. *A cover letter to accompany this document could request financial statements.*

4. *The form itself should request information about the type of organization: individual, partnership, limited liability corporation or corporation.*

5. *Some potential suppliers to dealers would also ask on the application about what other lines the dealer represents.*

6. *The company salesperson, whose name appears at the bottom of the form, should also be able to provide the company with some insight about the applicant.*

7. *Dealer credit applications require a higher degree of attention. Special care is placed on gathering data about the applicant's reputation and character since the dealer represents the company.*

8. *The credit manager can demand more information from the dealer-applicant than from a "regular" applicant for credit. For example, a company might require all its dealers to submit financial statements annually, as well as financial statements as a matter of course from a dealer/applicant.*

DEALER APPLICATION—BUSINESS CREDIT REFERENCES

NUMBER

Business Name	Street Address

City	State	Zip	Telephone No.

TO: Credit Manager

Dear Sir:

In consideration of our possible appointment as your dealer, we furnish the following preliminary credit references:

BANK REFERENCE

Bank Name _____

Street Address _____

City _____ State _____ Zip _____

Individual's Name _____ Position _____

MAJOR TRADE REFERENCES

Company Name _____

Street Address _____

City _____ State _____ Zip _____

Individual's Name _____ Position _____

Company Name _____

Street Address _____

City _____ State _____ Zip _____

Individual's Name _____ Position _____

Company Name _____

Street Address _____

City _____ State _____ Zip _____

Individual's Name _____ Position _____

Name of Representative Who Gave You This Form	Signed	Date
	Title	

Dealer Type Credit Application

Dun & Bradstreet Report

Comments

1. *The Dun & Bradstreet Company provides credit-reporting services on most companies in the United States. It is the nation's acknowledged leader in this field. The report on the following pages is about a fictitious company.*

2. *A D&B subscriber can obtain information online via terminal and modem, or call or write to Dun & Bradstreet for a particular report. If a report is not in file, D&B will assign an employee to gather information if the subscriber wishes the company to do so.*

3. *Because of similarities of names, it is usually wise to compare identification data (address, etc.) in the report with data in the credit department.*

4. *Of particular interest to credit professionals is the D&B rating found in the upper right-hand corner of the first page of the report. This rating is a snapshot of the creditworthiness of the company under review.*

5. *The first page contains a vast amount of valuable information, including the legal name of the company, its dba's, the complete address and telephone number, a description of the business the company is engaged in, the number of years in business, and the number of employees.*

6. *The first page also contains information about Special Events. This section might describe a change in ownership, a merger or a bankruptcy, a fire, a recent move, etc.*

7. *The Summary Analysis section provides an overview of the company's D&B ratings over time. This analysis is another quick way to evaluate changes in the creditworthiness of the company.*

8. *The Paydex score is a composite summary of the company's payment habits with creditors.*

9. *The aging analysis section provides a dollar-weighted average view of payments.*

10. *The payments reported section is obtained from the firm's suppliers. Those suppliers typically provide D&B with a disk or tape of their credit experience with customers each month. Thus, the information contained in this section is not handpicked data from creditors selected by the debtor company.*

Business Information Report

```
                                SUBSCRIBER:  123-4567L
                                PREPARED FOR:

                        ANSWERING INQUIRY
```

```
DUNS:  00-007-7743              DATE PRINTED              SUMMARY
GORMAN MANUFACTURING CO. INC.   OCT 30 199-       RATING    3A3
  (SUBSIDIARY OF GORMAN
   HOLDING COMPANIES INC.,      COMMERCIAL PRINTING
   LOS ANGELES, CA)             SIC NO.                 STARTED   1965
                                2752                   SALES F   $13,007,229
                                                       WORTH F   $2,125,499
492 KOLLER ST                                          EMPLOYS   105(100 HERE)
AND BRANCH(ES) OR DIVISION(S)                          HISTORY   CLEAR
SAN FRANCISCO CA 94110                                 FINANCING SECURED
    TEL: 415-555-0000                                  FINANCIAL
                                                       CONDITION FAIR
CHIEF EXECUTIVE: LESLIE SMITH, PRES
```
===
SPECIAL EVENTS
09/11/9-   On Sept 9, 199-, the subject experienced a fire due to an earthquake.
            According to Leslie Smith, President, damages amounted to $35,000, which
            was fully covered by their insurance company. The business was closed for
            two days while employees settled personal matters due to the earthquake.

03/17/9-   Subject moved from 400 KOLLER ST. to 492 KOLLER ST. on March 11, 199-.
===
                        * * * CUSTOMER SERVICE * * *
===
            If you need any additional information, would like a credit
        recommendation, or have any questions regarding this report, please call
        our Customer Service Center at (800) 234-3867 from anywhere within the
        United States.

===
                        * * * SUMMARY ANALYSIS * * *
===
RATING SUMMARY . . . .
        The "3A" portion of the Rating (Estimated Financial Strength) indicates
        that the company has a worth between $1 million and $10 million. The "3"
        on the right (Composite Credit Appraisal) indicates an overall "fair"
        credit appraisal. The "fair" credit appraisal was assigned because the
        company's overall payment record shows frequent slowness and because of
        D&B's "fair" assessment of the company's 12/31/9- fiscal financial
        statement.

        Below is an overview of the company's D&B Rating(s) since 1-1-91:
                RATING   DATE APPLIED
                ------   ------------
                3A3   09/11/9-
                --   01/01/91
===
                        * * * PAYMENT SUMMARY * * *
===

This Payment Summary section reflects payment information in D&B's file as of
October 29, 199-.

                The PAYDEX for this company is 67.

This PAYDEX score indicates that payments to suppliers average 18 days beyond terms,
weighted by dollar amounts. When dollar amounts are not considered, approximately
75% of the company's payments are within terms.

17G-1150

Dunn & Bradstreet Report

Business Information Report

Page 2

Below is an overview of the company's dollar-weighted payments, segmented by its suppliers' primary industries:

	TOTAL RCV'D	TOTAL DOLLAR AMOUNTS	LARGEST HIGH CREDIT	W/IN TERMS	DAYS SLOW			
					<31	31-60	61-90	91+
	#	$	$	%	%	%	%	%
Total in D&B's file	24	785,150	250,000					

Top 10 Industries:

1 Whol Printing Paper	8	747,500	250,000	64	18	18	-	-
2 Repair Service	2	7,500	7,500	-	100	-	-	-
3 Mfg Industrial Mach	2	2,000	1,000	50	50	-	-	-
4 Misc Services	2	750	500	33	67	-	-	-
5 Whol Non Durables	1	15,000	15,000	50	50	-	-	-
6 Air Courier Service	1	7,500	7,500	100	-	-	-	-
7 Mfg Service Ind Mach	1	2,500	2,500	50	50	-	-	-
8 Transportation Svcs	1	1,000	1,000	50	-	-	50	-
9 Mfg Photo Equipment	1	500	500	100	-	-	-	-
10 Mfg Plastic Products	1	250	250	100	-	-	-	-
11 Other Industries	1	100	100	100	-	-	-	-

Other Payment Categories:

Cash experiences	2	450	250	
Paying record unknown	1	100	100	
Unfavorable comments	0	0	0	
Placed for collection:				
with D&B	0	0		
other	0	N/A		

The highest "Now Owes" in D&B's file is $250,000
The highest "Past Due" in D&B's file is $90,000

The total dollar amount from the 24 trade experiences listed is 6.0% of this company's annual sales as presented in the Summary. D&B considers the trade experiences to be representative of this company's payment habits.

===

PAYMENTS (Amounts may be rounded to nearest figure in prescribed ranges)

  Antic - Anticipated (Payments received prior to date of invoice)
  Disc - Discounted (Payments received within trade discount period)
  Ppt   - Prompt   (Payments received within terms granted)

REPORTED	PAYING RECORD	HIGH CREDIT	NOW OWES	PAST DUE	SELLING TERMS	LAST SALE WITHIN
03/9-	Ppt-Slow 90	1000	500	-0-	N30	1 Mo
02/9-	Ppt	250	100			4-5 Mos
	Ppt-Slow 30	2500	2500	1000		1 Mo
	Slow 30	500	500			2-3 Mos
	(005)	200				
	Slow 30-60	70000	70000	6500		1 Mo

===

Dunn & Bradstreet Report (cont'd.)

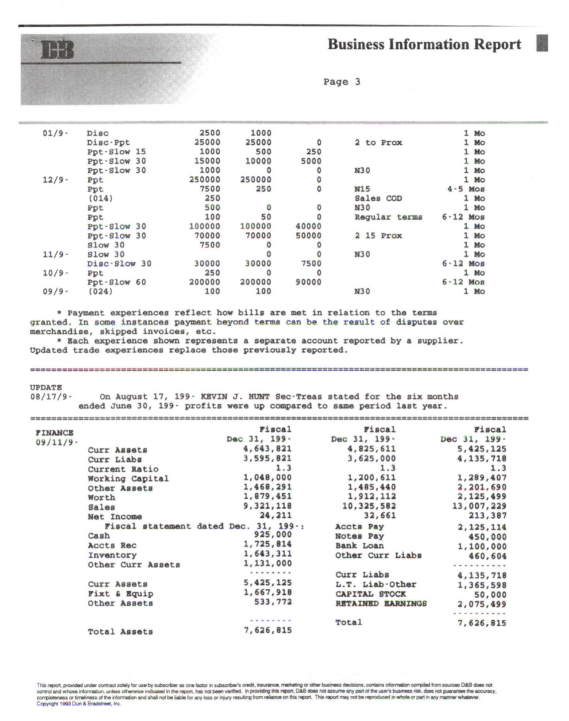

Business Information Report

Page 3

Date	Type				Terms	Duration
01/9-	Disc	2500	1000			1 Mo
	Disc-Ppt	25000	25000	0	2 to Prox	1 Mo
	Ppt-Slow 15	1000	500	250		1 Mo
	Ppt-Slow 30	15000	10000	5000		1 Mo
	Ppt-Slow 30	1000	0	0	N30	1 Mo
12/9-	Ppt	250000	250000	0		1 Mo
	Ppt	7500	250	0	N15	4-5 Mos
	(014)	250			Sales COD	1 Mo
	Ppt	500	0	0	N30	1 Mo
	Ppt	100	50	0	Regular terms	6-12 Mos
	Ppt-Slow 30	100000	100000	40000		1 Mo
	Ppt-Slow 30	70000	70000	50000	2 15 Prox	1 Mo
	Slow 30	7500	0	0		1 Mo
11/9-	Slow 30		0	0	N30	1 Mo
	Disc-Slow 30	30000	30000	7500		6-12 Mos
10/9-	Ppt	250	0	0		1 Mo
	Ppt-Slow 60	200000	200000	90000		6-12 Mos
09/9-	(024)	100	100		N30	1 Mo

    * Payment experiences reflect how bills are met in relation to the terms granted. In some instances payment beyond terms can be the result of disputes over merchandise, skipped invoices, etc.
    * Each experience shown represents a separate account reported by a supplier. Updated trade experiences replace those previously reported.

UPDATE
08/17/9-   On August 17, 199- KEVIN J. HUNT Sec-Treas stated for the six months ended June 30, 199- profits were up compared to same period last year.

FINANCE
09/11/9-

	Fiscal Dec 31, 199-	Fiscal Dec 31, 199-	Fiscal Dec 31, 199-
Curr Assets	4,643,821	4,825,611	5,425,125
Curr Liabs	3,595,821	3,625,000	4,135,718
Current Ratio	1.3	1.3	1.3
Working Capital	1,048,000	1,200,611	1,289,407
Other Assets	1,468,291	1,485,440	2,201,690
Worth	1,879,451	1,912,112	2,125,499
Sales	9,321,118	10,325,582	13,007,229
Net Income	24,211	32,661	213,387

Fiscal statement dated Dec. 31, 199-:

Cash	925,000	Accts Pay	2,125,114
Accts Rec	1,725,814	Notes Pay	450,000
Inventory	1,643,311	Bank Loan	1,100,000
Other Curr Assets	1,131,000	Other Curr Liabs	460,604
	--------		----------
Curr Assets	5,425,125	Curr Liabs	4,135,718
Fixt & Equip	1,667,918	L.T. Liab-Other	1,365,598
Other Assets	533,772	CAPITAL STOCK	50,000
		RETAINED EARNINGS	2,075,499
	--------		----------
Total Assets	7,626,815	Total	7,626,815

Dunn & Bradstreet Report (cont'd.)

Business Information Report

Page 4

From JAN 1, 199- to DEC 31, 199- sales $13,007,229; cost of goods sold $9,229,554. Gross profit $3,777,675; operating expenses $3,751,661. Operating income $26,014; extraordinary gain $187,373. Net income $213,387.

Submitted SEPT 11, 199- by Leslie Smith, President. Prepared from statement(s) by Accountant: Ashurst & Ashurst, PC. Prepared from books without audit.
-- 0 --
Accounts receivable shown net less $12,586 allowance. Other current assets consist of prepaid expenses $64,471 and $1,066,529 of a loan from an affiliated concern. Other assets consist of deposits. Bank loans are due to bank at the prime interest rate, are secured by accounts receivable and inventory, and mature in 3 years. Notes payable are due on printing equipment in monthly installments of $27,500. Other current liabilities are accrued expenses and taxes. Long term debt consist of the long term portion of the equipment note.
On SEPT 11, 199- Leslie Smith, president, submitted the above figure(s).
Leslie Smith submitted the following interim figures dated JUNE 30, 199-.

Cash	$ 1,011,812	Accts Pay	$ 1,932,118
Accts Rec	1,932,118	Owe Bank	1,100,000
Inventory	1,421,112	Notes Pay	350,000

Sales for 6 months were $7,325,001. Profits for 6 months were $103,782. Projected annual sales are $14,000,000.
He also stated operating profits were below average due to heavy price competition in the industry, higher operating expenses, and decreased advertising budgets following the nationwide move towards cost containment.
==
PUBLIC FILINGS

The following data is for information purposes only and is not the official record. Certified copies can only be obtained from the official source.
- -
* * * SUITS * * *
- -

DOCKET NO:	12345	STATUS:	Pending
SUIT AMOUNT:	$1,000	DATE STATUS ATTAINED:	03/25/199-
PLAINTIFF:	MAZZUCA & ASSOC.	DATE FILED:	03/25/199-
DEFENDANT:	GORMAN MANUFACTURING	LATEST INFO RECEIVED:	03/31/199-
	CO. INC.		
CAUSE:	Breach of contract		
WHERE FILED:	SAN FRANCISCO, CA		

- -
* * * UCC FILING(S) * * *
- -

COLLATERAL:	Accounts receivable · Inventory including proceeds and products		
FILING NO:	86188586	DATE FILED:	07/24/199-
TYPE:	Original	LATEST INFO RECEIVED:	10/04/199-
SEC. PARTY:	A.C. Paper, Palo Alto, CA	FILED WITH:	SECRETARY OF STATE/ UCC DIVISION, CA

==
BANKING
09/9-   Account(s) averages high 6 figures. Account open over 10 years. Loans granted to low 7 figures on a secured basis. Now owing low 7 figures. Collateral consists of accounts receivable and inventory. Matures in 1 to 5 years. Borrowing account is satisfactory. Overall relations are satisfactory.
==

Dunn & Bradstreet Report (cont'd.)

DB

Business Information Report

Page 5

HISTORY
09/11/9-

LESLIE SMITH, PRES   KEVIN J. HUNT, SEC-TREAS
DIRECTOR(S): THE OFFICER(S)
- -
BUSINESS TYPE: Corporation - Profit   DATE INCORPORATED: 05/21/1965
AUTH SHARES - COMMON: 200   STATE OF INCORP: California
PAR VALUE - COMMON: No Par Value
- -
Business started May 21, 1965 by Leslie Smith and Kevin J. Hunt.
100% of capital stock is owned by Parent Company.
SMITH born 1926. Married. Graduated from the University of
California, Los Angeles, in June 1947 with a BS degree in Business
Management. 1947-65 general manager for Raymor Printing Co., San
Francisco, CA. 1965 formed subject with Kevin J. Hunt.
HUNT born 1925. Married. Graduated from Northwestern University,
Evanston, IL. in June 1946. 1946-1965 controller for Raymor Printing Co.,
San Francisco, CA. 1965 formed subject with Leslie Smith.
RELATED COMPANIES: Through the financial interest of Gorman Holding
Company Inc., subject's parent company, the Gorman Manufacturing Co.
Inc., is related to two other companies:
1. Smith Lettershop Inc., San Diego, CA; commercial printing,
started 1972.
2. Gorman Suppliers Inc., Los Angeles, CA; commercial print, started
1980.
Intercompany relations consist of loans.
==

OPERATION
09/11/9-

Subsidiary of Gorman Holding Company Inc., Los Angeles, CA, started
1965 which operates as a holding company for its subsidiaries. Parent
company owns 100% of capital stock. Parent company has 2 other
subsidiaries. Intercompany relations: consist of loans and advances.
A consolidated financial statement of the parent company dated
Dec. 31, 199- showed a worth of $4,125,112, with an overall fair
financial condition.
Commercial Printing specializing in advertising posters, catalogs,
circulars and coupons.
Net 30 days. Has 175 account(s). Sells to commercial concerns.
Territory: United States.
Nonseasonal.
EMPLOYEES: 105 which includes officer(s). 100 employed here.
FACILITIES: Rents 55,000 sq. ft. on first floor of one story cinder
block building in good condition. Premises neat.
LOCATION: Central business section on well traveled street.
BRANCH(ES): Subject maintains a branch at 1073 Boyden Road, Los
Angeles, CA.

Dunn & Bradstreet Report (cont'd.)

Financial Information Statement (Front)

Comments

1. *The use of the creditor's name in the opening paragraph can make the information provided in the form representative with regard to a sales contract. In other words, the information provided is an inducement to do business, which, if materially false, may be cause for damages.*

2. *The financial statement information is requested in categories other than those on the conventional financial statement.*

3. *It might be better to number each question for ease of reference.*

4. *A cover letter could suggest that where there is insufficient space for a complete answer a blank page could be used for a rider to provide more complete information.*

5. *See page 56 for the back of the form.*

Firm name _____ Address _____

Members of firm _____

_____

Co-partnership or Corporation   Nature of Business

   For the purpose of procuring credit, and to induce SHARP TOOL CORP. of Wayne, Nevada to sell (me) (us) merchandise which (I) (we) may now or here-after purchase of them, or any individual, firm or corporation that they may be, or become factors for, do submit the following true statement of (my) (our) present financial standing, based upon (my) (our) INVENTORY TAKEN _____

                               Date

ASSETS		LIABILITIES
Cash in _____ _____ Bank		Accounts payable for mdse., not due _____
		Notes payable to_____ _____ } Bank ____ _____ }
Cash on hand _____		
Customers notes, not due_____		
Owing to firm by partners _____		Indebtedness for notes sold by firm _____
Accounts receivable good (not more than		Notes payable for merchandise _____
six months old) _____		
Accounts receivable doubtful _____		Amount owing for all other borrowed
Entire stock of manufactured merchandise		money including money on deposit with us___
figured at _____		Other liabilities _____
Entire stock of raw material figured at ___		
Machinery and fixtures _____		Total liabilities _____
Total assets in business _____		SURPLUS IN BUSINESS _____

Annual rental _____ $ _____		Amount of losses by bad debts Fire } Mdse. $ _____
Amount of sales last year _____ $ _____		last year _____ $_____ Insurance } Plant $ _____
Amount of expenses last year _____ $ _____		

[See other side for details of real estate and other holdings of firm or partfers thereof (or of the corporation) and indebtedness thereon].

Nature of security given to banks, or to others, as collateral against loans. _____

Are any of your accounts payable past due _____ (Yes or no) _____

Have you any contingent indebtedness as endorsers or guarantors _____ (Yes or no) _____

Did any member of your firm ever fail, or compromise his indebtedness _____ (Yes or no) _____

Amount owing for merchandise NOT included as an asset or liability _____ $_____

Are any merchandise creditors secured in any way _____ (Yes or no) _____

How much of the accounts receivable above mentioned represent goods out on memorandum _____ $_____

Were the accounts receivable above referred to, created by the sale and delivery of merchandise in the regular course of business?

                                                      (Yes or no) _____

Does the net worth indicated above represent your condition after deducting all accounts that are in bankruptcy

or in the hands of receivers or assignees, and after writing off all business and living expenses?   (Yes or no) _____

Have you transferred, cashed, pledged or borrowed any money upon any of your accounts or bills receivable at

any time up to the date of signing this statement?   (Yes or no) _____

Have you at any time pledged your merchandise or transferred any of the same as security for any debt, or given

chattel mortgage on it or sold any large portion of the same out of the ordinary course of business?   (Yes or no) _____

  Have you had any losses either by fire, water, smoke, theft, or otherwise, that have reduced your capital since

date of the last inventory?   (Yes or no) _____

  Suits pending and of what nature _____

  How often do you take an inventory and when _____

  Keep Bank account with _____

  What books of account do you keep in your business   Name each one _____

_____

  We, as individuals (or I) hereby agree and bind ourselves (or myself) unto

jointly and severally, that any and all real estate or personal property standing in our (or my) own name, shall at all times as we (or I) may be in debt to them, be subject to any and all sums owing by us (or me) to them.

  The above statement, both printed and written, has been carefully read by the undersigned, and is a full and correct statement of (my or our) present financial condition.

  This statement is considered as reiterated and applicable to each purchase until revoked in writing, and it is understood that in the event that we (or I) borrow any money hereafter by pledging our (or my) outstanding accounts or any part of them, we (or I) must notify at once.

                                     FIRM SIGNATURE _____

Witness _____   By _____

                                                    A member of the firm

Date _____   If individual sign here _____

Financial Information Statement (Front)

Financial Information Statement (Back)

Comments

1. *See page 55 for the illustration of the front of the form.*

2. *Additional details of the financial statement are requested.*

3. *The request for references could be more specific as to the number and types requested.*

4. *The form provides for credit department computations and remarks.*

5. *Some attempt should be made to state that the information sought will be kept in confidence.*

6. *The back of the form need not be signed in view of the fact that the front of the form is signed.*

Real Estate of Individual Partners Located at

_____ $_____

_____ $_____

_____ $_____

_____ $_____

_____ $_____

Total real estate_____ $_____

Total amt. of mortgages_ _____ $_____

Net amount of money invested in real estate _____ $_____

Other assets of firm or corporation $_____

_____ $_____

_____ $_____

Total other assets _____ $_____

Indebtedness on Real Estate by Mortgages or Otherwise

$_____

$_____

$_____

$_____

$_____

REFERENCES: _____

_____

_____

_____

_____

_____

_____

_____

_____

_____

_____

_____

NOT TO BE FILLED IN:

DATE	ASSETS	LIABILITIES	CAPITAL

REMARKS

Date submitted _____19_____

Have you had any serious losses through bad debts or otherwise between date of this inventory and present time? _____

If so please itemize _____

Signed _____

per _____

Financial Information Statement (Back)

Requesting Updated Financial Statements, Poor Results Reported

Comments

1. *Sometimes, when applicants or customers provide updated financial statements to the creditor or to a credit reporting agency, the statements indicate that the company might be in serious financial trouble.*

2. *No credit professional can afford to ignore this type of information.*

3. *Rather than jump to hasty conclusions, the more experienced credit professional will ask the debtor company to provide updated information. This more current information should enable the credit professional to make a better informed credit decision.*

4. *The letter should be carefully written to cause as little offense as possible. The letter should assure the debtor company that the creditor (a) is looking for additional information in order to continue to extend open account credit, and (b) is not looking for a reason or an excuse to withdraw the open account terms.*

5. *The salesperson and the sales manager should be copied on this type of letter.*

6. *If the debtor fails to provide the requested updated financial information, the creditor may have no choice but to withdraw or reduce the debtor's open account terms.*

[date]
[customer name]
[address]

Attention: Milt Gibson
       [title]

Dear Mr. Gibson:

Thank you for sending us a copy of your company's fiscal year end financial statements. We have analyzed those statements carefully. I hope you will understand that as an unsecured creditor we are concerned about the financial position of your company as reported in those financial statements. Specifically, your Income Statement shows a loss for the year of $XX,XXX.

I do not want to act hastily. Therefore, I would appreciate it if you would send me a copy of your company's interim financial statements for the first six months of the year. Please include copies of your Balance Sheet, Income Statement, and Cash Flow Statement.

I look forward to receiving this information shortly. If you have any questions or concerns about this request, please call me at (800) XXX-XXXX.

Thank you.

Sincerely,

Melissa Ryan-Bonhall
Corporate Credit Director
[creditor company name]

cc: salesperson
    sales manager
    credit file
    correspondence file

**Letter Requesting Updated Financial Statements,
Poor Results Reported**

Handling Retail Credit Card Request

Comments

1. *Prompt response. Try to answer a request for a credit card within two or three days.*

2. *Ask for simple-to-obtain data.*

3. *Use a form letter which is tailored to handle a variety of types of requests. However, have separate letters to distinguish business and nonbusiness accounts.*

4. *Note that this letter requests and audited balance sheet.*

5. *Assure the letter recipient that all information which is obtained will be held in confidence.*

6. *Thank the potential customer for his or her interest in doing business with your company.*

SLICK OIL COMPANY

CREDIT CARD CENTER
132 BROADWAY
TULSA, OK 74136

August 1, 19XX

XXXXXXXXXXXXXX
XXXXXXXXXXXXXXXXXX
XXXXXXXXXXXXX
XXXXXXXXXXXXXXXXXXXXX

   Thank you for your recent request for credit card accommodations. You can help us process your request by completing the enclosed application and forwarding it together with your certified fiscal year end Balance Sheet and accompanying Profit and Loss Statement.

   Let me assure you that all information supplied is held in the strictest confidence.

   Thank you for thinking of Slick Oil.

                        Sincerely,

                        C. E. Small
                        Commercial Credit

enc.

Reply to Corporate Credit Card Request

Credit Card Application

Comments

1. *Note that sections of the application are numbered in the left margin. This provides step-by-step ease in completing the application. It makes it look like a simplified application.*

2. *Sections 3, 4 and 5 contain the nitty gritty for credit investigation and evaluation. While 3 and 4 are for qualifying and identification, section 5 reveals who the applicant's other creditors are at present.*

3. *Other creditors could confirm information on the application as well as supply some indication as to the applicant's paying patterns.*

4. *The number (01-005-05) in the upper right section is for marketing purposes. It is a code used to reveal the source of the application. Sources could include insert in a magazine, direct mail solicitation from a particular mailing list, etc.* That coding may be indicative of the type of applicant for credit purposes.

5. *See Alternate Credit Card Application which is illustrated on page 65.*

GOURMAND NATIONAL CREDIT CARD

PERSONAL ACCOUNT APPLICATION

01-005-05

Please assist us in processing your application quickly by providing all requested information.

1. **Check One** ☐ Mail bill to home address ☐ Mail bill to business address ☐ Former Diners Club member? ☐ No ☐ Yes Acct. No. _____

2. **Courtesy title (optional)** ☐ Mr. ☐ Miss ☐ Dr. ☐ Mrs. ☐ Ms. ☐ Other_____ Name (First) (Middle) (Last)

Home Address   Apt. No.   City   State   Zip

3. Years at Present Address_____   Own Home ☐ Rent ☐   Home Telephone (Include Area Code)   Date of Birth   Month Day Year   Social Security Number   Number of Dependents

Previous Home Address Street   City   State   Zip   Years There

4. Firm Name or Employer   Business Telephone (Include Area Code)

Address   City   State   Zip

Nature of Business   Years with Firm   Your Position   Annual Employment Earnings $

Note: If employment earnings are less than $12,000, please show the amount and source of all other income (such as dividends, interest, etc.,) and at the right the name and address of the individual who can confirm. Income from alimony, child support or separate maintenance payments need not be revealed, if not relied upon for purposes of this application.

Amount and Source of Other Income

Name of Person to Confirm Other Income

Address   City   State   Zip

Previous Employer or College/University if Recent Graduate   Address   Yrs. with firm or yr. graduated

5. Name of Bank, Savings Bank or Credit Union and Branch Address   Other Credit Accounts   Account No.

Checking _____ (Name/Address)   Acct. No.   ☐ American Express _____

   ☐ Carte Blanche _____

Savings _____ (Name/Address)   Acct. No.   ☐ BankAmericard (VISA)_____

   ☐ Master Charge _____

Loan _____ (Name/Address)   Acct. No.   ☐ Other: _____

Department Store Accounts

Oil Company Accounts

Name and Address of Personal Reference (not living with you)

6. **Desired Monthly Billing Period** ☐ Between 1st and 12th ☐ Between 13th and 20th ☐ Between 21st and 31st ☐ No Preference

7. **Doublecard™ Embossing Instructions:** Please tell us how you want your Gourmand cards embossed. There is a limit of 25 characters per line including spaces. Leave one space between names or words. Omit periods and commas.

FIRST CARD: You may designate your business affiliation on the first card if you desire.

Line 1: Your name or your name and business title

| | | | | | | | | | | | | | | | | | | | | | | | |

Line 2: (optional): Your company or business title and company

| | | | | | | | | | | | | | | | | | | | | | | | |

SECOND CARD: The second card may be for your personal use or in the name of the below signed member of your family (co-applicant).

Only one line: Your name or name of co-applicant

| | | | | | | | | | | | | | | | | | | | | | | | |

8. **$30 FEE:** Covers 12 months' membership from date cards are issued plus a trial subscription of 3 issues of Glutton, the Gourmand Magazine. It is understood that you will be billed later for $4.50 for the remaining nine monthly issues of Signature. You receive a total of twelve issues for $4.50 (annual rate is $6.00). Or you may elect to write "cancel Glutton" across that bill and keep the 3 free copies with no further obligation. Do NOT enclose check —we will bill you later.

9. Please issue a third Gourmand Card at $10.00 to the below named member of my family (co-applicant):

First Name   Middle   Last

Please send me _____ forms for additional cards at $10.00 each for members of my family.

The applicant and each co-applicant authorize the investigation of their credit worthiness and the renewal of any cards issued and any Signature subscription not previously cancelled. The applicant and co-applicants will be individually and jointly responsible for all charges incurred with the cards.

X _____
Signature Of Applicant   Date

X _____
Signature Of Co-applicant from Section 7 above (second card)   Date   ☐ Spouse ☐ Other_____ Relationship to Applicant

X _____
Signature Of Co-applicant from Section 9 above (third card)   Date   ☐ Spouse ☐ Other_____ Relationship to Applicant

PLEASE BE SURE TO PRINT ALL REQUESTED INFORMATION CLEARLY.

Credit Card Application

Alternate Credit Card Application

Comments

1. *This is less detailed than the Credit Card Application illustrated on page 63.*

2. *Shaded areas containing bold print divide the form into important sections for easy reference by the applicant.*

3. *The form can be folded and actually used as an envelope. The back has preprinted addressing.*

4. *The form is used by Slick Oil Company and is ideal for gasoline credit card customers.*

5. *The information requested is for personal credit as opposed to the use of business or commercial credit.*

6. *Note the disclaimer in the bottom of the employment section related to alimony and other payments.*

PLEASE COMPLETE ALL SECTIONS

CREDIT CARD APPLICATION

PERSONAL HISTORY

NAME - FIRST MIDDLE LAST	SOCIAL SECURITY NUMBER

RESIDENCE - STREET ADDRESS	CITY	STATE	ZIP CODE

RESIDENCE AREA CODE + PHONE NO.	☐ OWN ☐ RENT	YEARS AT PRESENT ADDRESS

PREVIOUS ADDRESS, IF PRESENT ADDRESS IS LESS THAN 1 YEAR	YEARS AT THIS ADDRESS

IF YOUR SPOUSE WILL USE THIS ACCOUNT, PLEASE PROVIDE SPOUSE'S FULL NAME

NAME OF NEAREST RELATIVE NOT LIVING WITH YOU	RELATIVE'S AREA CODE + PHONE NO.	RELATIONSHIP

RELATIVE'S STREET ADDRESS	CITY	STATE	ZIP CODE

EMPLOYMENT

EMPLOYER	OCCUPATION	MILITARY RANK	HOW LONG

BUSINESS ADDRESS	BUSINESS AREA CODE + PHONE NO.	ANNUAL SALARY

IF PRESENT EMPLOYMENT LESS THAN 1 YEAR, GIVE PREVIOUS EMPLOYER, CITY AND STATE

OTHER INCOME SOURCE (ALIMONY, CHILD SUPPORT, OR SEPARATE MAINTENANCE INCOME NEED NOT BE REVEALED IF YOU DO NOT WISH TO HAVE IT CONSIDERED AS A BASIS FOR REPAYING THIS OBLIGATION.) ▶	ANNUAL AMOUNT

BANK REFERENCE

DO YOU USE BANKING FACILITIES?	☐ YES (IF YES, PLEASE COMPLETE BANKING ☐ NO INFORMATION BELOW.)

BANK NAME	TYPE OF ACCT. ☐ CHECKING ☐ SAVINGS	CHECKING ACCOUNT NO.
BANK ADDRESS		SAVINGS ACCOUNT NO.

CREDIT REFERENCES (CREDIT CARDS, BANKS, FINANCE COS. & DEPT. STORES)

DO YOU HAVE ANY CREDIT REFERENCES?	☐ YES (IF YES, PLEASE COMPLETE CREDIT ☐ NO REFERENCE INFORMATION BELOW.)

CREDITOR	ADDRESS	ACCOUNT NUMBER

MY CREDIT CARD WILL BE USED FOR	☐ Personal ☐ Business ☐ Truck ☐ Airplane	ESTIMATED MONTHLY CHARGES ▶ $	FOR SHELL USE ONLY

EVERYTHING THAT I HAVE STATED IN THIS APPLICATION IS CORRECT TO THE BEST OF MY KNOWLEDGE. I UNDERSTAND THAT YOU WILL RETAIN THIS APPLICATION WHETHER OR NOT IT IS APPROVED. YOU ARE AUTHORIZED TO CHECK MY CREDIT AND EMPLOYMENT HISTORY AND TO ANSWER QUESTIONS ABOUT YOUR CREDIT EXPERIENCE WITH ME. THE APPLICANT, IF MARRIED, MAY APPLY FOR A SEPARATE ACCOUNT.

NO. CARDS DESIRED	SIGNATURE (must be signed by above named applicant)	DATE

BE SURE APPLICATION IS SIGNED,
MOISTEN FLAP, FOLD APPLICATION, SEAL, STAMP, AND MAIL

Alternate Credit Card Application

Banking Information Request

Comments

1. *A preprinted letter should be avoided unless volume is excessively heavy.*

2. *This letter is generalized and is not specific as to the type of information sought. The benefit of a generalized letter is that unusual data is more likely to be reported.*

3. *Letters to a bank should be addressed to a specifically named individual. Only as an expedient would there be justification for addressing the letter to the "loan officer" or "credit officer."*

4. *The first paragraph of the letter explains who referred the company to the bank.*

5. *Creditors should include as part of their credit application a release specifically authorizing bank and trade creditors listed on the application to respond to the creditor's inquiry. This letter can make reference to that application and authorization. A copy of the signed application, with this section highlighted, could accompany the inquiry to the bank.*

6. *It is a good idea to include a stamped, self-addressed envelope for the bank's convenience in responding to this inquiry.*

7. *A seven-business-day follow-up should be set for this letter. Creditors should consider calling the bank for an update if they do not receive a response in seven business days.*

[date]
[security bank]
[address]

Attention: Warren Ettleman
          Assistant Vice President

Dear Mr. Ettleman:

Mr. Arthur Weber of Hardware Retailers Company recommended that we contact you regarding credit information about his company.

Kindly send to us as much information about your bank's relationship with Hardware Retailers in connection with our credit evaluation of this applicant.

A copy of Hardware Retailers Company's written authorization to you to release information to us is attached for your review. Any information you choose to supply will be held in strictest confidence.

Thank you for your prompt attention to this request.

Sincerely,

Emma Edison
Assistant Credit Manager
[creditor company name]

cc: credit file
    follow-up file

Letter to Request Banking Information

Bank Reference Check

Comments

1. *See page 68 for an alternate type of request for banking credit information.*

2. *This letter requests specific information from the bank reference.*

3. *By including the section "Any additional comments," creditors hope to gather useful information that they would otherwise not receive.*

4. *One can expect that bank officers will call their clients to advise them of credit information requests.*

5. *In order to evaluate other sources of information, a comparison of the bank's reply can be made to information supplied by credit reporting agencies. Any significant differences could be attributed to misinformation supplied by the account itself.*

6. *Compare this letter with the illustrated bank information request form on page 71.*

[date]
First National Bank
[street address]
Winnemuca, NV 89445

Attention: Burt Wilson
           Loan Officer

RE: Smith Retail Corporation

Dear Mr. Wilson:

We have been asked to extend an open account line of credit to the above referenced account in the amount of $XX,XXX. Please provide the information requested below:

Date account opened _____
Average account balance _____
Number of NSF checks in the last 12 months? _____
Is this a borrowing or nonborrowing relationship? _____
If borrowing, what is the credit limit? _____
Is the line secured or unsecured? _____
Is the customer in violation of any loan covenants
    at this time? _____
Any additional comments? _____
_____

Enclosed, please find a self-addressed, stamped envelope for your convenience in responding. If you have any questions, please fell free to call me at (800) XXX-XXXX.

Thank you for your assistance in this matter.

Sincerely,

Willis Wade
Credit Administrator
[creditor company name]

enc.

cc: credit file
    correspondence file

Letter to Request Bank Reference Check

Request for Banking Information Form

Comments

1. *The form is prepared in duplicate, one copy being retained by the bank.*

2. *Compare this form with the detailed request letter on the previous page.*

3. *The requesting credit department completes the upper half of the form. For new accounts, the experience portion can be omitted.*

4. *A cover letter could be used to explain that the bank is expected to complete the lower portion of the form.*

5. *While there is a general presumption to such effect, the cover letter could state that the information will be kept confidential.*

6. *It is desirable to include a stamped and addressed envelope for responding convenience.*

7. *Upon the return of the form, additional information can be sought via telephone. See page 72 for some guidelines when calling banks for information.*

TO: Bank _____

Address _____

City/State/Zip _____

ACCOUNT

Name _____

Address _____

City/State/Zip _____

REQUEST FOR BANK CREDIT INFORMATION

The above account has given the name of your bank as a reference in applying for credit. Following is our experience:

Sold Since _____

Now Owing $ _____

First Order $ _____

High Credit $ _____

Days Slow _____

We would greatly appreciate your completing the information below. All information will be held in strict confidence.

Very truly yours,

Company _____

Address _____

City/State/Zip _____

Signed by _____

Title _____

Date _____

Date Account Opened _____

Average   □ Low   □ Medium   □ High

Balance   □ Four   □ Five   □ Six Figure

Deposit Account Relationship Satisfactory? _____ _____

               Yes   No

Remarks: _____

Loans	High	Present
Unsecured	$ _____	$ _____
Secured	$ _____	$ _____
Mortgage	$ _____	$ _____
Installment	$ _____	$ _____

Line of Credit Available: _____ _____

            Yes   No

LOAN EXPERIENCE:

Satisfactory □

Unsatisfactory □

Remarks: _____

_____

_____

Bank Signature _____

Title: _____

Date _____

(white)

(BANK COPY)   **(pink)**

Title: _____

Date _____

Request for Banking Information Form

Effective Telephone Techniques to Secure Bank Information

Comments

1. *Of course telephone contact is much faster than relying on written communication. However, some banks will only supply information upon written request. See the letters and forms illustrated on pages 67, 69 and 71.*

2. *The best results are achieved on the telephone by the more experienced personnel. One can expect a lower level of the quality of response to inquiries that are made by those who are at a more clerical level.*

3. *Senior level personnel can permit the more junior level of credit personnel to listen in on an extension for training in the use of telephone inquiry techniques.*

4. *One can expect to sometimes have to make several calls before reaching the account officer to obtain information about the applicant company. Often, bank employees are reluctant to release sensitive information over the phone.*

5. *Bankers often ask trade creditors to put their requests in writing. As an expedient, creditors might want to fax their questions to the account officer.*

6. *Some banks never provide credit ratings to trade creditors. Instead, they will rate only to another bank; the creditor must arrange for its bank to contact the applicant company's bank for a rating.*

7. *Another popular twist involves banks charging creditors a fee to provide references on their clients. These fees typically range from $10 to $25.* Caution: *Paying for the bank reference does not make the reference any better or more detailed than one given for free.*

1. Prior to the call, completely familiarize yourself with account information so that you will ask intelligent and knowledgeable questions. Have the complete account file on your desk at the time of the call.

2. Try to get the actual account (or loan) officer who handles the client's account. Avoid speaking to secretaries or clerks who are merely familiar with the account and have little to do with the granting of credit to the client.

3. If the client's file is marked restricted or the account officer is unwilling to rate or provide you with relevant information about the customer, you might call the applicant and ask him or her to contact the banker to give permission for the account officer to answer your questions.

4. Tell the bank officer your name, your position, the name of your firm and its location. State the purpose of your call. Bank officers get scores of these types of calls each week and know the type of information you can use.

5. They should tell you the following information readily:
   a. Average cash account balance
   b. Secured loan balance
   c. Unsecured loan balance

6. Repeat that information over the phone so that you are sure that you have it correctly noted.

7. Using a professional manner, ask about the type of collateral used for secured loans, the credit limits the bank extends on various types of loans, guarantees and other possible loan data.

8. Ask about the loan pay-back history. "Satisfactory" means that loans have been liquidated on time. "Good" can be taken to mean that loans were liquidated prior to the due date. Try to elicit a distinction.

9. Inquire as to whether loans are cyclical or seasonal.

10. Ask bank officers if they have any other comments about the account, remembering that they may be hesitant about weak situations unless they are confident that you understand "generalizations." Be alert to grab the significance of well-chosen words.

11. Remember to thank the banker for his or her time and assistance. It is not only the right thing to do, but you might need the banker's help again in the future.

**Effective Telephone Techniques
to Secure Bank Information**

Using a Salesperson Credit Contact Report for Data

Comments

1. *The marketing organization of many companies require their salespeople to maintain records of all contacts—even those who are not currently customers of the company.*

2. *Forms and procedures can be developed that will help the credit department in the credit review process, whenever that information is actually needed.*

3. *One should not expect too much from a salesperson's contact report. Salespeople are optimists by nature. The contact reports are simply a starting point for the credit investigation.*

4. *Conflicts between the salesperson's report and other information on file should be resolved before there is new or further credit extended.*

5. *Once the initial report is reviewed, credit professionals might have additional questions they would like the salesperson to ask the potential customer.*

SALESPERSON CREDIT CONTACT REPORT

INSTRUCTION: *Complete as much of this report as possible without being too aggressive and forward to Credit Department.*

Complete Name of Firm _____

Names of Owners or Principals _____

Address _____

Corporation   _____   *   Manufacturing _____

Partnership   _____   *   Wholesale _____

Sole Owner   _____   *   Retail _____

Other   _____   *   Other _____

Year That Firm Was Established _____

Which Bank Does the Firm Use? _____

Bank Address _____

Estimate the Number of Employees _____

Estimate the Size of the Premises _____

Estimate the Annual Sales Volume _____

From Observation or Other Information List the Firm's Principal Suppliers _____

_____

_____

Which of Our Products or Services Can the Firm Use? _____

_____

Other Comments _____

_____

_____

_____

_____

Salesperson _____ Office _____ Date _____

Salesperson Credit Contact Report

Welcoming the Potential Customer

Comments

1. *The letter should thank the customer for his or her interest in doing business with your company.*

2. *It should advise the customer that the credit limit has been approved.*

3. *The letter should indicate that the creditor company looks forward to receiving the first order.*

4. *A copy of the letter to the sales manager may result in a push for the initial order.*

5. *New accounts need to be more closely monitored than established accounts. Credit professionals should find ways to manage and monitor newly established accounts closely to prevent the customer from developing bad habits.*

6. *See pages 79–87 for additional letters welcoming new customers under special situations.*

[date]
[customer name]
[address]

Attention: William Wybrand
          [title]

Dear Mr. Wybrand:

Thank you for your inquiry about establishing an open account with our company. I am pleased to report our credit investigation has been completed and the credit limit you requested is in place. Please ask your accounting department to note our terms of sale are net 30 days from date of invoice.

We look forward to receiving your opening order, and for the opportunity to be of service to you.

Sincerely,

Walter Smith
Credit Manager
[creditor company name]

cc: salesperson
    sales manager
    credit file

Letter Welcoming the Potential Customer

Welcoming New Customer—Advice of First Order

Comments

1. *This letter also advises the new account that open account credit has been approved.*

2. *The terms of sale are listed so that there is no misunder-standing now or in the future.*

3. *The customer is informed when the opening order will or did ship.*

4. *By a copy of the letter, the sales manager is advised of the extension of credit, the initial shipment and the credit limit of the account.*

5. *The follow-up file can be used to closely monitor new account activity.*

[date]
[customer name]
[address]

Attention: Sam Smith
      [title]

Dear Mr. Smith:

We are pleased to advise you that the $XX,XXX credit limit you requested has been approved. Our terms of sale are 2% 15 days, net 30 days from date of invoice. Please inform your accounts payable department that because the cash discount is so large the discount due date is rigidly enforced.

Your initial order under PO number 98831 was shipped on March 23rd.

We look forward to a long and mutually beneficial business relationship.

Sincerely,

Jane Clark
Credit Manager
[creditor company name]

cc: sales manager
    salesperson
    credit file

Letter Welcoming New Customer—Advice of First Order

New Account Processing—Reminder of Credit Terms

Comments

1. *The new customer is told when the opening order was shipped.*

2. *The company indicates that it is proud of its service to customers.*

3. *The customer is asked to notify his or her accounting department of the credit terms—in this case net 30 days from date of invoice.*

4. *By a copy of the letter, the sales department is advised of the action that has been taken as well as the credit limit imposed on the account.*

[date]
[customer name]
[address]

Attention: Richard Rogers
          [title]

Dear Mr. Rogers:

Thank you for your opening order. We are pleased to be given the opportunity to compete for your business. We find that most of our customers are happy with our products and our after-sales service. If there is anything I can do to assist you in any way, please don't hesitate to call on me. My direct telephone number is (800) XXX-XXXX.

Just as our customers expect good service, we would ask for your assistance and cooperation in observing our terms of sale, which are net 30 days from date of invoice.

Thank you for your confidence in this company, its products and services, and its employees!

Sincerely,

Wilma Sampson
Assistant Credit Manager
[creditor company name]

cc: salesperson
    sales manager
    credit file

**Letter for New Account Processing—
Reminder of Credit Terms**

New Account Processing—Reference Requested

Comments

1. *The letter should thank the customer for the order.*

2. *The customer should be told when the order will ship.*

3. *The new customer is told the tentative credit limit.*

4. *A request is being made for the name and phone number of a bank officer who handles the customer's account in order for the credit department to obtain additional information.*

5. *Apparently, the credit department has enough information upon which to approve the initial shipment and the granting of a temporary credit limit, but desires additional data. There is no reason why a sale should be refused or delayed because all of the desired information is not available as yet.*

6. *The salesperson should receive a copy of this letter as a courtesy.*

7. *An asterisk in the appropriate data field could indicate that the credit limit established is considered to be temporary.*

8. *A follow-up should be set for ten business days after the letter is sent.*

[date]
[customer name]
[address]

Attention: Tim Thomas

Dear Mr. Thomas:

We want to thank you for your confidence in our industrial products. Our shipping department informs me the order will be shipped tomorrow.

We have extended a preliminary credit limit of $XX,XXX based on the information we have been able to gather up until now. To complete our credit investigation, we need to contact your bank. Please provide me with the name and telephone number of your bank account officer. My telephone number is (800) XXX-XXXX.

Thank you for your prompt response.

Sincerely,

Ron Baker
Credit Manager
[creditor company name]

cc: salesperson
    credit file
    correspondence file

Letter for New Account Processing—
Reference Requested

New Account Processing—Explanation of Credit Limit

Comments

1. *The customer, along with the salesperson, is informed of the fact that an account has been established.*

2. *The customer is told the credit limit assigned to the account.*

3. *The customer is also told that he or she will need to pay COD on any orders over their credit limit.*

4. *The door is left open to the possibility that the credit limit might be increased.*

5. *There are two major risks associated with COD shipments. The first is that the customer's company check will bounce. The other is that the customer will refuse a COD delivery and the creditor will have to pay to get the goods returned.*

6. *The sales manager may want to help by encouraging the customer to provide the information necessary to increase the credit line. Otherwise, competitors might get the business because they aggressively sought out the additional information necessary to consider a larger line.*

[date]
[customer name]
[address]

Attention: Carl Quinces

Dear Mr. Quinces:

We are pleased to extend a credit limit of $XX,XXX to your company. If orders are received that would cause your account to exceed this credit limit, those orders can be shipped to you on a COD basis.

The credit limit was established on the basis of the limited information that was available to us through our normal sources. If you can provide additional informa-tion, such as your company's most current financial statements and additional trade references, then I would be pleased to evaluate your account for a larger credit limit.

We look forward to serving you, and thank you for your business.

Sincerely,

John Bowen
Credit Manager
[creditor company name]

cc: salesperson
    sales manager
    credit file

**Letter for New Account Processing—
Explanation of Credit Limit**

New Account Processing—Open Account Terms Rejected

Comments

1. *From time to time, a creditor has no choice but to reject an applicant for open account terms.*

2. *This is never a popular decision with the customer or with the sales department.*

3. *The salesperson should be notified before the applicant of the decision not to offer open account terms. The credit manager should take the time to explain the credit decision in detail to the salesperson.*

4. *The credit manager should be very careful about what information he or she shares with the salesperson. The salesperson should be reminded not to repeat anything to the customer about the credit department's reasons for the decision not to offer open account terms.*

5. *The letter to the customer should state clearly that the creditor has denied the request for open account terms. If appropriate, the credit professional should offer the customer alternatives, which might include sales against a standby letter of credit or COD terms.*

6. *The letter should indicate that the decision will be reevaluated from time to time as conditions change or as additional information becomes available.*

[date]
[customer name]
[address]

Attention: Jessica Weber
      [title]

Dear Ms. Weber:

Thank you for completing and returning our credit application. I have carefully reviewed your application. Unfortunately, I am unable to offer your company an open account credit line at this time.

If you wish, I would be happy to ship the order pending on terms of COD, company check. Another alternative would be to ask that you arrange for a standby letter of credit in the amount of $XX,XXX with this company as the beneficiary.

I will ask our salesperson to contact you as soon as possible to discuss the order pending. We will be happy to review this decision from time to time as conditions change at your company.

If you have any questions, please call me at (XXX) XXX-XXXX.

Thank you.

Sincerely,

Gillian Taylor
National Credit Manager
[creditor company name]

cc: salesperson
    sales manager
    credit file

Letter to Process New Account—
Open Account Terms Rejected

Chapter 3

Solving New Account Problems

Only an inexperienced businessperson would be unaware that getting open account credit terms from suppliers is not easy or automatic. In fact, only the most highly rated firms have an easy time getting the credit limits they need from new suppliers. Most applicants are required to complete a credit application and provide sufficient information to the potential supplier to justify the supplier's decision to offer open account terms.

That rejecting an order is better than having a bad debt loss goes without saying. However, the credit department should carefully consider whether there are alternatives to simply rejecting an order. For example, can COD terms be substituted for the open account terms requested?

At first glance, COD might seem to be an entirely unacceptable option to a buyer. However, if the COD term is combined with a cash discount for early payment, then COD might be a viable (and even attractive) alternative to not shipping the order. Another thing for credit professionals to keep in mind is that the applicant's request for open account terms has probably been rejected before by other creditors.

Of course, most applicants can read between the lines when they receive a letter from a creditor indicating the creditor would prefer COD terms to open account shipments. No matter how carefully worded, the message will be, "We do not trust you with open account terms."

Some companies accept small dollar volume orders from marginal accounts, even though the applicant may not be considered creditworthy and despite the fact that the small dollar amounts involved make the orders marginally profitable anyway. Why? These small "accommodation lines" of credit are extended as an investment in the future. The little acorn may one day grow into an oak. Even if it does not, the loss incurred is small because the credit exposure is carefully monitored.

Refusal to Give Away the Store

From time to time, accounts request a credit limit far in excess of the amount they really need or actually want. Often, customers believe that, by asking for far more than they need, they are more likely to get the credit limit they want.

"I need the entire order shipped right away or we cannot do business."

"If your company cannot ship x quantity on open account terms, then forget the whole deal."

Threats from customers must be taken seriously, but not so seriously that the credit department loses sight of its primary obligation: to properly manage credit risk. Evaluating credit risk must be done as if there were no threat. If possible, alternatives should be suggested that preserves goodwill with the customer. If not, the credit professional should try to find a way to solve the problem and allow the customer to save face. Partial shipments, shorter terms, guarantees and pledges of collateral are concepts that have to be sold to customers.

Handling Accounts That Refuse to Provide Information

Many companies know that their credit record does not speak well for their creditworthiness. Therefore, these accounts are often reluctant to comply with requests from creditors for information. Maybe every time they have submitted financial statements in the past or provided trade references, potential creditors have rejected their requests for open account terms.

If applicants refuse to provide the necessary information to allow the credit professional to make an informed credit decision, open account terms should not be offered. Rather than simply refusing to sell to the applicant, the savvy credit professional will offer terms that involve acceptable risk, including sales made on COD or cash in advance terms.

Some customers try to intimidate creditors into offering open account terms. These applicants might complain about the delay in making a credit decision to senior management, or they might pressure the sales department to press the credit department for an immediate approval. The applicant might simply call and try to bully the credit department into offering open account terms. As a general rule, the harder an account pushes for open account terms (and the more unreasonable the account becomes), the more cautious the credit professional should be about approving the credit risk.

New Businesses

Most new businesses start small. They lack a track record of open account purchases and are frequently undercapitalized. In addition, their management might be experienced, and they may have an unrealistic view of how open account terms are granted by creditors. Selling to such an account may prove challenging for the credit professional. For example, creditors might need to explain the terms of sale to the applicant, or they might need to remind the applicant every time an invoice comes due.

Extreme care has to be taken in extending open account credit to a new business. Even well capitalized start-up companies fail. Most credit professionals are aware that the majority of new businesses formed do not survive for even five years—and that many fail in less than a year.

Credit Fraud

Some criminals travel around the country using a creditor's willingness to offer open account terms to an apparently creditworthy applicant as a way to steal. There are a number of variations of the scam, but essentially it works this way. The criminal:

- Establishes a business location and opens a bank account.
- Arranges for co-conspirators to provide the company with phony trade references.
- Contacts a credit reporting agency to establish a credit report.
- Compiles a set of impressive but entirely fraudulent financial statements that will be sent to prospective creditors.
- Offers to sign a personal guarantee and be prepared to provide equally fraudulent personal financial statements.

For a period of time, the criminal may purchase goods and services on open account terms and pay creditors. The criminal then uses those legitimate references to get additional creditors to extend credit. Sooner or later, the debtor company begins to slow down on payments and eventually stops paying all together. In the meantime, all the product that is being delivered on open account terms is being sold as quickly as possible for cash. Eventually, the debtor skips town or even files for bankruptcy protection.

A careful check of the background of the owners of a company may reveal that the information they have provided is a clever work of fiction. The con artist relies on the fact that at least some creditors will grant open account credit terms because on the surface the applicant looks solid.

Credit Refused—Open Account Possible in the Future

Comments

1. *Credit refusals are distasteful letters to write. A credit person has to have significant justification for turning away business. However, all accounts cannot be readily accepted—otherwise, bad debt losses would make business prohibitive.*

2. *There is nothing wrong with suggesting to an applicant that open account terms might be offered at some point in the future. After all, sometimes even bankrupt companies turn themselves around. Possibly an account that looks untouchable today might be quite different in six months or less.*

3. *In many instances, an applicant has been bought out, merged, or received a cash infusion resulting in a far more creditworthy company.*

4. *Some companies do not like to write a credit refusal letter and prefer that the matter eventually be dropped, or the sales manager handle the refusal in person or by telephone.*

[date]
[customer name]
[address]

Attention: Bob Bernhart
            [title]

Dear Mr. Bernhart:

Thank you for your inquiry about opening an account with our company. Unfortunately, your company does not meet our current criteria for granting of open account credit terms.

I will be happy to reevaluate your request in six months or if conditions change. In the meantime, we would be happy to do business with your company on a cash basis.

Thank you for your interest in XYZ Corporation.

Sincerely,

Catherine Wilson
Credit Manager
[creditor company name]

cc: sales manager
    file

**Letter Refusing Credit—Open Account
Possible in the Future**

Refusing to Offer Extended Terms to a New Account

Comments

1. *Thank the applicant for the order.*

2. *The applicant has demanded 60-day credit terms. The industry norm is 30 days. The applicant apparently believes it is in a strong bargaining position.*

3. *Assuming the applicant company is otherwise creditworthy, a letter should be generated explaining that 60-day terms cannot be granted.*

4. *The creditor should require that the applicant acknowledge net 30-day terms in writing. Otherwise, the customer could claim that the matter was not addressed and resolved, and then delay payment.*

5. *Some companies try to demand net 60-day terms because this ploy works from time to time. However, the applicant company probably has more respect for creditors who do not waver in enforcing their terms of sale than those who agree to the demand for extended dating.*

[date]
[customer name]
[address]

Attention: Al Argus
            Buyer

Dear Mr. Argus:

Thank you for your initial order on purchase order #97-2281. We note that your purchase order lists terms of sale as "net 60 days." Our terms of sale are net 30 days from date of invoice.

Before we can process this order, we will need to receive a revised purchase order or a letter acknowledging the correct net 30-day terms on the order pending on the account.

We hope to hear from you shortly so that we can release this pending order without further delay. If you have any questions, please call me at (800) XXX-XXXX.

Thank you.

Sincerely,

Ed Burroughs
Credit Officer
[creditor company name]

cc: sales manager
    file

**Letter Refusing to Offer Extended Terms
to a New Account**

Limited Open Account Credit—
Partial Shipment Suggested

Comments

1. *Thank the customer for the order.*

2. *Indicate that a limited credit line is offered, one below the limit required to ship the order pending.*

3. *The customer is asked to rewrite the order so that it does not exceed the credit limit established.*

4. *An alternative is suggested: The customer is asked to provide additional information that could be helpful to the creditor in considering a larger credit limit.*

5. *A second alternative of a partial payment in advance may also be suggested.*

6. *The salesperson should be copied so that he or she can contact the customer and make arrangements as outlined in the letter.*

[date]
[customer name]
[address]

Attention: Lou Loveland
           [title]

Dear Mr. Loveland:

Thank you for your initial order and for your confidence in our company.

We have established an initial credit limit of $_____. As you know, this is below the amount of your initial order. I can suggest two alternatives to resolve this problem:

Please rewrite the order to reduce the dollar value to or below the credit limit, or

Please provide additional information—specifically your company's financial statements—so that we can evaluate your company for the larger credit limit you need.

A partial payment of $XXX made in advance would also allow the open order to be approved and released.

Please call me if you have questions at (800) XXX-XXXX.

Thank you.

Sincerely,

Jack Warren
Credit Administrator
[creditor company name]

cc: sales manager
    file

Letter to Limit Open Account Credit—
Partial Shipment Suggested

No Credit Information Available—Cash Terms Required

Comments

1. *Thank the customer for the order.*

2. *The letter provides a brief explanation of the credit evaluation process.*

3. *Advance payment is requested.*

4. *By being copied, the salesperson is made aware of the situation/problem and is invited to help expedite payment, if possible.*

5. *While at first glance cash in advance terms may seem unreasonable, chances are that the applicant has contacted other creditors, which have made the same request.*

[date]
[customer name]
[address]

Attention: Vanna Vogt
            [title]

Dear Ms. Vogt:

Thank you for your opening order on your purchase order #33903 and for your confidence in our ability to serve your organization.

At present, we cannot locate sufficient information in order to process the pending order on open account terms. We would be happy to ship your order upon receipt of a cashier's check or wire transfer for $_____.

Please feel free to call me at (800)XXX-XXXX if you have any questions. Thank you.

Sincerely,

Sara Walsh
Assistant Credit Manager
[creditor company name]

cc: sales representative
    file

Letter Explaining No Credit Information Available—Cash Terms Required

Credit Rating Poor—COD Recommended

Comments

1. *The letter thanks the applicant for the order.*

2. *The letter should not dwell on the negative aspects of the customer's credit history.*

3. *The applicant is asked to agree to accept the order pending on COD company check terms.*

4. *Experience indicates that customers are reluctant to respond to this type of letter.*

5. *The applicant may be "shopping" the order pending to try to find a creditor willing to offer open account terms.*

[date]
[customer name]
[address]

Attention: Max Maugh
          [title]

Dear Mr. Maugh:

Thank you for your initial order with our firm.

Unfortunately, we are not able to offer your company open account terms at this time. Upon receipt of written notice from you, we will be glad to ship this order promptly on a COD basis.

Please call me if you have any questions at (800) XXX-XXXX. Thank you for your interest in doing business with AAAA Best Inc.

Sincerely,

Mary Ward
Assistant Credit Manager
AAAA Best Inc.

cc: sales manager
    file

Letter Explaining Poor Credit Rating— COD Recommended

Missing Credit Information—Alternatives Suggested

Comments

1. *The customer is thanked for the order.*

2. *The letter should explain that open account terms cannot be granted at this time due to insufficient credit information.*

3. *The applicant is asked to provide additional trade references, financial statements or a new bank reference.*

4. *An alternative is suggested to expedite shipment—COD terms.*

5. *The salesperson is contacted and asked to follow up to make certain the applicant company sends the requested information.*

6. *The credit decision maker must take into consideration that risk is associated even with COD terms. The main risks are that (a) the order might be refused on delivery or (b) the customer's check might bounce.*

7. *If the credit decision maker is not confident that the customer's check will clear, then cash in advance terms should be requested.*

[date]
[customer name]
[address]

Attention: Chris Cobbler
            [title]

Dear Mr. Cobbler:

Thank you for your opening order with our company. Unfortunately, we are unable to process your order at this time due to a lack of information. Specifically, we would need _____ in order to consider releasing the order pending on open account terms.

Please send this information to my attention at the address shown below, or fax it to me at (800) XXX-XXXX.

If you need this order shipped immediately, please contact me and I will be happy to ship it on a COD basis. My telephone number is (800) XXX-XXXX.

Thank you.

Sincerely,

Joan Appley
Credit Manager
[creditor company name]

cc: sales representative
    file

Letter Explaining Missing Credit Information—
Alternatives Suggested

Adverse Credit Report—COD Requested

Comments

1. *The applicant is thanked for the opening order.*

2. *The letter is not specific about what sources were contacted, nor does it contain any specific responses or comments received in response to the credit inquiries sent. Providing the applicant with this type of information would be unethical and inappropriate.*

3. *Before offering COD terms, the credit grantor must make certain the applicant qualifies for COD terms. Otherwise, cash in advance terms must be requested.*

4. *Chances are that the applicant knows that the credit history is marginal. Therefore, the COD request will probably not come as a great surprise.*

[date]
[applicant company name]
[address]

Attention: Carl Crowley
            [title]

Dear Mr. Crowley:

Thank you for your initial order with our firm and for your confidence in our products.

Based on the information we have on file, we find that your company does not meet our credit-granting criteria at this time. We will be glad to ship the order pending on a COD basis.

Please let me know if these terms are acceptable to you. My telephone number is (800) XXX-XXXX.

Thank you.

Sincerely,

Arthur Stone
Assistant Credit Manager
[creditor company name]

cc: sales representative
    file

Letter Reporting Adverse Credit—COD Requested

Incomplete Information—Memo to Sales Representative

Comments

1. *A good rapport with the sales department can help the credit department.*

2. *Prompt notification about problems is essential. Faxing or e-mailing a request to the salesperson is more reliable than simply leaving a voice mail message. It is also less likely that your message will be misunderstood.*

3. *Internal memos should be succinct and clear. They should describe the problem in sufficient detail so that the salesperson understands the specific action he or she is being asked to take.*

4. *If an order is pending, be sure to state that fact clearly.*

5. *Remember, a cooperative working relationship with the sales department will result in a more effective and efficient credit department.*

INTERNAL MEMORANDUM

[date]

TO: George Jones

FROM: Bill Smith

SUBJECT: Order Pending for Sloe Bottling
             Company

George:

I received an order today from Sloe Bottling
for $_____. As you can see from the at-
tached correspondence, the applicant has
omitted several key pieces of information
from their credit application. As a result,
I am holding the order pending.

Please call the buyer and ask them to send
the information ASAP. To expedite the order,
I suggest you ask your contact at Sloe to
fax me the information. My fax number is
(XXX) XXX-XXXX.

Please call me if you have any questions.

Otherwise, I look forward to receiving the
information necessary to release the orders
pending.

Thank you.

Peter Lorry

attachment

cc: file

Incomplete Information—Memo to Sales Representative

Communication Breakdown—Memo to Sales

Comments

1. *Memos to sales should be brief and informal.*

2. *Credit managers should be specific about the type of information they need or the actions they want the salesperson to take.*

3. *With a vested interest in seeing the sale go through, the sales representative should be motivated to help resolve the problem.*

INTERNAL MEMO

[date]

TO: Wally Warren

FROM: Barbara Branch

SUBJECT: Stone Luggage

Hi Wally:

I have sent three requests for additional trade references to the purchasing agent for Stone Luggage. Unfortunately, she has not responded to these requests [copies attached].

I am puzzled by the lack of response. We all want to ship the pending order, but I simply cannot do so with the limited information we have on file at this time.

Any assistance you can offer in getting the information requested would be appreciated. Please call me if you have any questions or comments.

Thanks for your help.

Barbara

cc: file

Communication Breakdown—Memo to Sales

No Response from Customer—Second Request

Comments

1. *The applicant has not responded to a request for information.*

2. *If the order can be released without all the facts and a temporary credit limit can be established, then the credit professional has an obligation to do so. Otherwise, a second request should be sent.*

3. *The letter should mention that there was no response to a previous request.*

4. *If there is not enough information, a second request should be sent. It should briefly mention that there was no response to a previous request.*

5. *The letter should request a prompt response, and should assure the applicant that the information requested will be kept confidential.*

6. *The sales representative should be encouraged to put pressure on the applicant to respond promptly to the request.*

[date]
[applicant company name]
[address]

Attention: Wanda White
          [title]

Dear Ms. White:

Unfortunately, I have received no response to the attached request for additional trade references. I would
like to release the order pending, but I cannot do so
without additional credit information on file.

Your prompt response to this request will enable us to
provide the type of responsiveness our customers have
come to expect.

Thank you for your prompt attention to this request.

Sincerely,

Bill Bishop
Credit Manager
[creditor company name]

attachment

cc: sales representative
    file

Letter Reporting No Response from Customer—Second Request

Order Released and Shipped—
Additional Information Requested

Comments

1. *Thank the customer for the order.*

2. *Tell the customer when and how the order shipped.*

3. *The letter requests additional credit information or references.*

4. *The terms of sale are confirmed.*

5. *The sales representative is copied on the letter.*

6. *A prompt response from the customer is requested.*

7. *The credit manager sets a relatively short internal follow-up date on the request.*

[date]
[customer name]
[address]

Attention: Gary Cooper
            [title]

Dear Mr. Cooper:

Thank you for your initial order on purchase order #97-1189. That order was shipped on April 10th via Overleaf Overnight Transport.

At this point, our credit file is incomplete. Please send me a copy of your company's most recent financial statements so that I may evaluate your request for a $_____ credit limit.

Also, in reference to the order just released, please ask your accounts payable department to note our terms of sale as being net 30 days from date of invoice.

Thank you for your prompt response.

Sincerely,

John Woodbury
Credit Manager
[creditor company name]

cc: sales representative
    file

Letter Requesting Additional Information—
Order Released and Shipped

Requesting More Data from a Reference

Comments

1. *The letter thanks the reference for the information already supplied.*

2. *Additional specific information is requested.*

3. *Using a copy of the letter for a response saves the time of the reference and also makes it easier for a quick response.*

4. *The use of a business reply envelope is an appreciated convenience.*

5. *The follow-up in the event of no further reply can be made via telephone.*

[date]
[creditor name]
[address]

Attention: Bob Brown

Dear Mr. Brown:

Thank you for your prompt response to our recent request for credit information about your customer, Wooden Toy Company, located in Mobile, Alabama.

Please let me know the maximum amount of open account credit your company has granted to Wooden Toy Company in the last year. A self-addressed, stamped envelope is attached for your convenience in responding.

Thank you.

Sincerely,

Diane Ward
Credit Director
[company name]

enc.

cc: file

Letter Requesting More Data from a Reference

Using a Credit Report

Comments

1. *It is important to "qualify" the subject. In other words, is the subject of the report the* same *party about whom credit information is being sought?*

2. *To qualify the subject, compare the information in the file with the identify contained in the report. Is the date of birth, address or social security number the same as the file information?*

3. *For commercial reports, comparison should be made for addresses, names of principals, etc.*

4. *An experienced credit manager may be interested in accounting for the past seven years as to work history or residence.*

5. *To some credit personnel, a credit report is the starting point for securing further information. Some credit reports are not as complete as this one.*

6. *Credit reports do not report ratings. That is still the job of the credit manager, who has to form his own opinion.*

7. *Care should be taken concerning any adverse comments that are reported and can only be considered valid if supported by documents available to the public, such as court records.*

ORANGE COUNTY CREDIT BUREAU, INC.
999 OFFICE DRIVE
CULVER, IA 50701

SPECIAL REPORT 10/20/XX
For #1225

SUBJECT: Doe, John   (Mary A.)   SS# 113 18 7948
123 Elm St.   DOB 3/23/58
Orange, Iowa 50701

IDENTITY: Subject is married for about 10 years and
has 2 dependent children of school age.
Graduated University of Utah.

RESIDENTIAL HISTORY: Lives at above address for 7
years in home that he owns jointly with spouse. Previous address was a rented apartment at 777 Maple
St., Orange, UT for 3 years.

BUSINESS BACKGROUND: Currently employed by Pressed
Glass Corp., 111 Industrial Drive, Carmel, IA as a
Sales Manager for past 12 years. Reported annual
salary is $XX,XXX. Prior employment, Dixie Flag Co.
in similar capacity.

BANKING: Orange Natl. checking account in low 4 figures. Joint savings account in low 5 figures. Bank mortgage on above residence, remaining balance $23,000, monthly payments
$315 prompt.

LITIGATION: Clear

CREDIT HISTORY: Amex card since 1980. Joint Sears account maximum $1,500, payments satisfactory. GMAC
loan on late model car $4,000, payments prompt.

JH/jw

NOTICE The information obtained above was from
sources deemed to be reliable but for which there is
no guaranty as to accuracy. A condition of acceptance
of this report is that it is to be held in strictest
confidence except for any lawful requirements.

Using a Credit Report

Export Credit Guarantees Program

Comments

1. *To promote exports, a United States agency will guarantee the credit of foreign firms. Such guarantees remove the question of the creditworthiness of the foreign customer in consideration of the sale.*

2. *Any domestic exporter is eligible for the guarantee. Even payment for services can be guaranteed. A sole requirement is that products or services be of domestic origin.*

3. *The shipper is protected from a wide range of potential hazards including wars, civil commotion, etc.*

4. *The exporter may be required to carry a portion of the risk— from 10 to 30% depending on the type of customer and the nature of the transaction. Certain types of exports to certain types of foreign projects carry a lower exporter risk.*

1. *Scope.* U.S. exporters who sell capital goods abroad may have such credit protected for a period of from 180 days to five years. A U.S. commercial bank may finance such sales without recourse to the seller and can receive a guarantee from the U.S. Export–Import Bank. The guarantee covers the full term of hazards including war, political risks, as well as the usual commercial risks. A supplier may apply directly to the Eximbank for financing of a shipment after refusal by commercial banks.

2. *Eligible Companies.* Any corporation, individual or partnership doing business in the United States.

3. *Eligible Products.* Any product or service which is of U.S. origin. However, exceptions are made for products with foreign components depending on a number of factors.

4. *Transaction Limits.* No known minimum limits exist. Any transactions of $1,000,000 or more usually require particularly careful scrutiny. Contract price may include freight and insurance paid in U.S. dollars. Foreign currency payments are excluded.

5. *Cash Payment.* The foreign buyer must pay 20% of the contract price on or before delivery. Exceptions exist for a 15% cash payment.

6. *Exporter Retention.* Eximbank requires the exporter to carry a portion of the risk. Usually this is 10% of the financed portion, but may be as high as 20 or 30%, dependent on conditions.

7. *Promissory Notes.* The financed portion is represented by promissory notes payable in U.S. dollars at a specified U.S. bank in approximately equal installments not less frequent than semiannually. On an individual basis, the Eximbank will consider the use of drafts and a variety of terms depending on conditions.

8. *Guarantee Fee.* A flat is payable at the time of the drawdown on the commitment. The fee varies from $0.32 to $5.29 per $100 of the financed portion. The size of the fee is determined by the tenor of the promissory notes.

9. *Application.* Most U.S. commercial banks are familiar with export credit guarantee programs and their procedures. They can assist the exporter in the completion of the varied forms and provide technical advice to their customers.

Export Credit Guarantees Program

Chapter 4

Resolving Special Situations

A popular misconception is that the credit manager's function is to collect from delinquent debtors. In reality, a credit professional handles a variety of problems in the average day, including:

- Collection problems of varying degrees of severity.
- Making decisions about whether to release orders pending for customers.
- Reviewing applicants for open account credit terms.
- Dealing with irate customers.
- Negotiating with significantly delinquent accounts.
- Doing financial statement analysis.
- Notifying customers and sales about credit holds.

Security for Creditors

In a perfect world, trade creditors would be secured creditors. However, because of the competitive nature of business, there is a limit to the credit manager's ability to demand security or concessions from customers if other companies are not.

Without exception, when additional assurance of payment is necessary, it should be requested before the product in question is shipped. After title to the product has passed from the seller to the buyer, it is almost impossible to obtain concessions from the debtor.

Unsecured notes or postdated checks are no more than proof of the indebtedness. If the account wishes to ignore the due dates, the creditor still has the same collection problem. However, they are more of a lever in the collection effort.

Lately, an old tool, the seller's lien, is becoming more popular in many industries. Typically, the buyer of the merchandise has to agree that title is vested in the seller until the payment for the merchandise is made. This restricts the buyer-debtor to some degree as he cannot give good title upon resale of the merchandise to someone else.

Using Consignments

A consignment shipment requires that all of the elements of ownership are still vested in the shipper. While the shipment has been made, a sale has not been consummated. Usually, there is a requirement that consigned merchandise cannot be commingled with other inventory of the consignee.

The use of consignments places inventory at wide distribution points. Depending on the consignment agreement, when a customer of the consignee wishes to buy some of the material, it is sold to the consignee for resale.

From a working capital point of view, the use of consignments *increases inventory levels,* but keeps accounts *receivables at a lower level.*

In consignment arrangement, controls are important. The consignor must receive periodic inventory reports and have the ability to occasionally check the reports against physical inventories on hand. Negative differences should be reconcilable or be charged to the consignee.

Letters of Credit

With the growth of international trade has come a collateral rise in the use of *letters of credit* (L/Cs) by U.S. companies to safeguard their sales to foreign companies. The issuance of a letter of credit is not a guaranty of payment. An L/C is a mechanism for payment. Getting paid is largely a function of the seller's ability to conform to the terms and conditions specified in the L/C.

The actual procedure requires that the buyer and seller come to an agreement on the sale transaction pending the issuance of a letter of credit. The buyer submits an application for the L/C to his bank. The issuing bank reviews the creditworthiness of the buyer-applicant. The bank may have a secured interest in the material. Upon L/C issuance, the buyer's bank notifies the seller (beneficiary) or the beneficiary's bank if required to do so. The seller delivers the material to a freight carrier and obtains bills of lading and other documentation. The documents are forwarded to the issuing bank for examination. If all of the documents are satisfactory, the cash is remitted to the seller's bank.

Guaranties

The use of a guaranty is appropriate when a debtor or applicant is not sufficiently creditworthy to justify the credit limit and credit terms requested. A guarantor is found, typically an individual or corporation associated with the uncreditworthy debtor. That guarantor signs a contract in which the guarantor unconditionally agrees to pay the obligation of the debtor in the event the debtor company defaults on payment for any reason.

An iron-clad rule relates to the use of guaranties: Creditors must verify the creditworthiness of the guarantor as closely as they do the original customer or applicant. Otherwise, the creditor may not be reducing or controlling credit risk by getting a signed guaranty. A guaranty is valuable only if the guarantor is creditworthy.

Joint Guaranties

If the guarantor is an individual, ask that both the individual and his or her spouse sign the guaranty. In many states, community property laws and other laws make it difficult to collect from one spouse without a guaranty signed by the other. Joint guaranties should state that the parties are jointly and severally liable for the debt in the event the debtor (the customer or applicant) defaults.

Corporate Guaranties

Sometimes a corporation is not creditworthy, but it is an affiliate or a subsidiary of a corporation that is creditworthy.

In this situation, credit professionals can ask the creditworthy company to sign a contract called an *intercorporate guaranty*. Similar to a personal guaranty, an intercorporate guaranty *adds* rather than *substitutes* the creditworthiness of the guarantor to that of the debtor.

Promissory Note—Payable in Installments

Comments

1. *A local legal stationery store may have preprinted forms that conform to the requirements of state or local law.*

2. *Obtaining a verbal promise to pay from a delinquent debtor is not as psychologically or legally binding as a written commitment. A promissory note is proof of indebtedness.*

3. *Getting a debtor to sign a promissory note after shipment is difficult. Often, debtors will sign if they are offered additional open account shipments as an inducement.*

4. *Another reason debtors agree to sign is that creditors some-times offer this ultimatum: Sign a promissory note as a gesture of goodwill and a demonstration of your intention to retire the past due balance. If you do not, we will assume you do not intend to pay the balance due and will refer your account to a third party (a lawyer or to a collection agency) to enforce our legal right to payment.*

5. *A benefit of the promissory note over an open account debt is that it is frequently easier to discount or market a note.*

6. *The note can be guaranteed. See page 133 for an illustrated note guaranty.*

PROMISSORY NOTE

$_____   Date: _____

    FOR VALUE RECEIVED, _____ of _____ (Maker) hereby unconditionally promises to pay by this promissory note to the order of _____ located at _____ the principal sum of _____ dollars ($_____) in installments as hereinafter provided and to pay interest concurrently with each payment of principal at the rate of _____ percent (____%) per annum on the unpaid principal balance hereof from time to time outstanding.

    The principal hereof shall be paid in _____ (_____) installments, the first of which shall be in the sum of _____ dollars ($_____) and shall be due and _____ 19__. The remaining installments shall each be in the sum of _____ dollars ($_____) and shall be due and payable monthly thereafter.

    Upon default in the prompt and full payment of any installment of principal or interest on this promissory note, the entire unpaid principal hereof and interest thereon to the date of payment shall immediately become due and payable at the option and upon demand of the holder hereof.

    Diligence, presentment, demand, protest or notice of non-payment or dishonor with respect to this promissory note are hereby waived.

    The failure of the holder hereof to exercise any of its rights hereunder in any instance shall not constitute a waiver thereof in that or any other instance.

               Maker _____

                   By _____

             Title _____

Promissory Note—Payable in Installments

The Apology Letter

Comments

1. *No matter how careful and diligent credit department personnel are, mistakes will happen.*

2. *When the credit department finds that it has made a mistake, the credit manager should apologize to the customer on behalf of the credit department and the company. That apology should be sent promptly, and it should be sincere.*

3. *The salesperson should be sent a copy of the letter to assist in smoothing any ruffled feathers.*

4. *The credit department also has an obligation to take any steps necessary and reasonable to ensure that the problem does not recur. Most often, human error results from inadequate training or rushing.*

5. *The account of the debtor involved should be flagged by the credit department for special care and attention. The only thing worse than making a mistake is compounding the problem with another error.*

[date]
[customer name]
[address]

Attention: Herbert Mallary
          [title]

Dear Mr. Mallary:

You are absolutely right, and we were completely wrong! Your check number 5883 for $843.25 dated March 3rd was in fact received and deposited last week by us.

We have been training some new people in our accounts receivable department, and one of them clearly made a serious mistake. I want you to know that I am truly sorry for any inconvenience this may have caused.

I have flagged your account so that our accounting group gives it special care and attention. I will make certain we have our facts straight in the future before any calls are made.

Again, I am sorry we made this error, and I regret the fact that you were contacted for payment of a balance that was already paid.

Please call me at (800) XXX-XXXX if you have any questions or comments.

Thank you.

Sincerely,

Michael O'Rourke
Area Credit Manager
[creditor company name]

cc: sales manager
    salesperson
    credit file

The Apology Letter

Promissory Notes and Personal Guaranties

Comments

1. *See the promissory note on page 133. Often, promissory notes are required from debtor corporations. Promissory Notes from corporations are strengthened if the signer also personally guaranties the obligation.*

2. *The guaranty specifically identifies the note that is being guarantied.*

3. *The guarantor, by signing the guaranty, waives most defenses for nonpayment.*

4. *The purpose of having a note guarantied is that the notemaker may have insufficient assets in the event of default.*

5. *It is useful to have notes that are executed by corporations, whether of limited resources or not, to be* guaranteed by one or more of the principals.

6. *Guaranties that are revocable are pointless if the revocation be made retractive. Normally, guarantees are written so that the guarantor cannot make the revocation retroactive.*

G U A R A N T Y

FOR VALUE RECEIVED, the undersigned guar-antor, hereby unconditionally guaranties the prompt payment of principal and interest on a promissory note dated _____ in the amount of _____ dollars ($_____) of _____ (Maker) when and as due in accordance with its terms.

Further, the undersigned guarantor, here-by waives diligence, demand, protest, or no-tice of any kind whatsoever, as well as any requirement that the holder of said promis-sory note exhaust any right or take any ac-tion against the maker of said promissory note and hereby consents to any extension of time or renewal thereof.

This guaranty is irrevocable.

Date _____   Guarantor _____

By _____

Title _____

Promissory Note—Guaranty

Addressing Missed Payments on a Note

Comments

1. *Occasionally, a creditor will allow a debtor to convert an account payable into a note payable. This is normally done to allow the debtor more time to retire a past-due balance.*

2. *Missing a payment on a note payable is more serious than paying an invoice late.*

3. *The creditor should protest the late payment to the president of the debtor company or to whoever signed the note.*

4. *The letter should demand immediate payment. If the creditor is also selling on open account terms, the debtor should normally be told that account is on hold until payment on the note is received.*

5. *A follow-up call should be made in five working days if payment is not received.*

6. *The salesperson should be copied on this type of letter since it contains a credit hold notice.*

[date]
[customer name]
[address]

Attention: William Gennip
            [title]

Dear Mr. Gennip:

We did not receive payment last month of $1,800 against the outstanding note payable. As you know, our contract calls for monthly payments to be received by us on or before the 15th of each month.

At this point, we are concerned. Please call me to discuss payment status at (800) XXX-XXXX.

Until payment is received, any orders placed on your open account with us will be on credit hold.

Thank you for your prompt reply.

Sincerely,

Steve Posner
Credit Manager
[creditor company name]

cc: salesperson
    sales manager
    correspondence file

Letter to Address Missed Payments on a Note

Completed Trade Acceptances

Comments

1. *A trade acceptance, executed by the debtor, on the face or upon the reverse, can be presented to the debtor's bank for payment. The use of trade acceptance for domestic sales in the Unites States is uncommon.*

2. *If the account has the available cash, the acceptance will be honored at maturity.*

3. *Trade acceptances can be marketed and discounted depending on the credit of the debtor. Assuming good credit, the seller or shipper's bank would normally discount the acceptance.*

4. *The usual procedure is for the creditor (shipper) to prepare the acceptance and forward it to the customer for execution of the acceptance. The acceptance is returned to the creditor. Before the maturity date, the creditor sends the acceptance to the customer's bank.*

5. *In the illustration, the acceptance was accepted (executed) by the Texas Corporation on January 11th for presentation to the Miami National Bank on April 15th (maturity).*

6. *After January 11th, but prior to April 15th, the seller corporation could have discounted the acceptance at their own bank.*

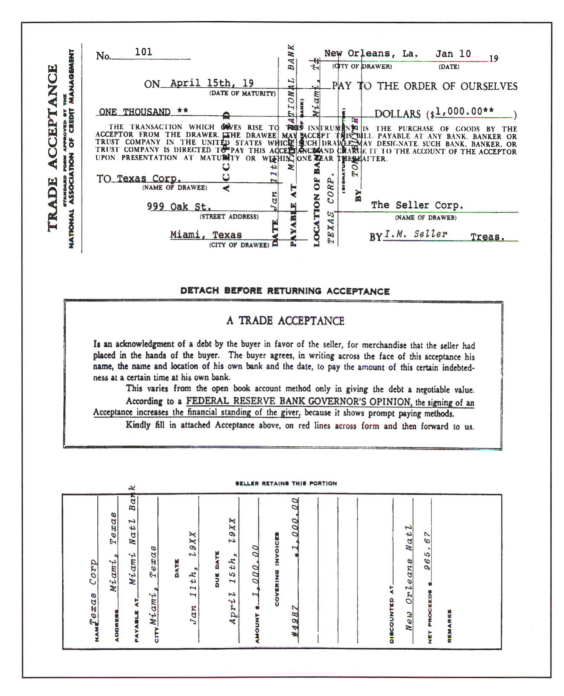

Completed Trade Acceptance

Memo to Sales Explaining a Credit Hold

Comments

1. *Salespeople should be notified as soon as possible of credit hold decisions.*

2. *Preferably, the salesperson should be informed about the credit hold before the customer.*

3. *Even if the salesperson is notified by phone or in person, it might be appropriate to confirm the credit hold in writing. Salespeople tend to develop selective amnesia: Without a written record the credit professional could be accused of not notifying the Sales Department in a timely manner.*

4. *An internal memo or e-mail need not be overly wordy or apologetic about the credit hold. A simple statement of the facts will suffice.*

5. *A copy of the memo or e-mail should be kept on file.*

INTERNAL MEMO

[date]

TO: David Strangeway

FROM: Judy Lewis

SUBJECT: Able Ink Company

David:

The attached letter will be mailed to the Able Company today. This account will remain on credit hold until the customer pays the $843.25 now seriously delinquent.

If payment is not made soon, I will have no choice but to consider reducing or withdrawing the open account all together.

Please call me if you have any questions.

Thanks.

Judy

Memo to Sales Explaining a Credit Hold

Low Credit—Guaranty Requested

Comments

1. *Thank the customer for the initial order.*

2. *Adverse comments about the potential customer are excluded from the letter. No reference is directly made regarding any poor credit standing.*

3. *"Standard form"* implies *that there is nothing unusual about the request.*

4. *A return envelope will help insure a more prompt return. Preprinted reply envelopes further indicate that the practice is common.*

5. *By a copy of the letter, the sales representative is notified of the situation, and should normally contact the applicant to make certain the personal guaranty is signed and returned promptly.*

[date]
[applicant company name]
[address]

Attention: Paul Phillips
          [title]

Dear Mr. Phillips:

Thank you for your initial order. A review of our credit records indicates that we would require a personal guaranty from you in order to consider releasing the order pending on open account terms to your company. Enclosed, you will find our standard form, along with a stamped and self-addressed envelope.

If you have any questions about this request or the guaranty, please call me at (800) XXX-XXXX. Otherwise, please arrange for your signature on this document to be notarized, and return this agreement to me at your earliest opportunity.

Thank you.

Sincerely,

Harry Oliver
Credit Director
[creditor company name]

enc.

cc: sales representative
    file

Letter for Low Credit—Guaranty Requested

Individual Personal Guaranty

Comments

1. *This guaranty is not given as an officer of the corporation.*

2. *See the personal guaranty illustrated on page 143.*

3. *The guaranty is irrevocable. Therefore, after shipment of the material, a revocation is of no effect.*

4. *The guarantor subrogates any claim that it may have against the debtor to the claim of the creditor.*

5. *Common defenses and jury trial are waived.*

6. *Note that the guaranty is without limit and is applicable to renewals of extensions of credit.*

7. *Upon default of any payments, the creditor can call upon the guarantor to make payments that are required.*

8. *The creditworthiness of the guarantor should be checked by the credit department before any shipments are made under this credit arrangement.*

Date _____

I, _____, residing at
_____ for good and valuable consideration do hereby personally guaranty and
promise to pay any obligation to [*creditor name*]
on demand any indebtedness of [*debtor name*] to
[*creditor name*] which may become due.

This guaranty shall be a continuing and irrevocable guaranty and indemnity to [*creditor name*].
Further I hereby subrogate any indebtedness of
[*debtor corporation name*] which it may have to
me to the indebtedness of [*creditor company
name*].

I do hereby wave notice of default, nonpayment
and notice thereof, and to a jury trial, and I
consent to all renewals of extension of credit.
Further, I agree that disputes over this guaranty are to be governed under the laws of the
state of _____ and that any litigation shall
be adjudicated in the county of _____,
state of _____ without regard to conflict of
jurisdiction.

Signature of Guarantor _____

Signature of Spouse _____

Notary Seal

Date: _____

Signature of Notary: _____

Personal Guaranty

Blanket Individual Personal Guaranty

1. This guaranty form is executed by someone who has an interest in the debtor.

2. See the personal guaranty illustrated on page 143.

3. The debt is not subrogated to any claims of the guarantor against the debtor as is the case of the guaranty illustrated on page 143.

4. A waiver of jury trial could be included in the guaranty. This will reduce collection costs and time. Similarly, a clause could be inserted calling for disputes to be submitted to binding arbitration in order to expedite the collection and recovery process.

5. No limit is set upon the amount of the guaranty.

6. The method of terminating the guaranty is explained in detail to prevent misunderstandings and problems.

Date _____, 19___

I, _____, residing at _____
for and in consideration of your extending credit at
my request to [*debtor company name and address*]
(herein after referred to as the "Company"), of which
I am _____,
            (Title)

hereby personally guarantee to you the payment of any
obligation of the Company. I hereby agree to bind myself and my heirs to pay you on demand any sum which
may become due to you by the Company whenever the
Company shall fail to pay the same.

It is understood that this guaranty shall be a continuing and irrevocable guaranty and indemnity for
such indebtedness of the company.

It is agreed that revocation of this guaranty may
only be made in writing. Such revocation may not be
made retroactive. Notice must be in the form of a
registered letter delivered to and signed by an officer of this Company. Termination of this guaranty
shall be effective upon receipt of such notification.

I do hereby waive notice of default, nonpayment and
notice thereof, and to consent to any notification or
renewal of the credit agreement hereby agreed.

_____   _____
Signature of Guarantor   Spouse's Signature

_____   _____
Date   Date

Notary Seal

Date: _____

Signature of Notary: _____

Individual Personal Guaranty

Limited Creditworthiness—Joint Guaranty Requested

Comments

1. *As always, thank the customer for the order.*

2. *No adverse comments are made about the credit standing of the debtor.*

3. *Both husband and wife are asked to execute the guaranty.*

4. *The letter makes the request seem like a normal procedure. Inclusion of a reply envelope makes the situation appear more normal.*

5. *The sales representative should be encouraged to help expedite the request for a signed personal guaranty.*

6. *The commingling of assets between spouses require the jointly executed guaranty. Frequently, collection is made easier when the spouse who is not active in the business is requested to make good under the guaranty.*

```
[date]
[applicant name]
[address]

Attention: Bill Bickoff
          [title]
```

Dear Mr. Bickoff:

Thank you for your first order and for your confidence in our company and our products. A review of the credit information for your company indicates we will require a joint personal guaranty from you and your spouse before we can process the order pending.

Enclosed you will find a stamped, self-addressed envelope for your convenience in returning the attached guaranty.

We look forward to your prompt reply.

Sincerely,

Martha Davies
Credit Manager
[creditor company name]

enc.

cc: sales representative
    file

Letter for Limited Creditworthiness— Joint Guaranty Requested

Threat to Notify Guarantor of Delinquency

Comments

1. *Occasionally, trade creditors will receive the personal guaranty of a third party guarantor and, on the basis of that additional assurance of payment, will extend open account credit terms to a debtor company.*

2. *There is a greater-than-normal likelihood that the debtor will at some point default on their open account obligation. (If that were not the case, the creditor would not have required a third party guaranty to begin with.)*

3. *It is appropriate to warn the debtor company that you intend to notify the guarantor if payment is not received within a specified time frame.*

4. *It would certainly be better for all parties concerned if the guarantor were not contacted—and the letter should make this point clearly and plainly.*

5. *The salesperson can be copied on this letter as a courtesy.*

[date]
[customer name]
[address]

Attention: Larry Friend
          [title]

Dear Mr. Friend:

Your account is seriously delinquent, and you have not responded to my calls and letters. As you may recall, before we established an open account for your company we received a personal guaranty from John Walker—one of your investors.

If payment is not received by [date], I will have no alternative but to contact Mr. Walker to demand payment under the terms of the personal guaranty. I dislike having to involve a third party in this matter, and I am convinced that it would be in all of our best interests if we did not need to do so.

We must have your payment by the above date to prevent this action. I urge you to give this matter your immediate attention.

Sincerely,

Mark Matrese
National Credit Manager
[creditor company name]

cc: salesperson
    credit file
    file

Letter for Threat to Notify Guarantor of Delinquency

Joint Personal Guaranty

Comments

1. This form of guaranty is not as an officer of the debtor company.

2. See the joint personal guaranty illustrated on page 151.

3. A guaranty that is revocable is of little or no value to a creditor. Only an irrevocable guaranty should be accepted.

4. Note that the guarantors subrogate any claim that they may have against the debtor.

5. A number of common defenses and right to a jury trial are waived.

6. The guaranty has no limit with respect to amount or duration of time.

7. The joint guaranty can be used for partners, investors or spouses.

8. The credit department must always evaluate the creditworthiness of the guarantor before shipping against a personal guaranty. Otherwise, the personal guaranty might be worthless.

9. A claim against the guarantors can be made either *jointly or separately.*

Date: _____, 19____

We, _____, and _____ residing at _____ and _____ respectively for good and valuable consideration including the extension of credit which we hereby acknowledge as having been received do hereby personally, jointly and severally, guarantee and promise to pay any obligation to [*creditor name and address*] on demand for any indebtedness of [*debtor name and address*] to [*creditor name*] which may become due.

This guaranty shall be a continuing and irrevocable guaranty and indemnity to [*creditor name*].

Furthermore, we jointly and severally, hereby subrogate any indebtedness of [*debtor name*] which it may have to us to the indebtedness of [*creditor name*].

We hereby waive notice of default, nonpayment and notice thereof and to jury trial and consent to all renewals of extension of credit.

Further, we agree to pay all reasonable attorneys costs and court costs that may be necessary to enforce this guaranty. We agree that any litigation involving this guaranty shall be adjudicated in courts in the County of _____, State of _____ irrespective of any disputes of jurisdiction.

Signature of Guarantor: _____

Signature of Guarantor: _____

Witnessed by: _____

Address of Witness: _____

Joint Personal Guaranty

Blanket Joint Personal Guaranty

Comments

1. *This form is for those who are officers of the potential customer (debtor).*

2. *See the joint personal guaranty illustrated on page 153 for comparison.*

3. *The guaranty is irrevocable which prevents subsequent changes of mind.*

4. *This form does* not *contain any provision with regard to subrogation of amounts owed to the guarantors.*

5. *While a number of rights are waived, the right to trial by jury is not. Creditors seeking judgments in jury trials typically increased collection effort, legal costs and delays experience.*

6. *Reference is made to a present credit agreement which may foreclose the use of extensions of credit.*

7. *Joint or separate court actions can be taken against the guarantors.*

8. *The creditworthiness of the guarantors as well as the debtor company should be evaluated when a guaranty is sought. Both the guarantors and the customers are jointly and severally liable for the entire obligation.*

JOINT PERSONAL GUARANTY

DATE _____19_____

We,_____ and _____, spouse,

residing at _____, for and in consideration of

your extending at our request credit to _____
_____
(Name of Company)

(hereinafter referred to as the "Company"), of which _____
_____
(Name)

is _____, hereby personally guarantee to you the pay-
_____
(Title)

ment at _____ in the State of _____

of any obligation of the Company and we hereby agree to bind ourselves to pay you on

demand any sum which may become due to you by the Company whenever the

Company shall fail to pay the same. If is understood that this guaranty shall be a

continuing and irrevocable guaranty and indemnity for such indebtedness of the

Company. We do hereby waive notice of default, non-payment and notice thereof and

consent to any modification or renewal of the credit agreement hereby guaranteed.

Signature _____

Signature _____

Witness: _____

Address _____

Blanket Joint Personal Guaranty

Personal Guaranty Withdrawn—Notice Sent That Credit Line Is to Be Reduced or Withdrawn

Comments

1. *As a condition for extending open account terms, some creditors require personal guaranties from their corporate customers.*

2. *Occasionally, a guarantor will want to revoke their guaranty.*

3. *When this occurs, the creditor must carefully reevaluate the credit risk. If the risk proves to be too high, the creditor must reduce or withdraw the debtor company's open account terms.*

4. *Notification of the decision to do so should be made in writing. The guarantor should be copied on the letter to the debtor company.*

5. *The salesperson needs to be notified of this decision also.*

[date]
[customer name]
[address]

Attention: Mary Forest
          [title]

Dear Ms. Forest:

As you may recall, before we established an open account for your company we requested and received a personal guaranty from Tim Brown. We recently received notice from Mr. Brown that he was withdrawing his personal guaranty effective [date].

We have evaluated your account with us in light of this decision by Mr. Brown. After careful consideration, I have decided that it is necessary to reduce your company's credit limit to $XX,XXX effective immediately.

Feel free to call me at (800) XXX-XXXX if you have any questions or concerns.

Thank you.

Sincerely,

Charles Winston
Assistant Credit Manager
[creditor company name]

cc: Tim Brown
    salesperson
    credit file

Letter for Personal Guaranty Withdrawn—Notice Sent That Credit Line Is to Be Reduced or Withdrawn

Financing Statement—The UCC-1

Comments

1. *States might have slightly different UCC-1 form layouts and processing requirements.*

2. *This form is useful for secured credit, but not for open account shipments where there is no seller's lien.*

3. *The UCC-1 form must be filed (perfected) in the state in which the goods or equipment is kept or located.*

4. *The Uniform Commercial Code, as adopted in each individual state, indicates the importance of the filing.*

5. *The filing is notice to other possible creditors of the lien held by the seller. It also provides a proof in court of the security interest.*

6. *The filing fee is a small price to pay for the opportunity to become a secured creditor.*

77336

IMPORTANT – READ INSTRUCTIONS ON BACK BEFORE FILLING OUT FORM – **DO NOT DETACH STUB**

THIS SPACE FOR USE OF FILING OFFICER

FINANCING STATEMENT – FOLLOW INSTRUCTIONS CAREFULLY
This Financing Statement is presented for filing pursuant to the Uniform Commercial Code and will remain effective, with certain exceptions, for 5 years from date of filing.

A. NAME & TEL. # OF CONTACT AT FILER (optional)	B. FILING OFFICE ACCT. # (optional)

C. RETURN COPY TO: (Name and Mailing Address)

D. OPTIONAL DESIGNATION [if applicable]: ☐ LESSOR/LESSEE ☐ CONSIGNOR/CONSIGNEE ☐ NON-UCC FILING

1. DEBTOR'S EXACT FULL LEGAL NAME - insert only one debtor name (1a or 1b)

1a. ENTITY'S NAME					
OR 1b. INDIVIDUAL'S LAST NAME		FIRST NAME	MIDDLE NAME		SUFFIX
1c. MAILING ADDRESS		CITY	STATE	COUNTRY	POSTAL CODE

1d. S.S. OR TAX I.D.#	OPTIONAL ADD'NL INFO RE ENTITY DEBTOR	1e. TYPE OF ENTITY	1f. ENTITY'S STATE OR COUNTRY OF ORGANIZATION	1g. ENTITY'S ORGANIZATIONAL I.D.#, if any ☐ NONE

2. ADDITIONAL DEBTOR'S EXACT FULL LEGAL NAME - insert only one debtor name (2a or 2b)

2a. ENTITY'S NAME					
OR 2b. INDIVIDUAL'S LAST NAME		FIRST NAME	MIDDLE NAME		SUFFIX
2c. MAILING ADDRESS		CITY	STATE	COUNTRY	POSTAL CODE

2d. S.S. OR TAX I.D.#	OPTIONAL ADD'NL INFO RE ENTITY DEBTOR	2e. TYPE OF ENTITY	2f. ENTITY'S STATE OR COUNTRY OF ORGANIZATION	2g. ENTITY'S ORGANIZATIONAL I.D.#, if any ☐ NONE

3. SECURED PARTY'S (ORIGINAL S/P or ITS TOTAL ASSIGNEE) EXACT FULL LEGAL NAME - insert only one secured party name (3a or 3b)

3a. ENTITY'S NAME					
OR 3b. INDIVIDUAL'S LAST NAME		FIRST NAME	MIDDLE NAME		SUFFIX
3c. MAILING ADDRESS		CITY	STATE	COUNTRY	POSTAL CODE

4. This FINANCING STATEMENT covers the following types or items of property:

5. CHECK BOX [if applicable]	☐ This FINANCING STATEMENT is signed by the Secured Party instead of the Debtor to perfect a security interest (a) in collateral already subject to a security interest in another jurisdiction when it was brought into this state, or when the debtor's location was changed to this state, or (b) in accordance with other statutory provisions [additional data may be required]	7. If filed in Florida (check one) ☐ Documentary stamp tax paid ☐ Documentary stamp tax not applicable

6. REQUIRED SIGNATURE(S)

8. ☐ This FINANCING STATEMENT is to be filed [for record] (or recorded) in the REAL ESTATE RECORDS Attach Addendum [if applicable]

9. Check to REQUEST SEARCH CERTIFICATE(S) on Debtor(s) [ADDITIONAL FEE] (optional) ☐ All Debtors ☐ Debtor 1 ☐ Debtor 2

(1) FILING OFFICER COPY

Financing Statement—The UCC-1

Financing Statement—The UCC in California

Comments

1. *To create a security interest, a creditor must simply arrange for a debtor to pledge assets as security against debts outstanding.*

2. *The pledge of assets must be made in writing.*

3. *The trouble is that other creditors may also have received as collateral the pledge of the same asset.*

4. *The Uniform Commercial Code (UCC) deals with this problem by creating a mechanism to identify which creditor's claim is superior to another's.*

5. *To "perfect" a security interest in the property of the debtor, the creditor has to file a financing statement, normally with an agency of the state government in the state in which the asset is located.*

6. *The effect of this financing statement is to put the notice of lien on official record. Any subsequent potential creditor can then examine the public records to determine if prior liens exist on the debtor's property or asset.*

7. *The earliest properly filed lien notice takes precedence.*

8. *See the UCC-1 form on the opposite page.*

STATE OF CALIFORNIA
UNIFORM COMMERCIAL CODE--FINANCING STATEMENT CHANGE--FORM UCC-2
IMPORTANT--Read Instructions on back before completing form

7 67775 82902 0

This **STATEMENT** is presented for filing pursuant to the California Uniform Commercial Code

1. FILE NO. OF ORIG. FINANCING STATEMENT	1A. DATE OF FILING OF ORIG. FINANCING STATEMENT	1B. DATE OF ORIG. FINANCING STATEMENT	1C. PLACE OF FILING ORIG. FINANCING STATEMENT

2. DEBTOR (LAST NAME FIRST)		2A. SOCIAL SECURITY NO., FEDERAL TAX NO.

2B. MAILING ADDRESS	2C. CITY, STATE	2D. ZIP CODE

3. ADDITIONAL DEBTOR (IF ANY) (LAST NAME FIRST)		3A. SOCIAL SECURITY OR FEDERAL TAX NO.

3B. MAILING ADDRESS	3C. CITY, STATE	3D. ZIP CODE

4. SECURED PARTY		4A. SOCIAL SECURITY NO., FEDERAL TAX NO. OR BANK TRANSIT AND A.B.A. NO.
NAME		
MAILING ADDRESS		
CITY	STATE	ZIP CODE

5. ASSIGNEE OF SECURED PARTY (IF ANY)		5A. SOCIAL SECURITY NO., FEDERAL TAX NO. OR BANK TRANSIT AND A.B.A. NO.
NAME		
MAILING ADDRESS		
CITY	STATE	ZIP CODE

6.

A. ☐ CONTINUATION—The original Financing Statement between the foregoing Debtor and Secured Party bearing the file number and date shown above is continued. If collateral is crops or timber, check here ☐ and insert description of real property on which growing or to be grown in Item 7 below.

B. ☐ RELEASE—From the collateral described in the Financing Statement bearing the file number shown above, the Secured Party releases the collateral described in Item 7 below.

C. ☐ ASSIGNMENT—The Secured Party certifies that the Secured Party has assigned to the Assignee above named, all the Secured Party's rights under the Financing Statement bearing the file number shown above in the collateral described in Item 7 below.

D. ☐ TERMINATION—The Secured Party certifies that the Secured Party no longer claims a security interest under the Financing Statement bearing the file number shown above.

E. ☐ AMENDMENT—The Financing Statement bearing the file number shown above is amended as set forth in Item 7 below. (Signature of Debtor required on all amendments.)

F. ☐ OTHER

7.

8.

(Date)_____19_____

By:_____
    SIGNATURE(S) OF DEBTOR(S)   (TITLE)

By:_____
    SIGNATURE(S) OF SECURED PARTY(IES)   (TITLE)

CODE
1
2
3
4
5
6
7
8
9

9. This Space for Use of Filing Officer (Date, Time, Filing Office)

10. **Return Copy to**

NAME
ADDRESS
CITY AND
STATE

UNIFORM COMMERCIAL CODE—FORM UCC-2

(1) FILING OFFICER COPY   Approved by the Secretary of State

Financing Statement—The UCC in California

Request for Information on Assignments
or Liens—UCC-11

Comments

1. *See page 161 for an illustration of the Uniform Commercial Code filing form.*

2. *This form is used for requesting either information or copies of filings.*

3. *This form may be useful in a credit investigation of a customer. However, as a practical matter, the Dun and Bradstreet Company credit reports contain information from a search of public filings and are sufficient for many credit purposes.*

4. *In most states, this form is submitted to the Secretary of State, along with the appropriate filing fee.*

5. *Copies of assignments typically require an additional fee be paid in advance. Most trade creditors are not particularly concerned about assignments.*

6. *The lower part of the UCC-11 form is to be completed by an official of the appropriate state office.*

STATE OF CALIFORNIA
UNIFORM COMMERCIAL CODE--REQUEST FOR INFORMATION OR COPIES--FORM UCC-3
IMPORTANT--Read Instructions on back before completing form

7 67775 82903 7

REQUEST FOR INFORMATION OR COPIES. Present in Duplicate to Filing Officer

1. INFORMATION REQUEST. Filing officer please furnish certificate showing whether there is on file any presently effective financing statement naming the Debtor listed below and any statement of assignment thereof, and if there is, giving the date and hour of filing of each such statement and the names and addresses of each secured party named therein.

1A.	DEBTOR (LAST NAME FIRST)		1B. SOC. SEC. OR FED. TAX NO.
1C.	MAILING ADDRESS	1D. CITY, STATE	1E. ZIP CODE

1F. Date_____19____ Signature of Requesting Party_____

2. CERTIFICATE:

FILE NUMBER	DATE AND HOUR OF FILING	NAME(S) AND ADDRESS(ES) OF SECURED PARTY(IES) AND ASSIGNEE(S), IF ANY

The undersigned filing officer hereby certifies that the above listing is a record of all presently effective financing statements and statements of assignment which name the above debtor and which are on file in my office as of_____19____ at_____ ___M.

_____19____
(DATE)

_____
(FILING OFFICER)

By:_____

3. COPY REQUEST. Filing officer please furnish_____copy(ies) of each page of the following statements concerning the debtors listed below ☐ Financing Statement ☐ Amendments ☐ Statements of Assignment ☐ Continuation Statements ☐ Statement of Release ☐ Termination Statement ☐ All Statements on file.

FILE NUMBER	DATE OF FILING	NAME(S) AND MAILING ADDRESS(ES) OF DEBTOR(S)	DEBTORS SOC. SEC. OR FED. TAX NO.

Date_____19____ Signature of Requesting Party_____

4. CERTIFICATE

The undersigned filing officer hereby certifies that the attached copies are true and exact copies of all statements requested above.

_____19____
(DATE)

_____
(FILING OFFICER)

By:_____

5. **Mail Information or Copies to**

NAME
MAILING
ADDRESS
CITY AND
STATE

UNIFORM COMMERCIAL CODE--FORM UCC-3

Request for Information on Assignments
or Liens—UCC-11

Confirmation Requests Using Business Reply Envelopes

Comments

1. *Outside auditors often request that confirmations of accounts receivable balances be received from debtors in connection with their annual audit of the creditor's books and records. Accounts receivable are often the largest asset of the creditor company.*

2. *The confirmation request on the opposite page is actually a business reply envelope.*

3. *A more typical form is described on pages 164–165.*

4. *While the confirmation is not normally used as a collection technique, differences between the creditor's records and those of the customer/debtor can be brought to light in this process.*

5. *Confirmation request may be sent by the internal audit staff or by the outside CPA firm.*

.............................19..........

TO...

....

....

We are auditing the books of our client...

as of the close of business..

In connection therewith, our records show a balance of $ ....

owed to our client by you.

Please inform us whether this balance is in agreement with your records. Indicate your answer below, sign and return this envelope to us as early as possible.

ANSWER: ☐ The balance shown is correct.
☐ The balance shown is NOT correct, and should be as follows:

....

Signed..

DO NOT WRITE IN THIS SPACE

Confirmation Request Using a Business Reply Envelope

Accounts Receivable Confirmation Request

Comments

1. *An important check of the internal controls of a company is the use of outside confirmation of the balances due from customers.*

2. *The form on the opposite page can be mailed with monthly statements or sent less frequently (for example, quarterly or even annually).*

3. *The accounts payable supervisor for the customer may review and take exception to the balance. Old outstanding items or differences may be reported to the auditors.*

4. *This form can be used by* either *an internal auditor* or *the public accounting firm.*

5. *The proper handling of the replies with respect to exceptions reported by customers can make the accounts receivable schedule and agings more accurate and reliable.*

6. *A business reply envelope addressed to the auditors will expedite reply processing.*

CONFIRMATION REQUEST

Our auditors are making an examination of our financial statements and for this purpose wish to obtain direct confirmation of your account with us. Please examine the accompanying statement carefully and either confirm its correctness, or report any differences to our auditors by completing and signing this form and returning it directly to our auditors in the enclosed stamped self-addressed envelope.

Our auditors will advise us of any discrepancy reported and the matter will have our prompt attention.

This is not a request for payment, and **remittances should not be made to the auditors.**

Your prompt attention to this request will be appreciated.

_____

No. _____

The balance of $_____ owing to the above named company at
_____ is correct except as noted below:

EXCEPTIONS: _____

_____

_____

_____

_____

_____

_____

Company

_____

Signature and Title

Date _____

Accounts Receivable Confirmation Request

Request for Invitation for a Credit Visit

Comments

1. *The letter should be addressed to a specific individual. Such person can either be in the customer's purchasing or financial department.*

2. *A brief explanation of the general purpose of the visit is appropriate. For example, the letter might indicate that the credit manager wishes to discuss the credit limit, or terms of sale, to review the customer's financial statements, or to discuss and resolve disputed items.*

3. *Generally speaking, credit managers should not make unscheduled visits. They tend to cause a good deal of concern on the part of the debtor, and they can damage the business relationship.*

4. *If the relationship has already been damaged by delays in payment, and assuming the debtor is not cooperating or returning calls, then a surprise visit might not be a bad idea.*

5. *Normally, the date and time for the meeting should be left up to the customer.*

6. *Some customers may request a reciprocal invitation to visit the supplier's facility. Creditors should be prepared to extend such an invitation.*

[date]
[customer name]
[address]

Attention: Rob Roe
            [title]

Dear Mr. Roe:

From time to time, I try to visit our key customers at their places of business. This allows me to get a first-hand view of how your business operates and to discuss certain issues that arise from time to time, such as your company's policy with respect to taking cash discounts on all invoices irrespective of when they are paid.

I would appreciate an invitation from you to visit your facility sometime next week. I would like to leave the time and date up to you.

Please call me at your convenience to discuss setting up an appointment. My telephone number is (800) XXX-XXXX.

Thank you.

Sincerely,

R. B. Reynolds
Credit Manager
[creditor company name]

cc: sales representative
    file

Letter to Request an Invitation for a Credit Visit

Requesting Financial Statements

Comments

1. *Requesting updated financial statements is a sensitive issue with some customers.*

2. *Credit professionals do not want to be overeager in their efforts to gather information about a customer. If the company does not share financial information with a credit bureau, however, it might be necessary to ask the customer directly for this information.*

3. *Some creditors give the debtor a lengthy explanation of their need for financial data.*

4. *Others simply assume the debtor is an intelligent business-person who probably does not want or need a detailed explanation about a request for current financial statements sent by a creditor.*

5. *The letter on the opposite page is deliberately brief and to the point.*

6. *It would be better if it were sent by mail than by fax. The letter itself should be sent to a decision maker, not to a clerk who might not have the authority to release financial statements.*

[date]
[customer name]
[address]

Attention: Robert Johnson
            [title]

Dear Mr. Johnson:

We periodically review our credit files on our active customers. When I reviewed your file, I noticed that the financial statements we have on file are more than two years old.

I would appreciate your sending me a current statement. It should help us to be more flexible in responding to your credit needs.

Thank you for your assistance.

Sincerely,

Ian Albright
District Credit Manager
[creditor company name]

cc: file
    credit file

Letter Requesting Financial Statements

Application and Agreement for Establishing an Irrevocable Letter of Credit

Comments

1. Many banks, particularly those with international trade departments, provide small booklets explaining the uses and benefits of letters of credit.

2. The basic process involves the customer going to its bank to establish a letter of credit. Upon issuance of the letter of credit, the bank substitutes its creditworthiness for that of the debtor company. Therefore, after issuance the creditor need not concern itself with the creditworthiness of the customer.

3. In the sample letter of credit on the opposite page, Japan Electronics Corporation can expect payment at sight (upon delivery of the specified documents to the issuing bank). The debtor and creditor might have agreed to terms such as 30 days or even 90 days or more after presentation of the documents to the issuing bank.

4. The matter of financing such payment is of concern between TV Importers and Bankers Trust Company.

5. The reverse of the application contains specific terms of the letter of credit.

IMPORTERS TRUST INC.
NEW YORK

APPLICATION AND AGREEMENT FOR IRREVOCABLE LETTER OF CREDIT
(PLEASE TYPE)

SHADED AREAS FOR BANK USE
• PROCEDURE: iip1
• ACCOUNT NO.:
04-999-123

DATE:
August 1st, 19XX

NOTIFY ——————

PLEASE FILL IN YOUR ACCOUNT NO. →

BENEFICIARY: (GIVE FULL NAME & ADDRESS)
Japan Electronics Corp.
100 Chome
Tokyo, Japan

← BENEFICIARY

7

BY: ☐ AIRMAIL (aml) ☐ CABLE (cab) ☒ AIRMAIL WITH PREADVICE BY CABLE (amc)
☐ AIRMAIL WITH PREADVICE BY PHONE (amp)

← CABLE CODE — — —

that you authorize them to value on yourselves (if in USA Dollars) or your correspondent (if in Foreign Currency) For:

ACCOUNT OF: (GIVE FULL NAME & ADDRESS, ZIP CODE)
TV Importers Inc.
123 Industrial Drive
Los Angeles, Calif.

ADVISING BANK
u / — — — / — — — —
c or o / — — — — — — — / — — — —
m / — — — — — — — / — — — —

NOT EXCEEDING: (AMOUNT)
FIFTY THOUSAND USD

NUMERIC AMOUNT:	BY THEIR DRAFTS AT:
$50,000.00	Sight

AMOUNT, CURRENCY — — —
TENOR
SHORT DESCRIPTION

ACCOMPANIED BY THE FOLLOWING INDICATED DOCUMENTS:

COVERING (SPECIFY COMMODITY, OMITTING DETAILS AS TO GRADE, QUALITY AND THE LIKE).

☒ COMMERCIAL INVOICE:
100 TV Sets model #475
240 TV Sets model #319

☒ COMPLETE SET OF CLEAN ON BOARD OCEAN BILLS OF LADING TO THE ORDER OF BANKERS TRUST COMPANY NOTIFY:

(NAME & ADDRESS OF NOTIFY PARTY)
AND SHOWING OUR L/C NO.

GIVE FULL NAME & ADDRESS INCLUDING ZIP CODE:
Fast Freight Forwarders Inc.
444 Harbor Drive
San Francisco, Calif

☒ SPECIAL CUSTOMS INVOICE

☒ INSURANCE POLICY OR CERTIFICATE COVERING MARINE INSURANCE ☒ AND WAR RISKS

☒ OTHER(S): 3 Originals of Statement of Country of Origin

SHIPMENT FROM:	SHIPMENT TO:
Osaka, Japan	Los Angeles, Calif
TRANSSHIPMENT PERMITTED ☐ YES ☒ NO	PARTIAL SHIPMENT PERMITTED ☐ YES ☒ NO
BILLS OF LADING — DATED NO LATER THAN	DRAFTS NEGOTIATED OR PRESENTED WITHIN 30 DAYS
August 31st	AFTER ISSUANCE DATE AS EVIDENCED BY THE SHIPPING
INSURANCE — TO BE EFFECTED BY:	DOCUMENTS BUT IN ANY EVENT NOT LATER THAN_____
Japan Electronics Corp.	
NEGOTIATING AND/OR DRAWEE BANK TO FORWARD ALL DOCUMENTS IN ONE AIR MAIL.	ALL NEGOTIATION CHARGES SHALL BE FOR THE BENEFICIARY'S ACCOUNT

SPECIAL INSTRUCTIONS:

If the credit is to be notified by Air Mail, you may forward original Letter of Credit directly to the beneficiary or to your Correspondent, at your option. (See "Special Instructions" for name of notifying bank, if any.)

We hereby certify that transactions in the merchandise covered by this application are not prohibited under the Foreign Assets Control Regulations of the United States Treasury Department and that any importation covered by this application conforms in every respect with all existing United States Government regulations.

In consideration of your opening, at our request, your Commercial Letter of Credit (hereinafter called the "Credit") substantially in accordance with the foregoing Application or as attached hereto, we hereby agree as follows:

**Application and Agreement for
Irrevocable Letter of Credit**

Prepayment Considerations

Comments

1. *For some industries, most notably the mail order business, prepayment before receipt of the merchandise may be the only safe way to sell to customers.*

2. *For some customers, especially customers who have never had trouble getting open account credit in the past, a request for prepayment may come as an unpleasant surprise.*

3. *There are some risks in the various prepayment methods. One that is notable is the possible bad check. A high credit risk account may have insufficient cash on hand to cover the check.*

4. *One of the biggest risks associated with COD shipment is the possibility that the customer may refuse the shipment resulting in the seller having to pay freight both out and back. Another risk is that the customer's check will not clear.*

5. *Another risk is that the merchandise in question could be lost or damaged in transit, either outbound or inbound.*

6. *Two of the safest methods of shipment are cash with the order or cash in advance. Under these terms, the creditor waits until the check clears before shipment is made.*

Prepayment Considerations

1. *Cash with order (CWO)*. The price of the order must be calculated and carefully compared to the payment received. Any difference must either be approved or resolved. Since cash with order is normally used only for marginal risks, the order should be held until the customer's check clears.

2. *Cash in advance (CIA)*. After receipt of the customer's order, it is priced and a check is requested prior to shipment. Questionable checks should await clearance before shipment. Freight and other charges should be included in the request for payment.

3. *Cash before delivery (CBD)*. Under these terms, the shipment is prepared, packaged and readied for shipment but is held pending the receipt of the remittance. If the remittance is not forthcoming, the seller loses his or her cost of shipment preparation.

4. *Cash on delivery (COD)*. The merchandise is shipped, but it is not released to the customer until the trucker receives payment in full. If a COD shipment is not accepted or paid for by the buyer, the seller can lose fright charges in both directions, packing costs, COD fees and suffer the possible deterioration of the merchandise. Such risks are not profitable to many industries and can only be considered in situations where the merchandise can readily be sold to another party.

5. *Sight draft*. Under such an arrangement, a bill of lading accompanied by an invoice and a sight draft drawn on the buyer is forwarded by the seller or his or her bank to the customer's bank. Upon the honoring of the draft, the shipment can be released to the customer. If the draft is not honored, the seller loses freight in both directions and other costs.

Consignment Considerations

Comments

1. *An alternative to shipping material on open account is to ship the material to the customer with title to the material being still vested in the seller.*

2. *Under such arrangements, the customer must pay for the material as it is used or sold.*

3. *Unless specified otherwise, using it (conversion) requires the customer to pay for the material according to the terms of the consignment agreement. With exceptions, conversions of the consigned material without the owner's consent may be a violation of law in certain states.*

4. *A resale of material that the customer does not own may be voidable by the owner of the material unless the consignment agreement states otherwise. In such event, the owner of the material* may *have a lien against the receivable from the third party.*

5. *Consignments are widely used in distributor types of operations where the manufacturer wishes the distributor to have a wide variety of inventory available to third parties but the distributor cannot carry a large inventory.*

Consignment Considerations

1. *Title*. The right of ownership remains with the seller. The material cannot be resold or pledged to another without payment or settlement with the seller. Nor can such material be converted into another form without the seller's permission.

2. *Insurance*. The seller should make certain it has sufficient insurance to cover the consigned merchandise. The seller should also make certain that their insurance covers consigned merchandise not in the seller's physical possession. The other alternative is to require the buyer to provide insurance for the consigned products.

3. *Agreement*. Care should be taken in the drawing of a consignment contract. Some courts have regarded such agreements as unrecorded conditional sales contracts. In such event, the material may belong to the other party.

4. *Segregation*. It would be desirable for the consigned material to be segregated and carefully labeled as belonging to the seller.

5. *Funds*. Proceeds from the sale of consigned merchandise must be segregated from other funds received by the debtor for the protection of the consignor/seller.

6. *Reports*. The consignee should provide to the consignor regular reports of removals from consignment stock and balances on hand and in transit at specified intervals.

7. *Taxes*. In certain states and jurisdictions, the presence of consignment stock may create "tax nexus" for the consignor, making them subject to, and liable for, local and/or state income taxes, franchise taxes, sales tax, and other taxes. Creditors should research this issue carefully before shipping on consignment.

Former Employee Loan Collection

Comments

1. *The collection of loans made to former employees is a difficult assignment. Frequently, the credit department gets into the matter very late.*

2. *If you are dealing with a disgruntled ex-employee, letters from a former supervisor or the accounting department will go unanswered. Telephone calls may not be of much help either.*

3. *The use of the credit department and its expertise in such matters is appropriate. The credit department tends to be more detached and professional, and is not uncomfortable about the process of contacting someone to collect money owed. The former employee must be told that the company does not intend to ignore the balance due, and will take any appropriate and necessary steps to collect the delinquent balance.*

4. *More frequently than not, payment plans have to be devised. Adherence to the plan has to be closely monitored by the credit department. Any delay in meeting a payment should result in a credit department follow-up.*

5. *For a variety of reasons, few companies like to sue former employees. However, collection procedures must run their course, and the credit department may be left with no alternative but to sue to collect from a former employee. However, this action will also send a message to other borrowers that the company is serious about having loans to employees repaid.*

[date]
[customer name]
[address]

Re: Unpaid Employee loan of $1,200.00

Dear Richard:

As you know, when you left the company there was a loan outstanding of $1,200.00 evidenced by a promissory note, copy enclosed. It was agreed when you left that this loan would be repaid within sixty (60) days. My records indicate that you resigned over 75 days ago and that no payment has yet been received.

As a former employee of this company, I want to extend to you every courtesy. I assume that the delay in payment is just an oversight. Please call me at your earliest opportunity to discuss this problem. I want to make sure this matter is resolved as amicably and as soon as possible. My telephone number is (800) XXX-XXXX.

I look forward to your prompt response.

Thank you.

Sincerely,

J. D. Selser
Credit Manager
[creditor company name]

cc: personnel manager
    file

Letter for Former Employee Loan Collection

Chapter 5

Collection Letters That Collect

Because there are varied types of collection problems and varied types of debtors, there is no one format or letter content that will work in each and every case. One has to analyze the nature of the debtor and the problem before a collection letter can be selected.

Type of Debtor

Does the account have the ability to pay, and are they just slow? Or, if they have limited ability to pay, are they just paying those who pose some sort of a threat? Perhaps, they lack liquid assets. Considerations such as these are used in determining the course of action to be used in effecting collection. *A credit manager will use a milder tone to an account who merely needs a reminder than to a debtor who probably ignores mere reminders.*

Continuing Sales

The duty of credit managers is to effect collections while trying not to damage the sales potential of their employers. If credit managers threaten legal action when a debtor goes past-due, goodwill will almost certainly be lost.

In most instances, collections can be effected quickly by the credit department without significant damage to goodwill between the buyer and the seller. Every attempt should be made to keep the customer and to keep them paying promptly.

Service Implications

While image might be difficult to convey, the credit department should try to present itself as a service organization to the customer and as a sales support organization to the Sales Department.

Early collection letters are sometimes signed by the "Customer Service Department." The designation of "credit department" can then be used for more strongly worded correspondence.

Most accounts will pay outstanding balances within a few days of receiving a first or a second reminder. It can be damaging to goodwill for the credit department to become involved too early or too heavily in collection matters.

Close Attention

A well managed company tries to keep cash flowing into the company to reduce borrowing costs and thereby increase earning by reducing interest paid on borrowed funds. The purpose of the credit department is to convert accounts receivable (A/R) into cash as quickly as possible. To do so, the credit manager must carefully monitor and manage accounts that go past due.

If collection efforts are sloppy or sporadic, then even good accounts might become slow payers. In fact, poorly managed collections results in a downward spiral in which good accounts become slow payers, slow accounts become problem accounts, and problem accounts become bad debts.

As a result of effective and professional monitoring and management of delinquent accounts, the seller:

- Needs to borrow less money, resulting in greater earnings.
- Is able to take cash discounts offered by its suppliers.
- Has the cash to take advantage of special deals offered by suppliers.
- Maintains a better credit rating because it is able to pay more suppliers on time, making it easier to obtain goods and services at competitive prices and on open account terms.
- Can borrow money more easily as a result of a better credit rating, as well as request and receive extended terms from its suppliers.
- Is better able to afford optimum inventory levels.
- Can provide better service and prices to its customers.

Many companies view the last benefit as the most important, since by satisfying its customers more fully the seller is able to be more successful and more profitable.

Management Image

The creditor who requires a rather strict observance of credit terms will, usually, have more respect in the business community. This respect develops and is inspired by the fact that others believe that *a well managed company is one that tries to collect its receivables promptly.* Thus, effective collection techniques while implying fewer overdue accounts, less bookkeeping, etc., also create the image that the management of the company is superior. An incompetent management team would have excessive receivables and an adverse bad debt experience.

The debtor should be seeing evidence of an efficient collection procedure system and, therefore, know that prompt payment is important to the creditor. The underlying effect of a credit department that knows what it is doing is increasing the image of competency of the creditor's management.

If a debtor has to choose which creditor to pay first, the creditor with the most efficient collection system most likely will be chosen.

Collecting on Small, Skipped Invoices

Comments

1. *Because of the size of small, skipped invoices, it is hard for creditors to find the time to address them. However, they must be addressed because skipped invoices cannot be wished away and will not go away if they are ignored.*

2. *A short, direct letter such as the one on the opposite page is a good way to collect small invoices.*

3. *Be certain to send a copy of the invoice in question with the letter.*

4. *Always include your telephone number in case the debtor wants to call you.*

5. *Sending this type of letter by fax is acceptable.*

6. *It is not necessary to copy the salesperson on this type of routine correspondence, unless your company requires it or the Sales Department has requested you to do so.*

[date]
[customer name]
[address]

Attention: Andy Gozlan
        [title]

Dear Mr. Gozlan:

Our records indicate that the attached invoice remains open and unpaid. It appears to be a skipped invoice. Please take a few minutes to review and resolve this minor problem today.

If you have any questions, please call me at (800) XXX-XXXX.

Thank you.

Sincerely,

Reece Prescott
Credit Administrator
[creditor company name]

cc: file

Letter Collecting on Small, Skipped Invoices

Establishing a Dialogue with a Delinquent Customer

Comments

1. *Every journey begins with a first step. Often, the first step in working out a collection problem involves getting the debtor to call you back.*

2. *Delinquent debtors soon become proficient at dodging calls from creditors. The purpose of the letter on the opposite page is to encourage the debtor to take the first step.*

3. *This type of appeal to fairness would be wasted on a chronic slow paying account, but it might work on an account that has run into some temporary difficulty.*

4. *The letter itself should be polite and professional. It should not accuse the debtor of anything.*

5. *This type of letter should suggest that at the very least the debtor should return the creditor's calls.*

6. *The salesperson should receive a copy of this letter. He or she should not be discouraged from contacting the customer and suggesting that someone give the credit manager the courtesy of a telephone call.*

[date]
[customer name]
[address]

Attention: Joy Bradley
            [title]

Dear Ms. Bradley:

People say that silence is golden—but when silence is
all we hear from our customers when we call them about a
past-due balance we become concerned.

Our records indicate that there is a past due-balance of
$843.25 over 30 days past due. We need to open a dia-
logue about this unpaid balance. Won't you please take a
few minutes and call me to discuss this situation?

My telephone number is (800) XXX-XXXX.

Thank you.

Sincerely,

Bryan O'Malley
Credit Manager
[creditor company name]

cc: salesperson

Letter Establishing a Dialogue with
a Delinquent Customer

Collection Letter—First Sale to New Account Gone Past Due

Comments

1. *It is especially important to set the tone early in a business relationship with the debtor by bringing the problem of the past-due balance to their attention firmly but professionally.*

2. *It is possible that the balance due was overlooked. It is also possible the debtor is testing the new creditor to see how sensitive the creditor is to delays in payment.*

3. *If an unearned cash discount was taken, it should be charged back. Even if it is not cost-effective to do so, it sends the wrong message to a new customer to simply allow the unearned discount to go unchallenged.*

4. *The debtor should be reminded of the correct terms of sale and asked to note them for future reference.*

[date]
[customer name]
[address]

Attention: Ron Darwin
             Accounts Payable Supervisor

Re: Invoice #21198

Dear Mr. Darwin:

According to our records, the above referenced invoice remains open and unpaid. This invoice represents our first sale to your company.

I think it is important that we start this business relationship properly. Please note in your records that our terms of sale are net 30 days from date of invoice.

Please remit payment immediately to clear this invoice, or call me at (800) XXX-XXXX if you have any questions or if you need any additional information or documentation.

Thank you.

Sincerely,

Michael J. Kinney
Credit Manager
[creditor company name]

cc: sales representative
    file

**Collection Letter—First Sale to
New Account Gone Past Due**

Request for Financial Statements

Comments

1. *Creditors often need updated financial statements to monitor and manage credit risk.*

2. *Analysis of a customer's financial statements (including a balance sheet, income statement and cash flow statement) makes it easier for a creditor to establish an appropriate credit limit for the account.*

3. *It is important that a creditor have current information on a debtor company's financial performance. Conditions change. A company that was doing well even as recently as a year or two ago may be in trouble now. Therefore, it is essential that creditors request updated financial statements periodically.*

4. *This letter is designed to suggest that the request for information is a routine part of the credit department's activities.*

[date]
[customer name]
[address]

Attention: Kim Bui
          Controller

Dear Ms. Bui:

A recent review of our credit file on your company reveals that it has been well over a year since we received updated financial statements from you. Please forward your company's most recent fiscal year-end financial statements to my attention at the address listed on the attached business card.

Any information you share will be kept in strictest confidence, and used only by the credit department.

If you have any questions or concerns about this request, please call me at (800) XXX-XXXX (ext. 7551).

Thank you.

Sincerely,

Jim Woods
Credit Manager
[creditor company name]

attachment

cc: file

Letter to Request Financial Statements

Past-Due Account—Alternate First Request 1

Comments

1. *The amount past due and the invoice number(s) should be apparent and readily available.*

2. *The letter should be sent to an individual in Accounts Payable identified by name and by title.*

3. *The letter contains a reminder of invoice terms.*

4. *A remittance is* not *specifically requested, only that the matter be researched.*

5. *Basically, the letter is a reminder.*

6. *No reply envelope is included as no attempt is being made at dunning for the money.*

7. *The sales representative would be copied on this letter as a courtesy, with no action required at this time.*

[date]
[customer name]
[address]

Attention: Amy Able
            Accounts Payable Supervisor

Re: Invoice #8735, for $843.25

Dear Amy:

Our records indicate that the above referenced invoice is now past due under our terms of sale of net 30 days from date of invoice.

Please review your records, and let me know if you need any additional information or documentation in order to set this invoice up for immediate payment. My telephone number is (800) XXX-XXXX.

Thank you.

Sincerely,

R. H. Gimbels
Credit Assistant
[creditor company name]

cc: sales representative
    file

Letter for Past-Due Account—Alternate First Request 1

Past-Due Account—Alternate First Request 2

Comments

1. *The reference section of the letter refers to the past due item.*

2. *The letter is addressed to a specific individual and it includes the person's title.*

3. *Even if the account pays by statement rather than by invoice, the letter should prompt some research into the delinquent balance.*

4. *Ms. Jones is being asked to process the account for payment.*

5. *A reply envelope is being included for convenience.*

6. *The letter is a little stronger than the one illustrated on page 193.*

7. *A serious payment problem does not yet exist with this account. Nevertheless, the sales representative should be copied on this letter as a courtesy.*

RE: 4/30 Statement
    $843.25 Balance

Attention: R.B. Jones, Accounts Payable Manager

We are enclosing a copy of the above statement which indicates that the balance is past due.

Kindly review your records and if the statement is correct, please remit.

An addressed envelope is enclosed for your convenience.

Sincerely yours,

C. D. Docker
Credit Reviewer

enc.

cc: credit files
    ten-day follow-up file

Past-Due Account—Alternate First Request 2

Past-Due Account—Alternate First Request 3

Comments

1. *The reference section of the letter refers to the past due item.*

2. *The letter is addressed to a specific individual and it includes the person's title.*

3. *The nature of the deduction that has been charged back has been explained to the recipient.*

4. *Shipping terms are listed and referenced in the letter.*

5. *A specific request for payment is made.*

6. *The letter is a little stronger than the one illustrated on page 195.*

7. *A serious payment problem does not exist with this account. Therefore, a copy of the letter need not be directed to the sales manager.*

[date]
[customer name]
[address]

Attention: C.B. Wheat
          Accounts Payable Supervisor

Re: Invoice #8735, $843.25
    Freight charges of $21.00

Dear C.B.:

We are in receipt of your recent payment on check number 12345 dated _____. We note that the freight charges of $21.00 on invoice #8735 were not included with the payment. This amount is now past due.

Please note that, by agreement, our shipping terms are FOB origin (shipping point) freight prepaid and bill. Please review your records and remit this $21.00 or call me if your records differ from ours. My telephone number is (800) XXX-XXXX.

Thank you.

Sincerely,

Richard Stone
Credit Analyst
[creditor company name]

cc: credit file

Letter for Past-Due Account—Alternate First Request 3

Past-Due Account—Alternate First Request 4

Comments

1. *The reference provides an immediate indication of the contents of the letter.*

2. *As distinguished from illustrations on the previous pages, this letter is directed to someone who should have more authority to cause payment to be issued.*

3. *The letter makes no demand for payment. It simply asks for the controller's assistance in resolving the problem. However, as a practical matter, the only assistance a creditor normally needs is assistance in getting a check cut, signed and mailed.*

4. *As a first request, no demand is made for any payment. After all, it is possible that the matter results from a discrepancy, such as a payment that has been misapplied.*

5. *A reply envelope could be included and may prompt a quicker response.*

6. *The ten-day follow-up file could trigger the mailing of a copy of the letter which has been stamped "Second Request."*

Re: $843.25 Past due

Attention: Fred Feidel
         Controller

Dear Mr. Feidel:

Our records indicate the amount referenced above is past due. Copies of the relevant invoices are attached for your review.

I would appreciate your assistance in resolving this problem. Please let me know if you need any additional information or documentation.

Thank you for your assistance and prompt response to this request.

Sincerely,

Mary Philips
Credit Manager
[creditor company name]

enc.

cc: file

Letter for Past-Due Account—Alternate First Request 4

Past-Due Account—Alternate First Request 5

Comments

1. *This letter is directed at the senior financial person in the organization. In theory, this individual will be concerned with the credit reputation of the debtor company.*

2. *The letter only "indicates" that an item is past due. There is no recrimination. As such, it allows for the possibility of an error on someone's part.*

3. *Once again, only information is requested. Nothing is strong or hard-nosed about the letter.*

4. *Invoice terms are reinforced. Chances are good that the treasurer may not be aware of terms.*

5. *An expectation of addressing the matter to an officer is that this person will pass it on to someone with an express or implied demand for research into the matter.*

6. *A self-addressed, stamped envelope is not required in this case.*

[date]
[customer name]
[address]

Attention: J. J. Sparks
          Treasurer

Re: $843.25

Dear Ms. Sparks:

Our records indicate that the above referenced invoice is past due. Our terms of sale are net 30 days from date of invoice.

Please contact me if there is any problem delaying payment. Otherwise, I would appreciate your assistance in resolving this problem.

Thank you.

Sincerely,

L. M. Becker
Credit Manager
[creditor company name]

cc: sales representative
    file

Letter for Past-Due Account—Alternate First Request 5

Past-Due Account—Alternate First Request 6

Comments

1. *This letter is better where an account usually pays on time—a reminder about the item may bring a quick payment.*

2. *For the more chronic problem account, such a letter would probably be routed to the wastebasket in short order.*

3. *The writer is fairly certain the past due balance is not the result of any error on the part of the seller such as a misapplied payment.*

4. *The use of a self-addressed, stamped envelope with this type of letter is appropriate.*

5. *Form letters should be personalized. Collection letters should be sent to a person, not simply a title such as Accounts Payable Manager.*

Re: $843.25

Attention: Bob Brown
          Accounts Payable Supervisor

Dear Mr. Brown:

I think you would agree that it is to our mutual advantage to keep your account current with us. Our records indicate the above referenced balance is seriously past due.

Please review your files and process a payment as soon as possible.

Thank you.

Sincerely,

Robert Watson
Credit Administrator
[creditor company name]

cc: sales representative
    file

Letter for Past-Due Account—Alternate First Request 6

Past-Due Account—Alternate First Request 7

Comments

1. *See the illustration on page 203, where a statement is not used. Both letters are more routine types of reminders.*

2. *The letter is used with accounts that, more often than not, pay on time.*

3. *It is probably a waste to use it with the chronic slow payer. Even as a first request, it is not strong enough to accomplish much, if anything.*

4. *This letter is considered mild because it merely states the creditor's records* indicate *that the account is past due.*

5. *This type of letter can be used as a form letter.*

6. *The letter makes no demand for payment.*

7. *The ten-day follow-up could trigger a telephone call or a more aggressive demand for payment letter.*

Re: $843.25

Attention: Accounts Payable Department

Please note that the attached statement indicates your account with us is past due.

Please give this problem your prompt attention.

Thank you.

Sincerely,

John Blocks
Credit Administrator
[creditor company name]

enc.

cc: file

Letter for Past-Due Account—Alternate First Request 7

Past-Due Account—Alternate First Request 8

Comments

1. *The illustrated letter is another type of short reminder.*

2. *For the chronic slow payer, this type of letter is a candidate for the wastebasket. It is more ideal for use with the account that usually pays promptly, but for this item something has gone amiss.*

3. *If every late payment was the fault of the U.S. Postal Service, as some debtors would ask you to believe, the American public would rise up and demand a new Postmaster General and a better postal system immediately.*

4. *In the letter on the opposite page, the creditor knows the facts but allows for the possibility that the payment was delayed in the mail.*

5. *Of course, a creditor's request for payment and a customer's check sometimes do cross in the mail. In that event, a simple thank-you should suffice.*

Re: $843.25
Invoice #8735

Attention: Mary Main
            Accounts Payable Representative

Dear Ms. Main:

If a check for the above referenced amount is in the
mail, please accept our thanks.

If there has been some delay in making this payment,
please expedite payment on this seriously past due item.

Thank you for your assistance and cooperation.

Sincerely,

Lori Wood
Assistant Credit Manager
[creditor company name]

cc: file
    seven-day follow-up

Letter for Past-Due Account—Alternate First Request 8

Past-Due Account—Alternate First Request 9

Comments

1. *The letter restates the invoice terms.*

2. *This customer is no different from any other debtor and should not be permitted to pay any slower.*

3. *The letter is deliberately brief and to the point.*

4. *Since a payment has been requested, a self-addressed and stamped envelope is enclosed.*

5. *If the customer fails to respond promptly to this letter by sending payment, the creditor should call the debtor.*

[date]
[customer name]
[address]

Attention: Jim L. Morse
         Accounting Manager

Dear Mr. Morse:

This letter is a reminder that our terms are net 30 days from the invoice date. As you probably already know, this is an industry norm.

Our records indicate invoice #8735 for $845.25 (copy enclosed) has not been paid within terms. Please investigate this matter, and forward your check to my attention at the address shown on the attached invoice as soon as possible.

Thank you.

Sincerely,

Al Martin
Commercial Accounts Credit Manager
[creditor company name]

enc.

cc: credit file

Letter for Past-Due Account—Alternate First Request 9

Past-Due Account—Alternate First Request 10

Comments

1. *The reference section of the letter indicates the purpose of the letter completely. The two small lines advise the reader that it is a collection letter.*

2. *The letter is addressed to the buyer. This is quite unusual. It is considered to be provocative—especially since this is the first letter sent. It is hoped that the buyer will not overreact to the letter.*

3. *An alternative to sending the exact letter on the opposite page would be for the letter to be signed by the customer service department.*

4. *Any follow-up necessary to this letter would not go to the buyer. It should be directed to the accounting or accounts payable department.*

5. *A copy of the latest account statement could be included with the letter.*

6. *No reply envelope is necessary.*

[date]
[customer name]
[address]

Attention: Eric Erikson
         Buyer

Re: Invoice #439881
    Due 4/30/XX
    $845.25

Dear Mr. Erikson:

First, a word of thanks for the business that you have given to this company.

Our Accounting Department reports that the above refer-enced invoice is past due. Please let me know if any problems with the product delivered or the invoice are causing a delay in payment. My telephone number is (800) XXX-XXXX.

Thank you.

Sincerely,

Steven Whist
Credit Administrator
[creditor company name]

cc: sales representative
    file

Letter for Past-Due Account—Alternate First Request 10

Past-Due Account—Alternate First Request 11

Comments

1. *This form can be a computer-generated dunning notice, printed automatically for all accounts over a certain number of days past due. Since the notices are automatic, they can be printed as often as the credit department and the creditor company believe is appropriate.*

2. *As a form letter, the only parts which require typing are the address (conforming with window envelope requirements) and the reference section as to invoice number and amount.*

3. *This type of letter may be of little use if it is sent to a chronically slow paying customer. The letter will simply be ignored, along with other collection letters from other creditors.*

4. *A self-addressed, stamped envelope can be included for the customer's convenience in remitting payment.*

[date]
[customer name]
[address]

Attention: Beth Bracken
            Controller

Re: Invoice #8745
     Due 4/30/XX
     $845.25

Dear Ms. Bracken:

Our records indicate that the above referenced invoice(s) remain unpaid. Our terms of sale are net 15 days from date of invoice. Please expedite payment to clear this invoice, and in the future please flag our account for more prompt payment.

A self-addressed stamped envelope is enclosed for your convenience in remitting payment.

Thank you for your assistance.

Sincerely,

Sam Alex
Credit Department
[creditor company name]

enc.

Letter for Past-Due Account—Alternate First Request 11

Past-Due Account—Alternate First Request 12

Comments

1. This letter is brief and to the point.

2. Including the days sales outstanding (DSO) shows the customer that the creditor is "on the ball" and watching accounts receivable carefully.

3. An immediate payment is requested, along with a request that the account be flagged for more prompt payment in the future.

4. Monitoring changes in customers' payment habits by monitoring account specific DSO is an excellent way to manage accounts receivable.

5. The notice can be faxed rather than mailed to the debtor company to save time.

[date]
[customer name]
[address]

Attention: Jan Walters
            Accounts Payable Manager

Dear Ms. Walters:

According to our records, invoice #8755 for $875.23 is now 20 days past due. This prompted me to review your account's payment history with us. According to our records, your account's average days to pay has slipped from nine days past due a year ago to 24 days as of the first of this month.

Please schedule the above referenced invoice for immediate payment. Also, please flag our account for more prompt payment in the future. If you have any questions, please call me at (800) XXX-XXXX.

Thank you.

Sincerely,

Walt Whitman
Credit Administrator
[creditor company name]

cc: sales manager
    credit file

Letter for Past-Due Account—Alternate First Request 12

Past-Due Account—Alternate First Request 13

Comments

1. *This reminder should be sent to someone with the authority to direct an immediate payment of the past-due balance.*

2. *The previous page contains an alternative to this letter.*

3. *Payment reminders (or dunning notices) are often computer-generated messages or form letters.*

4. *No specific demand for payment is made. Therefore, it should cause no offense even if the customer's payment and this letter cross in the mail.*

5. *This type of correspondence will probably be ignored by chronic slow paying accounts, but it is fine for the majority of customers as a friendly reminder that payment is overdue.*

6. *Based on industry norms, sending a self-addressed, stamped envelope is optional.*

[date]
[customer name]
[address]

Attention: Lou Williams
          Accounts Payable Supervisor

RE: Invoice #8735
    $843.25
    Due date 4/30/XX

Dear Mr. Williams:

Our terms of sale are net 10 days from date of invoice. Please review your records and determine if there is any reason that the above referenced invoice remains open and unpaid.

If there is a problem, please contact this department as soon as possible at (800) XXX-XXXX.

Thank you.

Sincerely,

Margaret Buckingham
Credit Department
[creditor company name]

Letter for Past-Due Account—Alternate First Request 13

Past-Due Account—Alternate First Request—Mailgram

Comments

1. *Sending a mailgram is more expensive than sending a letter, but it is less costly than sending a series of letters followed by a series of follow-up calls.*

2. *Mailgrams can be sent in bulk, which reduces their per-unit cost.*

3. *The text of a mailgram is normally transmitted via electronic data interchange to a company offering mailgram services. For a fee, that company processes a mailgram message that can be delivered via overnight courier or by first class mail, depending on the creditor's requirements.*

4. *The assumption is that mailgrams are more likely to be read than routine correspondence.*

5. *If mailgrams are used too often, they lose effectiveness. Customers soon recognize that the mailgram is basically a past-due notice.*

MAILGRAM

[date]

Ronnie Stokes
Glass Tool Company
Bridgeport, IL 62417

OUR RECORDS INDICATE INVOICE #9755 FOR $843.25 IS NOW
PAST DUE. PLEASE EXPEDITE PAYMENT OR ADVISE.

CREDIT DEPARTMENT
ABLEMAN SUPPLY CO.
ATLANTA, GA

Letter for Past-Due Account—Alternate
First Request—Mailgram

Alternate First Request—Past Due with Missed Discount

Comments

1. *Missing a discount is an indication that the debtor may be having cash flow problems, especially if the debtor company normally discounted invoices in the past.*

2. *Creditors should remind debtors that the discount terms are a business courtesy and that taking cash discounts requires prompt payment. Prompt payments reduce days sales outstanding.*

3. *The letter should make it clear that the cash discount is no longer available. After receiving this letter, if the customer takes a cash discount, it most certainly should be charged back.*

4. *The salesperson can be encouraged to try to get the customer to pay promptly and to take the discount since having the customer do so would benefit both the Credit and the Sales Departments.*

[date]
[customer name]
[address]

Attention: Luke Williams
            Accounting Manager

Dear Mr. Williams:

Invoice #8755 for $845.23 remains open and is now 21 days past due. Our terms of sale are 2% 15, net 30 days.

At this point, the cash discount is no longer available. However, it is important that you remit payment immediately to clear this open balance.

In the future, I would encourage you to consider taking advantage of our cash discount. To do so, it is necessary for payment to be received by our bank lockbox within 15 days of the invoice date.

Thank you for your prompt attention to this matter.

Sincerely,

Luke Skyrunner
Assistant Credit Manager
[creditor company name]

cc: sales representative
    credit file

Letter for Alternate First Request—
Past Due with Missed Discount

Alternate First Request—Reminder of Credit Terms

Comments

1. *If a customer was taking a cash discount but is not doing so now, the credit department should ask the customer to consider discounting again.*

2. *This should be a fairly easy "sale." Typically, a cash discount is a big incentive for customers to pay within the discount terms.*

3. *Often, the senior financial executive of the debtor company is unaware of the missed discounts. The only reason the debtor is no longer paying early and taking the cash discount may be simply that the accounts payable department is busy. It requires more work to process invoices fast enough to take the discount, and the A/P clerk is no longer doing so.*

4. *The letter is intended to be a friendly reminder. It contains no accusations or threats. It is an invitation for the debtor to take advantage of a program offered by the creditor to customers in return for prompt payment.*

5. *The letter should be sent to the CFO or to the Controller, since either is in a position to instruct the accounts payable department to remit payment quickly enough to qualify for the cash discount.*

```
[date]
[customer name]
[address]
```

Attention: K. M. Singh
            Controller

Dear Mr. Singh:

Our terms of sale are 2% 15, net 30 days from date of invoice. Up until about a year ago, your company normally paid within the 15-day discount period and took advantage of the discount. Since then, your company's payment pattern has changed, and payments are now made in about 42 days.

Please consider taking the 2% cash discount on future payment by scheduling our invoices for payment within 15 days.

Thank you.

Sincerely,

Steve Gardiner
Area Credit Manager
[creditor company name]

cc: file

Letter for Alternate First Request—
Reminder of Credit Terms

Past-Due Account—Alternate Second Request 1

Comments

1. *The reference section is a quick recap of the reason for the letter.*

2. *The letter should be addressed to a specific person who is able to authorize payment.*

3. *Payment is not demanded in the letter; it is requested. Therefore, this is a "soft" collection letter.*

4. *This letter will probably not work with chronic slow payers; so if you have a choice, send an alternative follow-up (second) letter to those accounts.*

5. *By copy of the letter, the salesperson is made aware of the problem. It is in his or her best interest to make certain the account remains current so that shipments can continue.*

6. *Credit professionals would do well not to underestimate the influence of the salesperson with the debtor.*

[date]
[customer name]
[address]

Attention: Jason McSweeney
            Accounts Payable Manager

RE: Invoice #8755
     $845.23
     Due date 4/30/XX

Dear Mr. McSweeney:

Two weeks ago, we wrote to your accounts payable department and indicated that the above referenced invoice was past due. As of this morning, we have received no response or payment.

We appreciate your business, but would like to clean up this matter quickly. We would appreciate your assistance in expediting payment.

Thank you.

Sincerely,

Sam Winston
Commercial Credit Manager
[creditor company name]

cc: sales representative
    follow-up file

Letter for Past-Due Account—
Alternate Second Request 1

Past-Due Account—Alternate Second Request 2

Comments

1. *The bold "SECOND REQUEST" provides a quick indication of the reason for the letter.*

2. *The first paragraph brings Ms. Amber up to date on the matter.*

3. *Late payment charges are explained to the account. However, no statement is made that the charge will actually be made.*

4. *State laws vary as to the legal limit of interest charges. Creditors must be certain to quote rates within the legal limits. Otherwise, they may be guilty of usury.*

5. *The account might reasonably believe that, by making payment promptly, they will avoid an interest charge on the past-due balance.*

6. *By copy of the letter, the sales representative's assistance is requested.*

SECOND REQUEST

[date]
[customer name]
[address]

Attention: Anne Amber
            Controller

Dear Ms. Amber:

Ten days ago, we notified your Accounts Payable Department there was an unpaid and past due balance of $845.23. As yet, we have had no reply to this letter.

A copy of your account statement is enclosed for your review.

The credit terms contained in our credit application and listed on each invoice provide for an interest charge of *x*% per month on any overdue balance.

We dislike imposing interest charges on our good customers. Please issue a check immediately to clear this past-due balance. A self-addressed envelope is enclosed for your convenience.

Thank you.

Sincerely,

Greg Fearing
Corporate Credit Director
[creditor company name]

enc.

cc: sales representative
    credit file
    follow-up file

**Letter for Past-Due Account—
Alternate Second Request 2**

Past-Due Account—Alternate Second Request 3

Comments

1. This letter is not addressed to a specific party as the two illustrations on pages 225 and 227.

2. The first paragraph starts out with a short question. This ploy tends to increase reader interest in the rest of the letter. The balance of the paragraph brings the reader up to date on the matter.

3. The recipient of this letter probably already knows that the creditor, Wilshire Leasing Partners, has had no response to the first letter and that no payment has been issued. Since this letter is being sent so soon after the first one, it should alert the debtor to the fact that someone is watching the account closely. This fact alone may prompt the customer to take action to clear the past-due balance.

4. Instead of concluding with a demand for payment, a simple question is being asked.

5. The chronic slow pay account will probably ignore this letter. However, the occasional problem account will probably issue payment fairly quickly.

6. It is unnecessary to include a self-addressed business reply envelope with this reminder.

7. A form letter of this type is best used when a relatively small balance is outstanding.

SECOND REQUEST

[date]
[customer name]
[address]

Attention: Accounts Payable Department

What happened? We sent a past-due notice a week ago regarding an unpaid balance of $843.25. In that letter, we
asked that the delinquent balance be paid or that someone contact us to discuss any problems.

Since then, we have heard nothing from you, nor have we
received your check. Can we expect you to issue payment
immediately?

Please call me at (800) XXX-XXXX if this presents a
problem.

Thank you.

Sincerely,

Carl Alatis
Credit Department
Wilshire Leasing Partners

cc: sales representative
    correspondence file
    five-day follow-up file

Letter for Past-Due Account— Alternate Second Request 3

Past-Due Account—Alternate Second Request 4

Comments

1. *By being addressed to a specific individual at the account, the letter may receive proper attention.*

2. *This type of request can be used when shipments are continuing and the account does not seem to be in any serious financial difficulty.*

3. *Since this is a second request for payment, it is reasonable to assume the past-due balance does not result from an oversight. Therefore, the warning contained in paragraph 2 is appropriate.*

4. *A self-addressed business reply envelope can be included with the letter.*

5. *The salesperson's assistance is not required but might be welcome.*

SECOND NOTICE

[date]
[customer name]
[address]

Attention: Derwin Snyod

Dear Mr. Snyod:

Our records indicate that this is the second request for payment of a past-due balance of $843.25 involving our invoice #8755.

I do not want to place your account onto our "slow payment" list. Please put a check in the mail today to clear the past-due balance.

Thank you.

Sincerely,

Tom S. Adair
Director of Credit
[creditor company name]

cc: sales representative
    correspondence file

Letter for Past-Due Account—
Alternate Second Request 4

Past-Due Account—Alternate Second Request 5

Comments

1. *This letter starts with a recap of the current problem.*

2. *The author allows for the possibility that payment has already been sent and was delayed in the mail.*

3. *The tone is mild. The letter is intended to prompt payment, not to threaten the customer in any way.*

4. *By copying Order Entry on the letter, the recipient may suspect that the account is being flagged and that orders may be held. However, a credit hold is never mentioned in the letter.*

5. *A reply envelope is not necessary.*

[date]
[customer name]
[address]

Attention: Ed Blist

Dear Mr. Blist:

Recently, we sent you a notice about a balance of $843.25 now almost 30 days past due. We hope a check is already in the mail to clear your account.

If that is not the case, can I ask that payment be sent immediately? Please call me if there are any problems at (800) XXX-XXXX.

Thank you.

Sincerely,

Evelyn Winters
Credit Administrator
[creditor company name]

cc: sales representative
    Order Entry
    correspondence file

**Letter for Past-Due Account—
Alternate Second Request 5**

Past-Due Account—Alternate Second Request 6

Comments

1. *The letter should be sent to a specific person rather than to a department or office.*

2. *A monthly statement could be mailed with the letter for quick reference by the recipient.*

3. *The account is given the benefit of the* cop-out *of "slow mails."*

4. *A return-addressed envelope is not necessary.*

SECOND PAST-DUE NOTICE

[date]
[customer name]
[address]

Attention: Carol Lopez
          Assistant Controller

Dear Ms. Lopez:

I have attached a monthly statement for your review along with a copy of our previous letter dated June 30th.

Admittedly, the mail may be slow and hopefully your check and this letter will pass in the mail. If this is not the case, please call me at (800) XXX-XXXX to discuss payment status.

Thank you.

Sincerely,

Fred Steir
Credit Manager
Anna's Wholesale Inc.

cc: sales manager
    correspondence file

**Letter for Past-Due Account—
Alternate Second Request 6**

Past-Due Account—Alternate Second Request 7

Comments

1. *The letter should be addressed to a specific individual. Only if the decision maker is not known by name should the letter be addressed to: The Accounting Department; or to Accounts Payable; or to the Controller.*

2. *The recipient is asked to investigate the situation, and then to call the creditor with payment status.*

3. *There is no threat to hold orders in the letter, but by copying the order processing department one might be inferred by the debtor.*

4. *By copy of the letter, the sales representative is invited to offer any assistance they can to influence the customer to pay what is due.*

SECOND REQUEST—IMMEDIATE ATTENTION REQUESTED

[date]
[customer name]
[address]

Attention: Jaime Martin
            Accounts Payable

Dear Jaime:

A review of our records indicates that we sent you a letter on [date] regarding a past-due balance of $843.25, but as of this morning we have received no response and no payment.

Please review our account and advise as to when you will be able to remit payment to clear this delinquent balance. My telephone number is (800) XXX-XXXX.

Thank you.

Sincerely,

Paul Barstow
Credit Administrator
[creditor company name]

cc: sales representative
    credit correspondence file
    Order Entry

Letter for Past-Due Account—
Alternate Second Request 7

Past-Due Account—Alternate Second Request 8

Comments

1. *The letter should be addressed only to a department such as Accounts Payable or to a position such as Accounts Payable Manager if the name of that person is not known. Normally, the name and title of a decision maker is only a phone call away.*

2. *Including a copy of previous correspondence is intended to show the debtor that the creditor is watching the account carefully, and is well organized and methodical in its collection efforts.*

3. *Rather than accusing the debtor of ignoring correspondence and delaying payment, the letter simply states that the creditor has no record of receiving payment from the debtor company.*

4. *The letter asks for an immediate response from the debtor. What that response should be is not defined, but the creditor expects an immediate payment. Failing that, a call from the debtor to explain why the balance due has not been paid is expected.*

SECOND REQUEST

[date]
[customer name]
[address]

Attention: Accounts Payable Manager

Dear Sir:

According to our records, we sent a letter to you on [date] (copy attached) regarding a past-due balance of $X,XXX.XX. Our Accounts Receivable Department reports they have received no payment from your company since [date].

Your prompt response to this letter would be appreciated. My telephone number is (800) XXX-XXXX.

Thank you for your assistance and cooperation.

Sincerely,

Karl Conner
Assistant Credit Manager
[creditor company name]

cc: sales representative
    follow-up file
    correspondence file
    Order Entry Department

Letter for Past-Due Account— Alternate Second Request 8

Past-Due Account—Alternate Second Request 9

Comments

1. *The first paragraph brings the reader up-to-date.*

2. *The second paragraph requests immediate action of some type.*

3. *The reference to the fact that the account is not on credit hold is intended to get the debtor company to think about the fact that they may soon be on credit hold. With any delinquent account, at some point the credit department must exercise the credit hold option to try to force the debtor to retire the delinquent balance.*

4. *The sales representative may also be more motivated to help once he or she realizes orders pending might be at risk.*

[date]
[customer name]
[address]

Attention: Tran Nguyen
            Accounts Payable

Dear Tran:

Previously, I sent you a notice regarding a past-due balance of $845.23, but I received no response to this notice.

Please call me to discuss the status of your account. My number is (800) XXX-XXXX. At this point, we are not considering this matter serious, and your account is *not* on credit hold.

Thank you.

Sincerely,

Kofi Witt
Credit Manager
[creditor company name]

cc: sales representative
    correspondence file

**Letter for Past-Due Account—
Alternate Second Request 9**

Past-Due Account—Alternate Second Request 10

Comments

1. *This request is fairly strongly worded. The phrase "seriously past due" is intended to convey that the creditor views the current situation with concern.*

2. *This type of letter should always be sent to the attention of a specific person. To save time, the creditor may want to fax this letter to the debtor and to the salesperson.*

3. *The salesperson should always be copied on this type of correspondence, since he or she might influence the debtor to get the account paid.*

4. *Copying the Order Entry Department is intended to suggest that the account's status is in jeopardy without making any overt threats of credit hold.*

[date]
[customer name]
[address]

Attention: Greg Paulson
            Assistant Controller

Dear Mr. Paulson:

Unfortunately, your Accounting Department has not responded to previous correspondence regarding an unpaid balance of $845.23.

This $845.23 is now seriously past due. I would ask that you give this matter your immediate attention and that remittance be made without further delay.

We look forward to receiving your payment.

Thank you.

Sincerely,

Darren Brown
Assistant Credit Manager

cc: sales representative
    correspondence file
    Order Entry Department

Letter for Past-Due Account—
Alternate Second Request 10

Past-Due Account—Alternate Second Request 11

Comments

1. *The letter should be addressed to a decision maker by name.*

2. *The letter can be faxed to save time.*

3. *The letter is deliberately brief. This allows the recipient to focus on the message without distractions.*

4. *A specific request for someone to call with payment status will usually result in the Controller delegating the task to someone in Accounts Payable. The fact the Controller is involved personally often results in payments being expedited.*

[date]
[customer name]
[address]

Attention: Candide Guerrero
          Controller

Dear Ms. Guerrero:

This is the second time I have written to request that invoice #8755 for $843.25 be paid. I am concerned that there was no response to the previous notice.

Please ask someone in your organization to call me as soon as possible with payment status. My telephone number is (800) XXX-XXXX.

Thank you.

Sincerely,

Randy Wykoff
Credit Manager
[creditor company name]

cc: sales representative
    correspondence file
    Order Entry Department

**Letter for Past-Due Account—
Alternate Second Request 11**

Past-Due Account—Alternate Second Request 12

Comments

1. *The first paragraph allows the customer a face-saving reason for not responding to the first letter and for not clearing up the past-due invoice.*

2. *The second paragraph is a straightforward request for immediate payment in full.*

3. *Since payment is being requested, sending a self-addressed envelope is appropriate.*

4. *This type of letter should be sent to a specific person in a position to authorize immediate payment. Collectors need to be working with decision makers, not message takers or clerks.*

5. *The salesperson is copied as a courtesy.*

SECOND NOTICE

[date]
[customer name]
[address]

Attention: Frank Fredonia
            Accounting Manager

Dear Mr. Fredonia:

These days, everyone is busy. This may be the reason you overlooked my letter of [date] regarding our past-due balance of $843.25 referencing invoice #8875.

Would you please take the time to issue and send a check today to clear this delinquent item? A self-addressed, stamped envelope is enclosed for your convenience.

Thank you for your assistance.

Sincerely,

Carol Simmons
Credit Manager
[creditor company name]

cc: sales representative
    correspondence file
    seven-day follow-up file

Letter for Past-Due Account—
Alternate Second Request 12

Past-Due Account—Alternate Second Request 13

Comments

1. *The letter refers to the fact that this is a second request, but gives no specifics as to when the first request was made.*

2. *The letter must be sent to a decision maker, not a clerk.*

3. *By enclosing supporting documentation, the creditor reduces the number of excuses the debtor can use to delay payment any further.*

4. *By involving the Treasurer or the CFO, the creditor expects to force the Accounts Payable Department to expedite payment.*

5. *The letter can be faxed to expedite payment.*

6. *If there is no response in a reasonable time frame—such as seven working days—the creditor must consider stronger measures to collect the unpaid balance, including telephone calls, personal visits and credit holds.*

SECOND REQUEST

[date]
[customer name]
[address]

Attention: Robert Chapman
            Treasurer

Dear Mr. Chapman:

Our records indicate the $843.25 past-due balance refer-enced in the attached statement remains open and unpaid. For your convenience, I have enclosed a copy of the rel-evant invoices making up this past-due balance.

Please expedite the processing of a payment to clear this delinquent balance. If there are any problems, please call me at (800) XXX-XXXX.

Thank you.

Sincerely,

Bob Dunn
Assistant Credit Manager
[creditor company name]

cc: credit file
    correspondence file
    Order Entry

**Letter for Past-Due Account—
Alternate Second Request 13**

Past-Due Account—Alternate Second Request 14

Comments

1. *This letter is clear and straightforward.*

2. *It refers to previous correspondence, but sending a copy of that document is not viewed as essential.*

3. *By stating that the invoice in question was for a rush order, the creditor is trying to get the customer to recognize a reciprocal obligation to expedite payment.*

4. *The second paragraph tries to eliminate the excuse that the order may not have arrived.*

5. *The letter requests a call from the debtor and an immediate payment. A payment is more likely than a call from the debtor, which is normally all the creditor actually wants anyway.*

6. *A business reply envelope can be included for the customer's convenience in remitting payment.*

[date]
[customer name]
[address]

Attention: Sandy Simca

Dear Ms. Simca:

Our records indicate invoice #8877 for $845.23 is now almost 30 days past due. This item was shipped within 24 hours of receipt of the order based on your company's request for expedited shipment.

We are not aware of any problems with this invoice. We have verified with the overnight delivery service that the order was received and signed for by [name] on [date] at [time].

Therefore, I can think of no reason why my previous letter about this past-due balance has been ignored. Please respond to the request I made two weeks ago for an update on the status of this open invoice. My telephone number is (800) XXX-XXXX.

I have enclosed a self-addressed, business reply envelope for your remittance. Thank you for your prompt response and immediate payment.

Sincerely,

Carol Sykes
Credit Administrator
[creditor company name]

enc.

cc: sales representative
    correspondence file
    follow-up file

**Letter for Past-Due Account—
Alternate Second Request 14**

Past-Due Account—Alternate Second Request 15

Comments

1. *The intent of the first line of the letter is to grab the reader's attention, to get him or her to read the letter and act on it immediately.*

2. *The tone of this collection letter is mild. No threats are made or implied.*

3. *A reply envelope should be enclosed for the customer's convenience in remitting payment.*

SECOND NOTICE OF PAST—DUE BALANCE

[date]
[customer name]
[address]

Attention: Ben Salgado
               Accounting Manager

Dear Mr. Salgado:

Nag, nag, nag!

That is the way some creditors treat their customers. That is not the way we want to treat our customers.

This is our second notice of a past-due balance of $843.25. I have enclosed a copy of the past-due invoices for your review.

While it may seem like nagging, we would like your account brought current. Please mail a check to us today. If this presents a problem, please call me at (800) XXX-XXXX.

Thank you.

Sincerely,

Theresa O'Donnell
Credit Director
Sharper Tool Company

cc: sales representative
    follow-up file
    correspondence file

**Letter for Past-Due Account—
Alternate Second Request 15**

Past-Due Account—Alternate Second Request 16

Comments

1. *These second request letters are designed to be progressively more assertive and direct, but none is belligerent, rude or unprofessional.*

2. *The message in the second paragraph is that the creditor wants to keep the business relationship working smoothly but that the debtor is endangering the relationship by delaying payment.*

3. *The phrase "seriously past due" is intended to send a message that the creditor is becoming increasingly concerned about the status of the account.*

4. *The letter requests immediate payment or an immediate response.*

URGENT

[date]
[customer name]
[address]

Attention: Mesia Saveng
           Assistant Controller

Dear Ms. Saveng:

Your account is important to us, and we appreciate your business. Unfortunately, your account is also seriously past due, and I have had no response to previous correspondence sent to your Accounting Department about this problem.

I would like to keep our business relationship on a mutually satisfactory basis. Therefore, I would appreciate any assistance you could offer in getting the past-due balance of $843.25 cleared immediately.

If this presents a problem, please call me at (800) XXX-XXXX.

Thank you.

Sincerely,

Gilbert Angeles
Senior Credit Representative
[creditor company name]

cc: sales representative
    correspondence file
    follow-up file

**Letter for Past-Due Account—
Alternate Second Request 16**

Past-Due Account—Alternate Second Request 17

Comments

1. *This letter should be addressed to a decision maker, not to a clerk. In most organizations, this means the letter should be sent to the Accounts Payable Manager, Controller, or Treasurer.*

2. *The tone of the letter is matter-of-fact. The history of the account is provided to present the facts and to demonstrate how carefully the creditor monitors collections.*

3. *It is hoped and expected that, once a customer realizes the account is being carefully watched, payment will become more prompt.*

4. *The concluding paragraph is an appeal and a request for immediate payment, along with a request that the creditor's account be flagged for more prompt payment in the future.*

[date]
[customer name]
[address]

RE: SECOND REQUEST FOR PAYMENT

Dear Mr. Simpson:

Our records indicate the following:

On May 6th, we received your rush order.
On May 10th, we shipped the order by overnight courier. We have confirmed through order tracking that your company received and signed for the shipment on the 11th.
On the same day, we invoiced you for $843.25 on net 30 day terms.
That invoice was due on June 10th.
On June 20th, we sent a notice to you about this past-due balance.
As of today, we have not received payment or any response to this notice.

Based on the above, I believe I am not out of line in asking for an immediate payment of this delinquent balance. Please call me if you are unable to schedule payment for any reason. My number is (800) XXX-XXXX.

Thank you.

Sincerely,

Karen Buckingham
Credit Manager
Family Food Wholesalers, Inc.

**Letter for Past-Due Account—
Alternate Second Request 17**

Past-Due Account—Alternate
Second Request—Mailgram

Comments

1. Obviously, mailgrams are more expensive to send than letters. However, if sending mailgrams results in more prompt payment from seriously delinquent accounts, then the creditor should continue to use them. Even chronically slow paying accounts may pay creditors more quickly.

2. Western Union has special rates for bulk mailgrams— particularly where the message is pretty much the same for all transmissions.

3. One advantage of a mailgram is that it normally arrives sooner than ordinary first class mail because it is sent from a location selected for its proximity to the debtor.

4. The real advantage is that, since mailgrams are used infrequently, the novelty of receiving one might prompt the debtor to pay more promptly than in response to collection correspondence.

MAILGRAM

Western Union

Mr. John Stacy
Sloe Wholesale Corp.
Springfield, MO

THIS IS A SECOND NOTICE THAT $843.25 IS PAST DUE. PLEASE
EXPEDITE PAYMENT.

THANK YOU.

CREDIT DEPARTMENT
CARDBOARD LUGGAGE INC.

Letter for Past-Due Account—Alternate
Second Request—Mailgram

Past-Due Account—Alternate Second Request—Telex

Comments

1. *Occasionally, companies use a telex machine as a collection tool.*

2. *Because it is so unusual, a telex message about a past-due balance can have a greater impact on the debtor than ordinary correspondence.*

3. *When sending a telex, keep messages brief and to the point.*

4. *To send a telex message, the customer and the seller must both have telex machines.*

5. *In most companies, fax machines have replaced telex machines. An advantage of fax over telex is that copies of supporting documents can be transmitted by fax.*

TELEX

Domestic WDI
TOFYSOC 252275 LA 7/25 1245

Accounts Payable Department
Faster Jobbers Inc.
New York, NY 10201

This is our second request for payment against a past-due balance of $843.25.

Please telex payment status.

Thank you.

Credit Department
Tool Supply Depot, LLC

FAJO 188877948 NYK

Letter for Past-Due Account—Alternate
Second Request—Telex

Past-Due Account—Alternate Third Request 1

Comments

1. *Third requests are intended to be no-nonsense requests for payment.*

2. *The salesperson should be encouraged to help, if possible, on any account that requires a third reminder letter.*

3. *At this point in the collection process, the credit department must be considering a credit hold. In fact, the question is not whether orders should be held, but rather whether there is any reason to release orders.*

4. *At this point, there is virtually no question of checks lost in the mail or of missing invoice copies.*

5. *If a balance remains unpaid, the debtor probably has a serious cash flow problem. To solve the problem, the debtor must establish contact with the customer or get the customer to recognize the account is seriously past due and take appropriate action.*

THIRD NOTICE OF PAST-DUE ACCOUNT

[date]
[customer name]
[address]

Attention: Steven A. Solochek

Dear Mr. Solochek:

I note with concern that your account has an $843.25 balance that is now over 30 days past due.

To meet our obligations to our suppliers, it is critical that we collect from our customers promptly. Unless we can do so, we will soon be in financial trouble.

Accordingly, we must request an immediate payment of this past-due balance. If this presents a problem, please call me at (800) XXX-XXXX.

Thank you.

Sincerely,

Dennis Gregory
Credit Manager
[creditor company name]

cc: sales representative
    sales manager
    correspondence file
    follow-up file

Letter for Past-Due Account—Alternate Third Request 1

Past-Due Account—Alternate Third Request 2

Comments

1. *Holding orders is a last resort. Debtors should be informed promptly of the credit department's decision.*

2. *Some companies want the sales staff to deliver credit hold notifications. Whether this is a good idea depends on the skill of the salespersons and their influence with the debtor.*

3. *A third reminder should include a demand for immediate payment in full. Excuses—such as, "The check must have been lost in the mail"—are not plausible.*

4. *Creditors should also consider whether to continue to extend open account terms if or when the account pays the past-due balance.*

5. *At the very least, creditors should seriously consider reducing the credit limit since the debtor company is obviously having cash flow problems. Otherwise, why would they be so far past due and ignore so many letters?*

[date]
[customer name]
[address]

Attention: Carol Coughran
            Controller

Dear Ms. Coughran:

We have sent your company two previous requests for payment of a past-due balance of $842.35. This balance is approaching 75 days past due.

As yet, we have received no reply or any check. Nor have we received any indication that the delinquent balance is disputed.

Based on these facts, I have no alternative but to hold orders and to ask that payment be made as soon as possible. Please call me to discuss payment status at (800) XXX-XXXX (ext. 7001).

Thank you.

Valarie Dale
Corporate Credit Director
[creditor company name]

cc: sales representative
    sales manager
    correspondence file
    follow-up file

Letter for Past-Due Account—Alternate Third Request 2

Past-Due Account—Alternate Third Request 3

Comments

1. *This letter is sterner than the one on page 265. This is an example of what happens when creditors get fed up with being ignored by a customer.*

2. *Presumably, the customer will want the order pending badly enough that the debtor will immediately pay the past-due balance.*

3. *The letter does not promise that the order pending will be released if payment is made. The decision to release the order should be made (a) after payment is received, (b) the creditor has updated the customer credit file, and (c) the creditor has evaluated the customer to determine if he or she still qualifies for open account terms.*

4. *Occasionally, a debtor will try to get a concession from the creditor in exchange for payment. Specifically, the customer may be willing to pay only if given assurance that a pending order will be released. Credit professionals should not make such a commitment unless they are convinced of the debtor's creditworthiness.*

THIRD REMINDER!!!

[date]
[customer name]
[address]

Attention: Jimmy Lopienski
            Controller

Dear Mr. Lopienski:

This is our third letter regarding your company's past-due balance. In addition, our calls to your Accounts Payable Department have gone unanswered.

We need to see a check from your company in the next few days. At this time, your account and the orders pending are on credit hold.

Please contact me if you have any questions at (800) XXX-XXXX.

Thank you.

Morris Field
Commercial Credit Manager
Fast Foodshops, Inc.

cc: sales manager
    credit file
    sales representative
    follow-up file

Letter for Past-Due Account—Alternate Third Request 3

Past-Due Account—Alternate Third Request 4

Comments

1. *The creditor should seriously consider withdrawing the open account credit line.*

2. *The first two paragraphs describe the recent history of the account. The creditor has been fair, even lenient until now.*

3. *A customer that cares about its reputation will respond to this letter. The accounts that do not, will not.*

4. *The salesperson and the sales manager should be copied on this type of letter.*

5. *The creditor should consider holding all orders, including orders for replacement products and for promotional materials, until the balance due is paid.*

6. *The letter can be faxed to save time.*

[date]
[customer name]
[address]

Attention: Claudia N. Matty
          Accounting Manager

Dear Ms. Matty:

Last year, I extended to your company an open account
with a credit line of $X,XXX. At this point, I am won-
dering whether or not this decision was a mistake.

We have sent two letters concerning a delinquent balance
of $843.25. This amount is now almost 60 days past due.
In addition, I have left several messages for you and
for your subordinates that have gone unanswered.

Based on these facts, we are holding two orders pending.
A final decision about your account's status depends on
your response to this letter. Please call me at (800)
XXX-XXXX to discuss payment status.

Thank you for your prompt attention to this serious
problem.

Sincerely,

Elsa Blocker
Senior Credit Manager
[creditor company name]

cc: sales representative
    sales manager
    correspondence file
    seven-day follow-up file

Letter for Past-Due Account—Alternate Third Request 4

Past-Due Account—Alternate Third Request 5

Comments

1. *The first paragraph brings the debtor up-to-date. It shows that the creditor has waited patiently for payment.*

2. *The letter explains one of the penalties for slow payment—a "slow payer" credit rating.*

3. *The high-risk, chronically slow paying account will not be overly concerned about any ratings creditors provide unless you happen to be a very large creditor of theirs.*

4. *The sales department must be kept informed of the status of the delinquent account, especially at this critical stage of the collection process. Ironically, this is the point at which communication between sales and credit break down; yet it is still in the salesperson's best interest to try to get the customer to pay the debt as soon as possible. Even if the open account terms are withdrawn by the credit department, chances are that the account will be reviewed more favorably in the future if the debt is retired soon.*

[date]
[customer name]
[address]

Attention: Tom Paney
            [title]

RE: Past-due balance of $843.25

Dear Mr. Paney:

We have sent two monthly statements and two other reminders about the above referenced past-due balance. As
of this morning, the balance remained unpaid.

We provide information to two credit reporting agencies,
and dislike having to report your account as being slow
paying to them each month.

I encourage you to issue a check to clear this balance
before month-end when our next report to these agencies
is due.

Please call me if you have any questions at (800) XXX-
XXXX.

Thank you.

Sincerely,

Kristin Alfonso
Credit Manager
[creditor company name]

cc: sales representative
    credit file

Letter for Past-Due Account—Alternate Third Request 5

Past-Due Account—Alternate Third Request 6

Comments

1. *The customer is told to expect a visit from the local salesperson. The rapport between the salesperson and the customer may result in a payment.*

2. *Salespersons are not necessarily the best of collection people. They were hired for their sales ability, not their collection experience. However, personal contact by one who may be familiar with the account could produce the desirable result—while, at times, still retaining the account—even on a COD basis.*

3. *The down side is that the customer is likely to delay payment until the salesperson comes to visit.*

4. *Before this type of letter is sent, the credit department should have a firm commitment from the salesperson about how soon he or she can visit the account.*

5. *The salesperson should be told to report the results of the visit immediately—and reminded not to "shade" the truth about what was said during the meeting.*

6. *In the meantime, the account must remain on credit hold.*

[date]
[customer name]
[address]

Attention: Faith Crosset

Dear Ms. Crosset:

By copy of this letter, I am asking our sales representative to stop by your office at her earliest opportunity to discuss the status of the past-due balance of $843.25.

As you know from my prior correspondence and from my voice mail messages to you, this balance is almost 70 days past due.

I will ask [name of salesperson] to schedule this visit as soon as possible. In the meantime, the four orders pending will remain on credit hold.

Thank you.

Sincerely,

Irene Messerli
Credit Manager
Alt's Wholesale, Inc.

cc: sales representative
    sales manager
    correspondence file
    five-day pop-up file

Letter for Past-Due Account—Alternate Third Request 6

Past-Due Account—Alternate Third Request 7

Comments

1. *The customer's purchasing manager normally dislikes having to get involved with creditors. Sending a letter to the purchasing manager might put some heat on the Accounts Payable Department to clear up the problem.*

2. *The purchasing manager will be not be happy to hear that orders are on credit hold. The order could be placed with another vendor, but your company was selected for a reason. The Purchasing Department will be particularly unhappy if they learn they must change vendors because their Accounts Payable Department could not resolve a problem in a timely manner.*

3. *Once the letter is sent, any follow-up should be directed to Accounts Payable rather than to the purchasing manager.*

4. *To save time, this letter can be faxed to the Purchasing Department. The salesperson should be able to give you the fax number and the name of the purchasing manager.*

5. *Fax messages are often thought of as more public than a letter or a telephone call. If a debtor is having trouble paying its bills, it is not the type of news employees should know about. Therefore, sending a fax rather than a letter can have a psychological impact on the debtor, especially if it is a small company.*

[date]
[customer name]
[address]

Attention: Joe Raines
          Purchasing Manager

Re: ORDER HOLD

Dear Mr. Raines:

Your account with us is over 60 days past due. Your company's Accounts Payable Department has not responded to any of the calls or letters we have sent about this serious problem.

Unfortunately, we have no alternative but to hold orders at this point. I regret having to do so, but candidly I see no alternative.

If we were to receive an immediate payment in full, I would be prepared to release the two orders pending on open account terms.

Please call me if you have any questions at (800) XXX-XXXX.

Thank you for your assistance.

Sincerely,

William White
Credit Manager
[creditor company name]

cc: salesperson
    sales manager
    correspondence file
    credit file

Letter for Past-Due Account—Alternate Third Request 7

Past-Due Account—Alternate Third Request 8

Comments

1. *Another way to encourage delinquent accounts to pay is to charge interest on past-due balances.*

2. *Purchase orders, acknowledgments, statements, etc., can carry an insert as to interest charges for late payment. Interest charges to consumers are another matter discussed later in this book.*

3. *This letter uses a "good cop, bad cop" approach: "If you pay now, we will not charge interest. If you do not, interest charges will appear on your next invoice and must be paid along with the past-due balance before shipments can resume."*

4. *The salesperson should certainly be copied on a letter of this type.*

5. *At this point, the account should almost certainly be on credit hold.*

[date]
[customer name]
[address]

Attention: Jackie Peralta
            [title]

Dear Ms. Peralta:

INTEREST CHARGE NOTICE

Our terms of sale are net 30 days from date of invoice. Your account balance is now over 45 days past due. Our arrangement with your company also provides for an interest charge of 1% per month on any past-due balance.

We have sent two statements, two reminder notices and made at least two calls about the past-due balance of $X,XXX. At this point, we are holding orders and considering accruing interest charges on this open balance.

If you wish to avoid this interest charge—which would have to be paid before any orders could be released—please issue payment. If payment arrives by [date], the interest charge will not be added to your account balance.

Please call me at (800) XXX-XXXX if you have any questions.

Thank you.

Sincerely,

Ernie Olmedo
Zone Credit Manager
[creditor company name]

cc: sales representative
    credit file
    follow-up file

Letter for Past-Due Account—Alternate Third Request 8

Past-Due Account—Alternate Third Request 9

Comments

1. *There is nothing wrong with notifying the customer's Purchasing Department that the account is on credit hold.*

2. *The letter is brief and to the point.*

3. *The creditor hopes that the purchasing manager calls the Accounts Payable Department and brings additional pressure to bear to get the account cleaned up.*

4. *Delays in payment that result in orders being held are a major irritant to the Purchasing Department. This department understands that the company wants to hold onto its cash for as long as possible, but when doing so damages the purchasing agent's ability to obtain goods and services, then the Accounting Department has gone too far.*

5. *The salesperson should always be copied on this type of letter. Often, the purchasing agent will call the salesperson after receiving the letter rather than the credit department. It would not be good if the call came as a surprise.*

6. *This letter can be faxed to save time and to draw attention to the problem.*

[date]
[customer name]
[address]

Attention: Rick Sadoski
            [title]

Dear Mr. Sadoski:

Your company has an unpaid balance of $X,XXX that is now more than 60 days past due. Several calls have been placed to your company's Accounts Payable Department. Those calls have gone unanswered.

Unfortunately, I have no choice but to put your account on credit hold. I would appreciate any help you can offer in getting your Accounting Department to call me to discuss this serious problem.

If you have any questions, please call me at (800) XXX-XXXX.

Thank you.

Sincerely,

Joe Rifka
Credit Manager
[creditor company name]

cc: salesperson
    sales manager
    credit file
    follow-up file

Letter for Past-Due Account—Alternate Third Request 9

Past-Due Account—Alternate Third Request 10

Comments

1. *This letter is being addressed to a senior executive in the debtor company. The creditor should know the exact name and title.*

2. *It is assumed the executive cares about the credit reputation of the company. Of course, a hard-core slow paying account may not care what creditors think or do.*

3. *The letter can be faxed because it saves time and because, psychologically, a fax message is seen as more public than a letter or a telephone call.*

4. *The letter is brief and mild. Senior executives are rarely intimidated, especially by a letter. It is hoped this appeal to common sense will prompt the executive to order a payment issued immediately.*

[date]
[customer name]
[address]

Attention: Bart Salmons
          Controller

Dear Mr. Salmons:

Your company owes us $XX,XXX and this balance is now over 60 days past due. We have addressed this matter in writing several times, and left numerous messages with your Accounts Payable Department. Those calls and letters have gone unanswered.

Unless payment is received within the next few days, I will have no alternative but to put your account on credit hold.

I would appreciate your assistance in resolving this problem.

Sincerely,

John Weinstein
Credit Manager
[creditor company name]

cc: salesperson
    sales manager
    credit file
    follow-up file

Letter for Past-Due Account—
Alternate Third Request 10

Past-Due Account—Alternate Third Request 11

Comments

1. *A letter should be sent to the president of the debtor company only when the situation is serious.*

2. *The president of the company may never see this letter. It will probably be passed along to the Accounts Payable Department by the president's secretary with a note asking them to take care of the problem.*

3. *If the matter is this serious, the account should almost certainly be on credit hold.*

4. *Creditors should be aware that writing to the president of the debtor company is an unusual step. The credit professional must be sure of the facts, and it is probably a good idea to notify the Sales Department before the letter is sent.*

[date]
[customer name]
[address]

Attention: Kevin Evans
            President

Dear Mr. Evans:

I don't know whether this matter has come to your attention, but your company owes us $XX,XXX and this balance
is now over 60 days past due.

I have received no commitment from anyone in your Accounting Department about when this seriously past-due
balance will be paid.

Can you ask someone to review our account and to expedite payment to us?

Thank you.

Sincerely,

Fred Valdez
Corporate Credit Director
[creditor company name]

cc: sales manager
    salesperson
    credit file

**Letter for Past-Due Account—
Alternate Third Request 11**

Past-Due Account—Alternate Third Request 12

Comments

1. *The first paragraph is intended to catch the reader's attention.*

2. *It is assumed that every customer values its credit reputation.*

3. *No threat is made that the creditor will no longer offer the debtor company open account terms. The letter simply states that the account is on hold until the past-due balance is retired.*

4. *The Sales Department may be able to help. That department should be told that, by the time a third reminder is sent, any assistance they can offer will be welcomed.*

5. *The letter can be faxed to save time.*

[date]
[customer name]
[address]

Attention: Mark Raymont
           Accounts Payable Manager

Dear Mr. Raymont:

This is the third letter we have sent about a past-due balance of $XX,XXX. Your company's orders are now on credit hold with us. I'm sure your Purchasing Department and my Sales Department are not pleased about that.

As you know, I have called you several times already to try to discuss this past-due balance. For whatever reason, you have not returned any of my calls.

At this point, we are still prepared to offer your company open account terms if the past-due balance is cleared up quickly. The next step is up to you.

Please issue payment today. If you have any questions, please call me at (800) XXX-XXXX.

Thank you.

Sincerely,

Ogden Hasher
Credit Manager
[creditor company name]

cc: sales manager
    salesperson
    credit file
    follow-up file

**Letter for Past-Due Account—
Alternate Third Request 12**

Past-Due Account—Alternate Third Request 13

Comments

1. *This letter is straightforward. The creditor wants payment, and the customer wants shipment.*

2. *Even if the debtor pays, the creditor has not agreed to release the order on open account terms. That decision should be made only after payment is received and the credit manager updates and reviews the credit file.*

3. *There is no need to recite the history of the problem.*

4. *The Sales Department should be told that, even if payment is received, the order pending may not be released on open account terms.*

5. *It would not be unusual for someone on the sales force to follow up—not necessarily based on the letter but rather by inquiring what Ms. Cranforde wants to do about the pending order.*

[date]
[customer name]
[address]

Attention: Carla Cranforde
          [title]

Dear Carla:

As you know from our recent conversations, your account has a seriously past-due balance of $X,XXX. I was surprised to see an order submitted today by your company under purchase order #2309-98.

As soon as I receive your payment in full for the above referenced past-due balance, I will consider releasing this order that is now on credit hold.

Please notify your Purchasing Department about the credit hold. If you have any questions, please call me at (800) XXX-XXXX.

Thank you.

Sincerely,

Roger Williams
Assistant Credit Manager
[creditor company name]

cc: salesperson
    sales manager
    credit file

**Letter for Past-Due Account—
Alternate Third Request 13**

Past-Due Account—Alternate Third Request 14

Comments

1. *Sending the letter by certified mail is another technique to get correspondence noticed. It is especially effective if the debtor is avoiding your calls.*

2. *Mr. Centers now knows that his creditor is going to receive a little green card from the post office which indicates that this letter has been delivered.*

3. *It is hoped the certified letter will at least be opened and read. If so, it was worth the extra cost.*

4. *The debtor should be told that the account is on hold. Why keep it a secret?*

5. *The Sales Department should be encouraged to get involved at this point in the collection process. A copy of the letter should be sent by regular mail, just in case the debtor will not sign for a registered letter.*

CERTIFIED MAIL

[date]
[customer name]
[address]

Attention: Doyle Centers
            [title]

Dear Mr. Centers:

Unfortunately, I have had no response to previous correspondence and to my telephone calls to you regarding a
past-due balance of $X,XXX.

At this point, your account is on credit hold. I urge
you to issue payment immediately to clear up this delinquent balance. At this point, our decision to continue
to offer your company an open account depends on how
quickly the past-due balance is paid.

Thank you for your prompt attention to this problem.

Sincerely,

Joan Simpson
Credit Administrator
[creditor company name]

cc: salesperson
    sales manager
    credit file

**Letter for Past-Due Account—
Alternate Third Request 14**

Past-Due Account—Alternate Third Request—Mailgram

Comments

1. *Mailgrams may be more expensive than letters, but letters are a complete waste of time and effort unless they are read.*

2. *A mailgram may lend more credence to any threat to the debtor.*

3. *Only a brief summary of prior collection efforts is necessary. That summary is contained in the first paragraph.*

4. *The last paragraph demands payment.*

5. *By using Western Union services, it is possible to send a great number of such mailgrams at bulk rates. Consideration has to be given to standardization to some extend of the content of the message. The past-due balance can be in a reference area near the addressee. Western Union can be given a list of addresses and related amounts due plus one copy of the message. Compare the costs of sending 300 separate collection letters versus permitting Western Union to do it automatically on their equipment.*

```
                        MAILGRAM

WESTERN UNION

JOHN WILKER
WOODEN MACHINERY INC.
INDUSTRIAL DRIVE
CLAREMONT, CA

PRIOR LETTERS ABOUT $843.25 PAST DUE REMAIN UNANSWERED.

KINDLY REMIT PAYMENT IMMEDIATELY TO PREVENT FURTHER
PROBLEMS.


JIM MESTON
CREDIT MANAGER
STONE TOOL CO.
```

Letter for Past-Due Account—Alternate
Third Request—Mailgram

Delinquent Account—Alternate Final Demand 1

Comments

1. *The creditor has been patient long enough.*

2. *The debtor company has not even had the courtesy to respond to previous calls and letters.*

3. *Statistics show that the longer a creditor holds onto a seriously past-due account, the lower the likelihood of recovery when that account is eventually turned over to a collection agency or to an attorney.*

4. *The debtor might offer a compromise payment plan. That might be acceptable to the creditor as an alternative to suing the debtor or placing the account for collection. However, the first step is to open a dialogue with the debtor. If that cannot be accomplished, there is no reason to hold onto the account any longer.*

5. *This letter can be sent by fax to save time.*

6. *Whenever you threaten to place an account for collection, the top executive of the debtor company should receive a copy of the letter.*

[date]
[customer name]
[address]

Attention: Saul Sweeper
        [title]

Re: Past-due balance of $843.25

Dear Mr. Sweeper:

The above referenced balance is now 90 days past due. During that 90-day period, we have sent numerous reminders and made numerous calls to you about this matter. All of our calls and letters have been ignored.

Unless we receive payment in full by [date], we will have no alternative but to place your account for collection with [name of agency].

I urge you to give this matter your immediate attention.

Sincerely,

Nigel Cecil
Credit Manager
[creditor company name]

cc: [name], President, [debtor company]
    salesperson
    sales manager
    credit file
    follow-up file

**Letter for Delinquent Account—
Alternate Final Demand 1**

Delinquent Account—Alternate Final Demand 2

Comments

1. *Typically, the treasurer has the job of being sure that D & B and other credit reporting agencies cast a fair light on the operation. Therefore, addressing this type of letter to the treasurer may create the desired impact and a payment may follow.*

2. *If the Treasurer was not aware of the problem prior to receiving this letter, chances are good that the problem will soon be resolved.*

3. *Even if the debtor company is having cash flow problems, the Treasurer will almost certainly want to avoid the stigma of being placed for collection. Other trade creditors would view a creditor placing the company for collection with concern.*

4. *The tone of the letter is not strong, just matter-of-fact. There is no need to make any appeals. The letter states that a) this is what has happened, b) this is what should have happened and c) this is what is going to happen in five days, unless a check is received.*

5. *The letter should be sent by fax or by overnight delivery.*

[date]
[customer name]
[address]

Attention: D. Mark Moore
            Treasurer

Dear Mr. Moore:

We have called your Accounting Department a number of times about an unpaid balance of $XX,XXX. In addition, we have sent several letters about this seriously past-due balance. To date, these efforts have not even been rewarded with a telephone call to discuss the past-due balance.

With these facts in mind, I have no alternative but to inform you that if payment is not received by [date], your account will be placed for collection with [name of agency].

I urge you to take the necessary steps to prevent this since the only party that wins if this happens is the collection agency. Please call me at (800) XXX-XXXX if you have any questions or wish to discuss this matter.

Sincerely,

Bill Camelot
Credit Manager
[creditor company name]

cc: [name], President, [debtor company]
    salesperson
    sales manager
    credit file
    follow-up file

**Letter for Delinquent Account—
Alternate Final Demand 2**

Delinquent Account—Alternate Final Demand 3

Comments

1. *This letter is sent to the president of the company. The president may also be the owner of the company and therefore the person with the most to lose if the company's credit reputation is damaged.*

2. *Of course this person may not read the letter, as it may get forwarded by a secretary to the appropriate authority. Even if that is the case, a letter passed down from the office of the president may receive priority attention.*

3. *The line has been drawn in this letter: payment or legal action. The decision is up to the debtor.*

4. *The debtor may call and try to stall the creditor. If the creditor backs down, it may send the wrong message.*

5. *The letter should be sent by fax or overnight delivery to save time.*

[date]
[customer name]
[address]

Attention: John Wenzel
           President

Dear Mr. Wenzel:

You may be unaware of a serious problem involving a delinquent balance of $XX,XXX. We have been trying without success for the last two months to get your accounting department and your Controller to clear this balance.

At this point, we are prepared to turn your account over to an attorney to file suit unless payment is received by [date]. As President of [name of debtor], we thought you would want to know, and that you might want to intervene to prevent this from happening.

Please ask your accounts payable department to issue payment immediately to clear the past-due balance. If you have any questions, please feel free to call me at (800) XXX-XXXX.

Thank you.

Sincerely,

Sam Wilts
Corporate Credit Manager
[creditor company name]

cc: salesperson
    sales manager
    credit file
    follow-up file

**Letter for Delinquent Account—
Alternate Final Demand 3**

Delinquent Account—Alternate Final Demand 4

Comments

1. *The underlined caption is intended to grab the reader's attention.*

2. *The Treasurer may pay upon receipt of this letter, or the company may want to go to court to settle the matter.*

3. *A law firm in the debtor's immediate locality should be used, if possible.*

4. *The letter should be sent by fax or by overnight delivery.*

5. *The president of the debtor company should be sent a copy of this letter.*

6. *The credit manager must be certain of the facts before sending any final demand letter.*

NOTIFICATION OF LAWSUIT

[date]
[customer name]
[address]

Attention: Robert Moran
           Treasurer

Dear Mr. Moran:

I have called you a number of times, but have not received a return call. As you know, your account with this company is seriously past-due.

Because we have not heard from you, and since we have received no commitment for payment of the past-due balance of $XX,XXX, we are now considering placing your account with a third party for collection.

If payment is not received by [date], your account will be turned over to our attorney, Scotter and Company, located in Glendale.

I hope this will not be necessary, but that is up to you. If you have any questions, please call me at (800) XXX-XXXX.

Sincerely,

Juanita Rojas
Director of Credit and Collections
[creditor company name]

cc: [name], President, [debtor company]
    salesperson
    sales manager
    credit file
    follow-up file

Letter for Delinquent Account—
Alternate Final Demand 4

Delinquent Account—Alternate Final Demand 5

Comments

1. *The caption above the body of the letter is intended to create interest in the letter. A little curiosity may make the recipient read the entire letter. Remember that a truly bad credit risk may receive several collection letters each time the mail is delivered.*

2. *The debtor may have made previous commitments of payment, and may have intended to keep them until another creditor contacted the debtor who was more creative or persuasive.*

3. *The debtor may have limited cash and often chooses to use that cash to "grease the squeakiest wheel." Therefore, one tactic used with success in collections involves being the loudest complainer and therefore the squeakiest wheel.*

4. *Some collection agencies specialize in a particular industry. Their reputation precedes them, both with creditors and debtors. Their familiarity with the industry may be particularly effective in a last ditch collection effort.*

$843.25 Past Due

COLLECTION NOTICE

[date]
[customer name]
[address]

Attention: Anne Abler
            Controller

Dear Ms. Abler:

We have sent several notices to you regarding the above referenced past-due balance. As you know, we received a commitment that the balance due would be paid. That commitment was made two weeks ago.

At this point, I have no alternative but to turn the account over to Bates and Bates, a collection agency in our industry, unless we receive payment in full within five (5) days.

I urge you to give this matter your immediate attention.

Thank you.

Sincerely,

Russ Wilmas
Credit Manager
[creditor company name]

cc: sales representative
    file
    five-day follow-up

**Letter for Delinquent Account—
Alternate Final Demand 5**

Letter to Be Sent before Placing with an Attorney

Comments

1. *A customer's credit can be seriously affected by a decision by one of its creditors to file suit to collect an unpaid debt. Filing a lawsuit is a matter of public record, something debtor companies normally try to avoid.*

2. *The key elements of the letter on the opposite page are (a) a simple and direct appeal to the debtor's common sense and (b) a reminder of the value of a good credit reputation.*

3. *Once such a threat is made, credit professionals must follow through or they will lose credibility and be seen as indecisive and ineffective.*

4. *The letter requests payment in full by return mail. This is not the time to suggest payment plans.*

5. *The salesperson should always be copied on a final demand letter such as this one.*

6. *This letter could be sent by fax to increase its impact and visibility.*

[date]
[customer name]
[address]

Attention: Andrew Smillie
            [title]

Dear Mr. Smillie:

As you know, we have been trying for some time to collect a past-due balance of $842.35 from you. Our efforts
to date have failed completely. This has prompted us to
consider asking our attorney to file suit against your
company.

Since suits are a matter of public record, I wanted to
be sure to give you this last opportunity to clear this
balance before we initiate a lawsuit. I believe it is in
your best interest and ours that this matter be resolved
outside the court system.

Please send your payment by return mail. A self-addressed stamped envelope is included for your convenience.

This will be our final letter to you about this matter.
If payment is not received by [date], your account will
be referred to our attorney.

The decision is yours to make. I urge you to give this
matter your immediate attention.

Sincerely,

Andrea Minor
Western Regional Credit Manager
[creditor company name]

enc.

cc: salesperson
    sales manager
    credit file
    correspondence file

Letter to Be Sent before Placing with an Attorney

Chapter 6

Other Effective Credit Letters

Writers of any business correspondence have to know how to influence others to see their point of view. The key in credit letter writing is that the letters must be especially well written since they are supposed to encourage a reluctant debtor to do something they do not want to do—pay up!

Avoid Business English

Any book or seminar on letter writing will stress a conventional approach to business correspondence. Unfortunately, standard or conventional collection letters are frequently ignored. One way to improve letter-writing skills is to save copies of letters that you feel are especially effective. From time to time, credit professionals must review each of their form letters and revise them in order to make them as effective as possible.

Experienced credit professionals know that effective letters:

- Are concise, direct and easy to understand.
- Request immediate action.
- Include all relevant information.
- Have all relevant documentation attached.
- If appropriate, give the debtor company a face-saving way out.

Brevity

Are there paragraphs, sentences or even words that do not contribute to accomplishing the goal of the letter? If so, remove them. Less is sometimes better.

Recommendation: Rarely is a carefully crafted credit or collection letter more than one page.

Documentation

A credit or collection letter can reference other documents (with copies attached). Supporting documentation should be attached to remove excuses for additional delays in payment.

Minimize Form Letters

Every businessperson recognizes that form letters are a useful shortcut. Form letters can be most effective when they do not look like form letters—when they are personalized. If a nonpersonalized form letter is used, the recipient will probably dismiss the creditor as not a serious threat since the method of delivering the message is so weak and impersonal.

With the widespread use of personal computers, it is normally possible—even simple—to customize and personalize letters that are, generally speaking, form letters. With that in mind, there are very few good reasons to use a form letter that looks like a form letter to the reader.

Be a Salesperson

Many credit professionals do not view themselves as having much in common with salespeople. However, if creditors are going to collect using letters, those letters must sell the idea that it is in the debtor's best interest to pay the creditor as soon as possible. The reader should be told how cooperation is in the best interest of all parties concerned.

Misuse of Tone

All the facts contained in the letter may be correct. The creditor may be justified in sending a letter to the debtor; yet the reader may take the letter the wrong way. Why? Perhaps the letter rubbed the debtor the wrong way. Some common problems are that the letter:

- Is more demanding or threatening than required.
- Stresses the creditor's needs more than the debtor's.
- Conveys a condescending attitude.
- Repeats points.
- Is discourteous.
- Is unprofessional.
- Lacks tact.
- Is not truthful.
- Is not accurate.

The tone of a letter should avoid unnecessarily antagonizing the debtor, no matter how severe the collection problem.

Observation: A professional approach displayed in the credit letter will further support the facts contained in the letter and the serious nature of the problem. Therefore, the debtor should be more likely to respond appropriately.

Collection Communication Checklist

Comments

1. Reference. *Collection letters should always include debtor's name, address, invoice date, description of merchandise or service and amount due.*

2. Personal attention. *Avoid form letters. Tailor the letter to the individual situation. Try to address the letter to a particular individual at the debtor firm.*

3. Affix responsibility. *Note the fact that the debtor signed an order or accepted the merchandise or service.*

4. Motivation. *Appeal to honesty, fair play, valued reputation, desire to avoid disputes, goodwill and maintaining vendor relationships.*

5. Face saving. *Consider phrases such as "inadvertently overlooked," "earlier letters not referred to you," etc. Do not imply that an invoice was deliberately bypassed.*

6. Urgency. *The tone should indicate that the matter should be settled quickly but avoid an indication of panic. Sometimes letters mailed about a week apart can be creating a sense of urgency.*

7. Attention formats. *Use different types of letters, shapes, sizes, colors, etc. Intersperse with mailgrams, telegrams and telephone calls. Similarity of communications can counter the sense of urgency. Routine letters defeat any motivation to settle the matter.*

8. Heightened impact. *Sending a document by registered letter with return receipt requested will assure that the debtor received the letter and indicates urgency. Collecting more quickly and with less follow-up can easily offset the added cost of mailing such letters.*

9. Promises. *Remind debtors that they agreed to pay within certain credit terms.*

10. Time element. *Affix a limit as to when a response is desired. "Return mail," "promptly," or "within seven days" can reinforce a sense of urgency.*

Collection Communication Checklist

1. *Courteous*. Concentrate on the tone of your letter or memo so that it is well received.

2. *Conversational*. A collection letter should not be stiff and formal. It should be conversational because conversational letters are more easily understood.

3. *Correct*. Check the facts. Do not mail a letter until you are sure the facts are correct.

4. *Concise*. Unnecessary details should be avoided. Every attempt should be made to make letters explicit and exact.

5. *Clarity*. Plan the letter. Continue from point to point in a logical order. End with a conclusion and a request for specific action from the debtor.

6. *Consideration*. Look at the matter in question—and the letter—from the reader's perspective. Stress the points that interest the reader. Invite the reader to call you if they have any questions or comments.

7. *Completeness*. Leaving out an important fact or failing to include copies of appropriate documents can unnecessarily delay payment. Before signing a letter, make certain all the facts are included. Use the "idiot test." Ask yourself if anyone who reads this letter will understand the points made and the requested action.

Explanation of Incorrect Credit Deduction

Comments

1. *A customer has two accounts, a foreign and a domestic account. A payment was apparently applied to the wrong account.*

2. *While the letter writer might well understand the situation, the reader might not. The letter can explain the situation in step-by-step fashion or provide a reconciliation of the customer's foreign and domestic accounts.*

3. *Of course, the real solution is to make certain that payments are not misapplied to begin with. Even if credit managers do not supervise the Accounts Receivable Department, they should make certain that safeguards are in place so that this serious error does not occur frequently.*

4. *Credit managers should keep records of this type of posting error. If a pattern emerges, or it turns out that one cash application clerk is responsible for the majority of these errors, then the credit manager has the information necessary to recommend corrective action.*

[date]
[customer name]
[address]

RE: Invoice #9731 dated 8/31/XX for $831.25

Dear Mr. Jones:

Please be advised that a credit of $823.71 was applied in error to your domestic account rather than to your international account with us. As a result, the above referenced invoice was cleared on your check number 9113 dated 7/4/XX.

This transaction has been reversed. The credit now appears on your international account statement (copy enclosed). The invoice listed above again appears on your domestic account—and is now past due. A statement of your domestic account appears for your review.

We apologize for any inconvenience this matter may cause you. However, in light of the facts outlined in this letter, and supported by the attached documents, we must ask that invoice #9731 be placed in line for payment.

Please call me if you have any questions about this matter.

Thank you.

Sincerely,

Rick Crawford
Credit Supervisor
[creditor company name]

enc.

cc: file

Letter Explaining Incorrect Credit Deduction

Declining a Request for Credit Limit Increase—
Increase Is Unnecessary

Comments

1. *Once a customer has reached the credit limit, the credit manager has a decision to make about whether to continue to support the growth in sales with a larger credit limit.*

2. *It is always easier to say "yes" to such a request than it is to say "no." However, certain accounts simply do not qualify for a larger line of credit. In particular, customers that need a larger credit limit because they do not pay their bills on time are not particularly good candidates for a credit limit increase.*

3. *Rather than simply declining the increase, the experienced credit professional can use the request for a larger credit limit to bring to customers' attention their payment pattern. Customers should be delicately told that, if they paid more promptly, there would be no need for a larger credit line.*

4. *The letter should begin by acknowledging the increase in sales volume and by thanking customers for their business.*

5. *The salesperson should be copied on this type of letter, along with the sales manager.*

[date]
[customer name]
[address]

Attention: Ross Armstrong
            [title]

Dear Mr. Armstrong:

Thank you for the orders you have been sending us. There has been a substantial increase in business with your company over the last three months. Because of this increase in business, our Sales Department has approached me to request that your credit limit be doubled to $XX,XXX to accommodate sales increases.

In reviewing your account, we note that your company does not take advantage of the cash discount we offer. Our terms of sale are 2% 15 days, net 30 days, but your company pays invoices in an average of 55 days. If you were to take advantage of the cash discount and pay within 15 days, it would more than triple the amount you could buy at your present credit limit.

Even if you simply paid within the net 30-day terms, you would almost double the amount of purchases you could make. Therefore, we believe your present credit limit should meet your needs.

If you have any questions, please call me at (800) XXX-XXXX.

Thank you.

Sincerely,

Matthew Perrault
Controller
[creditor company name]

cc: salesperson
    sales manager
    credit file

**Letter Declining a Request for Credit Limit Increase—
Increase Is Unnecessary**

Partial Payment Received—No Explanation

Comments

1. *Occasionally, a delinquent debtor will attempt to satisfy more than one creditor by making partial payments. They may have every intention of paying creditors and may be trying hard to catch up.*

2. *Unfortunately, it is probably equally likely that they will fall further behind as it is that they will eventually catch up.*

3. *While it is sometimes difficult to "look a gift horse in the mouth," creditors must try to retain as much control over the collection process as possible. Therefore, creditors who do not challenge and require debtors to provide them with specific payment commitments tend to receive partial payments more and more sporadically and might eventually end up with a bad debt.*

4. *When a partial payment is received, the payment should be acknowledged, and the debtor should be asked to provide a realistic schedule for retiring the remainder of the balance due.*

5. *If the debtor does not respond to the letter, the creditor must not hope (or assume) that additional payments will follow periodically.*

6. *Unless a commitment is received, the creditor must proceed in an orderly manner toward placing the account with a third party for collection.*

7. *This letter can be sent by fax to expedite the collection process.*

[date]
[customer name]
[address]

Attention: James S. Bailey
            [title]

Dear Mr. Bailey:

We recently received your payment of $843.25 on check number 34993. Thank you for that payment.

Your payment did not contain any explanation about why the remaining past-due balance of $4,201.67 was not paid or when it will be paid. However, the fact that you sent a payment is an indication that you want to resolve this problem.

Naturally, we are anxious to resolve this problem as quickly as possible. Therefore, please call me upon receipt of this letter to discuss the remaining balance of $4.201.67.

Thank you.

Sincerely,

Malcolm Davis
Credit Manager
[creditor company name]

cc: salesperson
    credit file

Letter for Partial Payment Received—No Explanation

Refusal to Increase Credit Line

Comments

1. *Naturally, a company wants to do more business with its existing customers by expanding their credit limits. However, as painful or as unpopular as the idea might be, there must be a limit to credit extensions.*

2. *Before deciding not to increase a credit limit, every argument must be heard and every fact carefully considered.*

3. *Sales personnel have a vested interest in getting their customers' credit limits increased. On the other side of the fence is the credit professional. But who gets the blame if something goes wrong? Certainly not the salesperson!*

4. *When a decision not to increase a credit limit has been made, it is expected that the decision can easily be explained and justified. However, the best way to avoid arguments with customers is not to get into the specifics about why a larger credit line was not offered.*

5. *Of course, if the customer's situation changes for the better, you might reconsider your decision. Any communication about a decision not to expand the line should state that, if conditions change, the decision would be revisited.*

[date]
[customer name]
[address]

Attention: Wally Warlow
            Senior Buyer

Dear Mr. Warlow:

Thank you for your recent inquiry regarding your current credit line. We have carefully reviewed the information you provided to us. However, at present we must continue to offer the credit line of $XXXXX, which was extended to your company on March first of this year.

This decision is based on the information you provided to us along with our own inquiries. If in the future your company's financial condition changes significantly, we would be happy to review your account at that time for a larger limit.

Please feel free to call me if you have any questions. My telephone number is (800) XXX-XXXX.

Thank you.

Sincerely,

Sandra Sumer
Assistant Credit Manager
[creditor company name]

cc: sales representative
     file

Letter Refusing to Increase Credit Line

Explanation of a Decision Not to Increase Credit Limit

Comments

1. *It is never easy to decline to offer the credit limit the customer or the salesperson requests.*

2. *Trade creditors are not required to share their sources of information or what they might have said about the customer/applicant when declining an increase.*

3. *This letter tries to turn down the request as tactfully as possible. Once again, the goal is to convey the news and to retain the customer.*

4. *The customer/applicant is told that, if conditions change, the decision not to increase the line can and will be reconsidered.*

[date]
[customer name]
[address]

Attention: Wayne Waldec
          Controller

Dear Mr. Waldec:

Thank you for your recent letter requesting an explanation about why your company was denied the increase to your open account credit limit that you requested. It would be difficult to try to explain in any detail our current credit granting philosophy. Therefore, rather than trying to do, so allow me to simply state that your company does not meet our current criteria for extending $XX,XXX in open account credit as you had requested.

We will be happy to review this decision again in six months or if conditions change within your company.

Thank you for your continued interest in this company and its products.

Sincerely,

Mike Glenn
Director of Credit
[creditor company name]

cc: credit file

Letter Explaining Why Credit Increase Was Denied

Moratorium Denied, Partial Payment Requested

Comments

1. *Delinquent accounts cost trade creditors money. That cost comes in the form of additional handling, additional bad debt losses, and lost interest in money that should have been in your bank rather than in the customer's.*

2. *Before considering any moratorium on payments, ask yourself these simple questions: Have any other creditors been approached for extended dating? Are they selling on open account terms with extended dating?*

3. *Rather than continuing to borrow from its trade creditors, the debtor really should try to borrow from those that know what they are doing in this area—specifically, banks, factors, finance companies, and flooring companies.*

4. *Even if cash is tight, the debtor should be urged to remit a partial payment. The failure to receive a check is indicative that the account is going to be a serious problem, and follow-up in seven days must be strong.*

[date]
[customer name]
[address]

Attention: Robert Wilson

RE: $842.25 past due

Dear Mr. Wilson:

Thank you for your recent letter regarding your company's current financial problems.

Unfortunately, we cannot grant your request for a moratorium on payment of the outstanding balance. As you know, the product in question was delivered on time in good condition, and our shipment was made based on the agreed terms of sale of net 30 days from date of invoice. The outstanding amount is now over 60 days past due.

We must have your account brought more current immediately. Please send an immediate payment of $250.00 as an indication of your goodwill, and let's discuss a realistic repayment schedule on the remaining balance owed.

My telephone number is (800) XXX-XXXX. Thank you.

Sincerely,

Jack Springer
Collections Manager
[creditor company name]

cc: credit file
    sales representative

Letter Denying Moratorium, Partial Payment Requested

Moratorium on Payment Denied, Partial Payment Requested

Comments

1. *Occasionally, customers ask for an open-ended moratorium on payment of a past-due balance. They normally indicate that the problem is temporary, but at the same time they offer no commitment at all for payment.*

2. *From the creditor's perspective, this request is unreasonable. The letter explains this position in a manner that is neither threatening nor condescending.*

3. *When considering any payment moratorium and/or payment plan, the creditor should always request a "good faith" payment as well as a realistic and reasonable payment plan.*

4. *By asking the debtor to call, the creditor allows them time to consider the counterproposal being made.*

[date]
[customer name]
[address]

Attention: Stan Turner

Dear Mr. Turner:

I just received your letter dated [month] and [date] requesting a moratorium on payment of the outstanding balance due of $845.25. I am pleased to learn that your cash flow problem is only temporary and, while I can sympathize with your company's current dilemma, I cannot grant an indefinite moratorium on payments to you or to any other debtor. As a business owner, I am confident you understand the logic behind this decision.

Please call me at your earliest opportunity to discuss a realistic payment plan. My telephone number is (800) XXX-XXXX. I would also ask that you send an immediate payment of $250.00 as a demonstration of your goodwill.

Thank you.

Sincerely,

Jack Springer
Collection Manager
[creditor company name]

cc: credit file
    sales representative

**Letter Denying Moratorium on Payment,
Partial Payment Requested**

Delinquent Account—Installment Payment Plan Approved

Comments

1. *In considering a payment plan offered by the debtor, the creditor must try to remain in control of the situation. Otherwise, the creditor is relegated to the position of a child waiting to receive a monthly allowance.*

2. *The payment plan should be put into writing. Once a debtor has begun to slip behind, it becomes easier and easier to miss other commitments and deadlines.*

3. *The agreement (or contract) should state (a) the date and the amount of future payments and (b) that, if payments are not made as agreed, the entire balance becomes immediately due and payable.*

4. *Installment payment agreements often include a provision for the payment of interest on the past-due balance. Sometimes, this interest charge is waived if the debtor makes the payments as agreed.*

5. *If debtors refuse to sign the letter shown on the opposite page, they may not be sincere about their desire and/or ability to retire the debt. The installment plan may be nothing more than a delay tactic. Therefore, the offer letter contains a "drop-dead" date after which the proposal to accept partial payments is withdrawn and the entire amount is once again due and payable.*

6. *If a creditor threatens to place an account for collection unless the debtor agrees to a proposal, the creditor either follows through on the threat or loses credibility with the customer and possibly with the Sales Department.*

[date]
[customer name]
[address]

Attention: Karl Kravitte
              [title]

Dear Mr. Kravitte:

I have just received your recent letter outlining your company's financial problems and suggesting that the past-due balance of $845.25 be paid on an installment basis over the next four months.

While we do not normally agree to accept any installment payment proposals, your letter indicates that you are sincere in your desire to retire this past-due balance as quickly as possible.

Therefore, we would agree to the following payment program:

- An immediate payment of $200.00.
- Two monthly payments of $200.00 due on the tenth of next month and on the 10th of the month after.
- A final payment to clear the remaining balance of $245.25 due by the 10th of [month].

In the event that any payment is more than five (5) days past due, it is agreed that the entire balance open will become due and payable immediately. If this occurs, we will take all reasonable and prudent steps to protect our right to payment.

If this agreement is acceptable to you, please sign below and return this document to me in the envelope provided. If I do not receive this document within 10 (ten) days, I will assume you are unwilling to agree to this proposal, which will then be withdrawn. At that point, we will have no alternative but to refer your account to a third party for immediate action.

I urge you to give this proposal your serious and immediate attention. Please feel free to call me at (800) XXX-XXXX if you have any questions.

Thank you.

Sincerely,

Leo Starre
Credit Manager
[creditor company name]

Agreed and accepted by: _____

                    Date: _____

Letter for Delinquent Account—Installment Payment Plan Approved

Long Installment Plan Rejected

Comments

1. *Occasionally, a customer will propose a payment plan that is far too protracted to be acceptable.*

2. *When such an offer is received, the credit professional must respond with a strongly worded letter rejecting the offer.*

3. *At the same time, the credit professional can offer an "olive branch" of sorts by making a more realistic counterproposal.*

4. *The counteroffer letter should contain a "drop-dead" date on which the offer is withdrawn.*

5. *If the letter is sent by someone other than the president or the chief financial officer of the debtor company, the creditor's response letter should be copied to the debtor company president.*

6. *Creditors should remember that often a proposal from a debtor with an unusually long payback period is nothing more than a trial balloon. The debtor can expect that for every ten of these letters sent, at least one creditor will agree without protest to the extended payment plan.*

[date]
[customer name]
[address]

Attention: Fred Snow
          [title]

Dear Mr. Snow:

I just received and reviewed your letter of [date] containing your proposal for payment of the outstanding balance of $845.25 over a six-month period. This payment proposal is unacceptable. Simply stated, it is unrealistic to ask that we accept such a protracted payout on a balance that is already over 60 days past due.

I am prepared to make the following counteroffer:

- An immediate payment of $200.00.
- Progress payments of $200.00 per month beginning next month and due by the tenth day of each month until the entire past-due balance is cleared.

If this proposal is acceptable to you, please sign below and return this agreement in the envelope provided. If I do not receive your written response within ten days, this offer is withdrawn. At that point, your account will be referred to a third party for immediate collection or legal action.

I urge you to give this letter and offer your serious and immediate attention.

Thank you.

Sincerely,

Robert Sutton
Corporate Credit Director
[creditor company name]

Agreed and accepted by: _____

          Date: _____

enc. copy of letter and return envelope

Letter Rejecting Long Installment Plan

Letter to Attorney Turning Over an Account

Comments

1. *If possible, select an attorney who is in the immediate locale of the debtor company. A local firm may be familiar with the account or may have a good rapport with the local courts.*

2. *A telephone call with the law firm should precede any decision to place the account for collection.*

3. *The fee arrangement can be a percentage of the collected amount or be based on an hourly arrangement.*

4. *The letter to the attorney should be completely forthright. For example, if the debtor has raised an objection to the debt or a counterclaim, the law firm should be so informed.*

5. *All necessary facts and supporting documentation should be included with the letter to the attorney. Any requests for additional information or documentation should be answered promptly.*

6. *Some law firms charge only a nominal amount if the debtor company responds with payment within a specific, short period of time after receiving the attorney's letter. Such a policy should be discussed and agreed on in writing and in advance of any placement.*

[date]
Morgan and Stevens
Attorneys at Law
123 Juris Drive
Chicago, IL 60609

Re: The Gorter Co.
   999 Third Street
   Garfield, IL 60701

Dear Ms. Morgan:

We are turning the above referenced account over to you for collection. Enclosed are the relevant documents in support of our claim. Please let me know if you need any additional information.

This customer has been given every opportunity to pay us. Therefore, we are not interested in offering or accepting any additional promises from this debtor short of payment in full.

I am not aware of any counterclaims or offsets by the debtor. Further, I have spoken recently with the debtor and can confirm the company is still in business and at the address listed above.

As usual, settlement should include payment of the debt plus legal costs, court costs, and interest on the debt (based on the terms contained in our credit application, which the debtor did sign).

Please keep me up-to-date as this situation develops. Feel free to call me if you have any questions.

Thank you.

Sincerely,

Roger Wales
Credit Manager
[creditor company name]

enc. statement, invoice copies, signed credit application

cc: bad debt credit file

Letter to Attorney Turning Over an Account

Response to a Debtor's Call After Referral to an Attorney

Comments

1. *Occasionally, after an account has been placed with an attorney for collection, the debtor will contact the creditor to try to negotiate a settlement.*

2. *It is rarely a good idea to respond to these settlement offers. Often, the debtor is simply responding to the pressure from the attorney.*

3. *Often, the debtor's offer or proposal is not sincere. It is simply another effort to delay payment.*

4. *The debtor may also be calling simply because the pressure is mounting. Of course, as a creditor, this is exactly the response you wanted when the account was placed with an attorney and a lawsuit was filed.*

5. *The creditor's best course of action is to refer the debtor back to the attorney. If there is a settlement or compromise, the attorney can structure it to protect the creditor's interests.*

[date]
[customer name]
[address]

Attention: Wayne Morse
          [title]

Dear Mr. Morse:

I am in receipt of your letter dated [date], in which you explain why your account became delinquent and ask that we accept a payment of $XXXX.XX as full and final settlement of the balance due.

As you know, your account has been placed with the law firm of George and Kahn of Seattle, Washington. We have found from experience that it is best not to interfere with the efforts of our attorneys once suit has been filed, unless of course we receive payment in full from the debtor company. Since you are not proposing payment in full, I have forwarded your letter to our attorneys without comment.

Please feel free to contact Mr. Kahn at (800) XXX-XXXX if you wish to discuss any offer of settlement.

Thank you.

Sincerely,

James Dell
Credit Manager
[creditor company name]

enc. letter from debtor

cc: Jim Kahn
    George and Kahn, LLC

Letter Rejecting a Settlement Offer

Follow-up Letter to an Attorney

Comments

1. *Lawyers, like anyone else, are busy and place certain priorities on their various requirements for time. Therefore, an occasional progress report is desirable.*

2. *In addition, the law firm may have hit a snag in its collection efforts and the creditor could be of some assistance.*

3. *A follow-up after one month is appropriate if the law firm has not already provided the creditor with an update. A letter from the creditor indicates to the attorney handling the case that the creditor company considers the matter to be important, even urgent.*

4. *Creditors should obtain relevant information such as:*

   - *When the debtor company was contacted.*
   - *Their response, if any.*
   - *The next step in the process.*
   - *When their next step will be taken.*
   - *What, if anything, the creditor can do to assist or to expedite the collection process.*

[date]
George and Kahn
Attorneys at Law
123 Office Drive
Seattle, WA 20122

Re: Cowletter Corporation
    999 Orchard Ave.
    Seattle, WA 20220

Dear Mr. George:

Last month, we turned over the above referenced customer
to you for collection. The unpaid balance remains
$9,123.77.

Please give me an update as to the status of your collection efforts on our behalf.

Thank you.

Sincerely,

Jennifer Mover
Credit Manager
[creditor company name]

cc: credit file

Follow-up Letter to an Attorney

Counterclaim Denied—Attorney Letter

Comments

1. *Often, after internal collection efforts have failed and an account has been placed for collection, the debtor company will assert some reason or excuse for nonpayment.*

2. *One popular reason/excuse is that the merchandise sold was not satisfactory. Even if the counterclaim is entirely unjustified, the claim must be answered. Any relevant documentation supporting the merchantability of the product in question should be provided.*

3. *If the customer failed to assert that the product in question did not conform to requirements prior to the account being referred and a lawsuit being filed, that information should also be shared with your attorney.*

4. *Often, the purpose of a counterclaim is to muddy the waters and further delay payment or settlement of a claim. Sometimes when a counterclaim is filed, attorneys representing the creditor will ask their clients to consider an out-of-court settlement.*

5. *Of course, the creditor may elect to proceed with the lawsuit and to have their day in court. The fact that a counterclaim was filed means the trial will be longer, more complex and, of course, more costly.*

[date]
Corten & Smythe, LLP
Attorneys at Law
123 Court Plaza
Austin, TX 52112

Re: Fennsing Corporation
    1408 A. Sunset Drive
    Bearsville, TX 52118

Dear Mr. Corten:

Thank you for your recent letter regarding the above referenced account and the counterclaim the debtor recently filed. The debtor has asserted that the material we delivered to them was not in accordance with the sample.

First, at no time prior to the filing of this counterclaim did the debtor ever complain about the product received. The customer signed the delivery document without protest or comments. I have spoken with the salesperson and the sales manager, and both of them report that the customer never complained about the quality of the product we sold. In fact, the customer always said the reason for the delay in payment was their cash flow problems.

In my opinion, the claim is totally without merit, and therefore it should be denied.

Please file the appropriate response, and let me know if you have any questions or require any additional information or documentation.

Thank you.

Sincerely,

Joseph Flatt
Director of Credit
[creditor company name]

cc: credit file

Counterclaim Denied—Attorney Letter

Information Letter to a Credit Guarantor

Comments

1. *Preferably, the debtor pays its own bills, and the creditor does not have to get embroiled in trying to enforce a personal guaranty.*

2. *The letter on the opposite page is not a demand for payment to the guarantor. Instead, it is a warning that such a demand may be made.*

3. *The letter is intended to prompt the guarantor to contact the debtor and pressure the debtor to pay the creditor immediately.*

4. *The tone of the letter is professional and courteous. It does not preclude payment coming from either the debtor or the guarantor.*

5. *If no payment is received within ten days, the creditor must act promptly.*

[date]
[guarantor name]
[address]

Re: Wooden Tool Company
    $845.25 past due

Dear Mr. Davidson:

As you know, our files contain your personal guaranty for the above referenced account, The Wooden Tool Company. The guaranty requires that we seek payment from you for any amounts that may become past due.

Unfortunately, the amount referenced above is seriously past due and Wooden Tool Company has been unable to make a commitment for payment.

If we do not receive payment within the next ten days, we will have no alternative but to demand payment from you under the terms of the personal guaranty.

Please take any action you feel is appropriate in order that this demand need not be made.

Thank you.

Sincerely,

John Rodes
Area Credit Manager
[creditor company name]

cc: credit file

Information Letter to a Credit Guarantor

NSF Check Put in for Second Presentment

Comments

1. *Occasionally, a customer's check will bounce due to insufficient funds (NSF).*

2. *Most creditor companies have an arrangement with their bank that NSF checks will be redeposited automatically.*

3. *It is important that debtors be called as quickly as possible so that they have time to make the necessary arrangements with their bank to be sure the check clears.*

4. *This letter may be faxed to the customer for expediency.*

5. *Multiple NSF checks are a clear indication that the debtor company is either in financial difficulty or at the very least is a poor recordkeeper. With this in mind, creditors should track the number of NSF checks they receive from each debtor and act appropriately to manage credit risk.*

[date]
[customer name]
[address]

Attention: John Dean
          [title]

Dear Mr. Dean:

We recently received and deposited your check number 7223 for $845.25. We received notice today from our bank that this check was returned due to insufficient funds. Per our instructions, our bank has redeposited that check.

Please make any necessary arrangements so that the check clears on the second presentment to your bank.

Thank you.

Sincerely,

Sam Walter
Assistant Credit Manager
[creditor company name]

cc: sales representative
    credit file

Letter for NSF Check Put in for Second Presentment

NSF Check Put in for Bank Collection

Comments

1. *A check may be returned by the debtor's bank when there were not sufficient funds to cover the check at the time it was presented for payment.*

2. *One ploy is not to redeposit the check. Instead, it can be sent to the debtor's bank for collection.*

3. *This particular technique provides for the debtor's bank to hold the check until there are sufficient funds to cover the check. The holding period varies from bank to bank, but is normally about five working days.*

4. *The letter requests that, if the check clears during the holding period, the bank remit its own check for the amount collected less their charges for the collection service.*

5. *Of course, the check may not clear during the holding period. At that point, little will have been lost. The dishonored check will be returned to the creditor who may then pursue collection through other means.*

[date]
[bank name]
[address]

Re: Check #8877 for $843.25
    Customer—Fast Warehouse, Inc.

Gentlemen:

Enclosed is the above referenced check that has been returned because of insufficient funds. Kindly accept this
item for collection. Upon clearance, please send your
check to the address shown below, less your normal collection charges.

Please contact me at (800) XXX-XXXX if you have any
questions or comments. Thank you for your assistance in
this matter.

Sincerely,

Joan Murphy
Credit Director
[creditor company name]

cc: sales manager
    sales representative
    credit file

Letter for NSF Check Put in for Bank Collection

NSF Check Handling

Comments

1. *The purpose of this document is to notify the debtor that the check has been redeposited. The debtor may already have received notification from its bank that the check has not cleared.*

2. *Most firms have the policy of disallowing cash discounts taken on an NSF check.*

3. *A special note: Customers often blame an NSF check on a bank error. In reality, banks make fewer and fewer mistakes of this type, if for no other reason than to prevent potential lawsuits.*

4. *When a bank does make an error resulting in an NSF check, the bank is normally willing to provide recipients of those NSF checks with a letter of confirmation or apology.*

[date]
[customer name]
[address]

Attention: Wally Worthy
            [title]

Dear Mr. Worthy:

Your check number 4545 for $845.23 dated 4/30/XX was re-
turned by your bank due to insufficient funds. We have
redeposited the check on the assumption that it will
clear the second time. Please give this matter your immediate attention.

Our bank has charged us a $15 handling fee. In addition,
you took a $16.06 cash discount on that check. These two
amounts will be charged back to your account, assuming
the check clears on the second presentment.

Please contact me at (800) XXX-XXXX if you have any
questions. Thank you for your assistance.

Sincerely,

Alan S. Williams
District Credit Manager
[creditor company name]

cc: credit manager
    sales representative
    cash application department

Letter for NSF Check Handling

How to Handle Two NSF Checks

Comments

1. *Occasionally, a debtor will send two checks within a few days of each other and each will bounce. One bounced check could be a bank error, but two returned checks normally indicates that the debtor is in trouble.*

2. *Most creditor companies arrange with their banks to automatically redeposit checks returned due to insufficient funds. Assuming that both checks have been redeposited and both failed to clear the second time, the creditor potentially has a serious collection problem with the debtor.*

3. *A letter should be addressed to the debtor as quickly as possible to protest the fact that NSF checks are being returned and to demand immediate payment in clear funds.*

4. *The fastest and safest way to get paid is to include a copy of your wire transfer instructions and to ask your customer to wire the money. Your bank will be able to provide you with all the specific information required to enable a customer to send you a wire transfer.*

5. *With two NSF checks, the account will probably already be on credit hold. Occasionally, the debtor will offer to pay cash for new shipments. The creditor should hold out for cash to clear the NSF checks instead.*

6. *The letter on the opposite page can be sent by fax to save time and to increase visibility.*

7. *The salesperson should be copied on this type of letter.*

8. *If and when the balance due is paid, the creditor should carefully reevaluate the decision to extend credit on terms other than cash in advance.*

[date]
[customer name]
[address]

Attention: Roy Hales
          [title]

Dear Mr. Hales:

You will be disappointed to learn that both your checks, #2331 and #2339 have been returned to us by your bank due to insufficient funds. As we discussed last week, both checks were redeposited after bouncing the first time. Unfortunately, they did not clear.

Will you please arrange with your bank to issue a wire transfer to us today to clear the balance due of $843.25. Our wire transfer instructions are attached for your convenience.

Please call to confirm when this wire transfer has been sent.

Thank you.

Sincerely,

Randy Emerson
Credit Manager
[creditor company name]

enc.

cc: salesperson
    sales manager
    credit file
    correspondence file

Letter to Handle Two NSF Checks

Request for a Replacement Check

Comments

1. *Sometimes, a customer will claim a check was mailed when it never was. After a week or so, the debtor may claim the check may have been lost in the mail.*

2. *While creditors might suspect that the customer is "exaggerating," they must be certain the check was not received, deposited, and somehow misapplied.*

3. *Once creditors are certain payment was not received, they can send the letter on the opposite page suggesting that the customer immediately contact its bank to determine if the check in question has been presented for payment.*

4. *If the check has not been cleared, the creditor requests issuance of an immediate replacement check.*

5. *The time delay can be kept to a minimum by tight follow-up on the check allegedly mailed by the debtor and by making a prompt request for the replacement check to be issued.*

6. *If the creditor offers a cash discount, the letter may also include an offer to allow the cash discount even though payment is late if the debtor sends the replacement check by overnight courier.*

[date]
[customer name]
[address]

Attention: Faith Field
        [title]

Dear Ms. Field:

Thank you for advising us that you mailed check number 8877 for $847.25 on the tenth of the month. A review of our records indicates that this check has not been received. Therefore, it appears the check may be lost in the mail.

Please contact your bank and put a stop payment on the check, and then issue a replacement immediately. If your replacement check is received by [date], we will allow the cash discount this payment would have earned had the check been received.

Please call me if you have any questions.

Thank you.

Sincerely,

Mary Worth
Assistant Controller
[creditor company name]

cc: sales representative
    credit file
    Cash Application Department

Letter to Request a Replacement Check

Alternative Request for Replacement Check

Comments

1. *Occasionally, a marginal credit risk will tell you that a check has been mailed to clear a seriously past-due balance when in fact it has not yet been mailed.*

2. *In contrast to the letter on page 349, the following letter is a more no-nonsense approach.*

3. *The debtor is asked to (a) immediately call the bank to place a stop payment order on the check and (b) issue an immediate replacement check.*

4. *The creditor does not state a credit hold is imminent, but the threat is implicit in the final paragraph of the letter.*

[date]
[customer name]
[address]

Attention: Dorothy Spiegel
         [title]

Dear Ms. Spiegel:

In our recent conversation, you indicated that your check number 8877 for $847.25 was mailed on [date]. As you know, we verified that the remittance address in your accounts payable system is correct, so I can think of no reason our bank's lockbox would not have received this payment.

Please contact your bank and arrange for an immediate stop payment on this item. Once you have confirmed the stop payment is in place, please immediately issue a replacement check and have it sent by overnight delivery to my attention at the address listed below. Doing so will ensure that we are able to continue to process your orders without delay.

Please let me know if you have any questions or concerns.

Thank you.

Sincerely,

Grace Hidalgo
Area Credit Manager
[creditor company name]

cc: sales representative
    credit file

Alternative Letter to Request a Replacement Check

Letter Addressing a Series of Lost Checks

Comments

1. *Sometimes, a customer will develop a pattern of making and then breaking payment commitments.*

2. *Often, the debtor blames the delays on checks lost in the mail. Creditors would do well to carefully document situations in which the excuse that "the check must be lost in the mail" is wearing thin.*

3. *When creditors document such abuses of open account terms, it is far more difficult for customers to claim they were blameless.*

4. *Pointing out a pattern of deception also makes it easier to justify credit holds in the short term, as well as a decision to withdraw open account terms in the longer term.*

[date]
[customer name]
[address]

Attention: Gilbert Nguyen
        [title]

Dear Mr. Nguyen:

According to our records, invoice #564311 was paid over sixty days late. It was paid on your check number 7766, which we received and deposited yesterday.

According to my notes, in a telephone conversation last week you told me the check had been mailed on [date]. When I reviewed the postmark on the envelope containing the check, it showed your payment was actually mailed three days ago. A similar situation happened last month involving your check number 7322.

The date the check was issued by your Accounts Payable Department is not relevant to us if someone in your organization is holding the check. In the future, please let me know when the check is [or will be] mailed. Your cooperation will ensure that there are no unnecessary delays in processing your company's orders for shipment.

Thank you.

Sincerely,

Steve Kozan
Director of Credit and Treasury
[creditor company name]

cc: sales representative
    file

Letter Addressing a Series of Lost Checks

Customer Inquiry—Proof of Delivery

Comments

1. *After the item has been on the statement for a number of months and after some dunning notices, the account advises that there is no record of receipt of the merchandise.*

2. *Is the request for proof of delivery legitimate or a delay tactic? If the request occurs shortly after the invoice is mailed, or shortly after a monthly statement is generated and mailed, perhaps it is legitimate.*

3. *If the request occurs months later, and after several calls and/or dunning notices, there is a good chance the customer is stalling.*

4. *Credit professionals recognize a big difference between what you think the debtor is doing and what you know they are doing. Therefore, each request for proof of delivery must be treated as legitimate.*

5. *Fortunately, obtaining proof of delivery can often be done on line and in real time using a computer connected to the carrier company. This technology has reduced the cycle time on getting proof of delivery from weeks to minutes, possibly even seconds.*

6. *When a customer asks for proof of delivery, the creditor should ask for a specific commitment that, once proof of delivery is provided, payment will be expedited.*

7. *To expedite payment, the letter can be faxed.*

[date]
[customer name]
[address]

Attention: Kim Bell
            [title]

Dear Ms. Bell:

Please find attached the proof of delivery you requested for our invoice #45588. As you can see, the order was signed for as complete on [date] by [name].

As we discussed and agreed in our conversation on [date], please place this invoice in line for immediate payment. I look forward to receiving payment in the next five days.

Thank you for your cooperation.

Sincerely,

Mark Green
Assistant Credit Manager
[creditor company name]

cc: credit file
    sales representative

Letter for Customer Inquiry—Proof of Delivery

Restrictive Endorsements

Comments

1. *Occasionally a customer with a disputed balance will issue a check to its creditor with a restrictive endorsement.*

2. *A typical restrictive endorsement might indicate that the check represents "Payment in Full for All Obligations."*

3. *While case law on the issue of depositing checks with restrictive endorsements is confusing and contradictory, creditors should not accept or deposit a check with a restrictive endorsement before consulting with legal counsel.*

4. *If a company uses a bank lockbox system, the bank should be informed in writing not to deposit any check received in the lockbox with a restrictive endorsement. Instead, the bank should be told to send the check to the creditor company for review.*

5. *If an attorney advises that the check be returned to the debtor, a cover letter such as the one on the opposite page is appropriate.*

[date]
[customer name]
[address]

Attention: Valarie Mack

Dear Mrs. Mack:

We are returning your check number 334 dated [date] in the amount of $845.23. You issued this check with a restrictive endorsement. Please reissue the check without this type of endorsement. As you know, the balance due according to our records is over $2,100. For obvious reasons, we are not prepared to accept $845.23 as full and final payment.

If you have any questions, please call me at (800) XXX-XXXX.

Thank you.

Sincerely,

Tim Selleck
Assistant Credit Manager
[creditor company name]

enc.

cc: file

Letter for Restrictive Endorsements

Customer Makes Frequent Request for Proof of Delivery

Comments

1. *Occasionally, a customer will make frequent requests for proof of delivery on various invoices.*

2. *When the number of requests is excessive, the creditor should document the situation.*

3. *A carefully worded letter may convince debtors using these requests as a way to delay payment that they are skating on increasingly thin ice.*

4. *If the debtor company legitimately needs the proofs of delivery, the letter may point out a problem that the management of the company may want to be made aware of. If it is a delay tactic, sending this letter may send the message that the creditor is watching.*

5. *The letter should be addressed to an individual at least one level above the level of the person the collector normally interacts with.*

6. *The letter should be sent by the senior credit representative of the creditor company.*

[date]
[customer name]
[address]

Attention: Ann Palmer
         Accounting Manager

Dear Ms. Palmer:

My collector, Jackie Martin, has brought to my attention an unusual situation. In the last three months, your Accounts Payable Department personnel have requested proof of delivery on 17 invoices. That is more than 25% of the total number of invoices generated to your company during that three-month period.

In each case, we were able to provide clear proof of delivery, and in every case the invoice in question was paid. However, each invoice was significantly past due by the time it was cleared.

I wanted to bring this matter to your attention in the hope that you may be able to resolve the apparent problem between your Receiving Department and your Accounts Payable group.

Please feel free to call me if you need any additional information.

Thank you.

Sincerely,

Michael Kinney
Credit Manager
[creditor company name]

cc: credit file

**Letter for Customer Making Frequent
Request for Proof of Delivery**

Skipped Invoice—Old Invoice Overlooked

Comments

1. *Frequently, the slow payer picks out the small invoices for payment and chooses to ignore one or more large ones. This customer may believe that skipping around is not noticed.*

2. *Whether it is a chronic situation or a once-in-a-while ploy, it need not be overlooked. A quick response is required.*

3. *The debtor will have more respect for creditors that are well managed, and call promptly to address both large and small past due balances.*

4. *A brief letter or fax may be all that is necessary to remind the customer that you are carefully monitoring the accounts receivable aging.*

5. *The omission of one or more invoices in a payment may be indicative that the account has cash flow problems. A review of the credit line which had been granted is therefore in order.*

[date]
[customer name]
[address]

Attention: Greg Hadek
        [title]

Dear Mr. Hadek:

Thank you for your recent payment on check number 8971. Your payment cleared the entire past-due balance with the exception of the following invoices:

#34588
#34621

For your convenience, I have enclosed copies of these open invoices as well as proofs of delivery. Please place these past-due items in line for immediate payment.

If you have any questions or concerns, please call me at (800) XXX-XXXX.

Thank you.

Sincerely,

Steve Vega
Assistant Treasurer
[creditor company name]

enc.

Letter for Skipped Invoice—Old Invoice Overlooked

Letter Appealing to Mutual Interest in Releasing an Order

Comments

1. *If a customer has a past-due balance and a creditor has an order pending, then each party has something the other one wants. There is nothing wrong with pointing this fact out—as long as it is done tactfully.*

2. *The goal of the letter on the opposite page is to remind debtors gently that whether an order pending is released depends on their actions with respect to the past-due balance.*

3. *Generally, the letter should not make an unqualified commitment to release the order on receipt of payment. What would happen if the debtor company took another 60 days to pay? The creditor would not want to have made a written offer that says, "If you pay the past-due amount, we will release the order pending for $X,XXX."*

4. *This letter can be sent by fax to the customer to save time.*

5. *The salesperson should be sent a copy of this letter. It is important that the salesperson be informed of an order hold before the customer is notified.*

[date]
[customer name]
[address]

Attention: Tony Griffin
             [title]

Dear Mr. Griffin:

We received an order today referencing your PO number 97-403C. I note your account has a past-due balance of $8,443.25.

It occurs to me that each of us has something the other wants and needs. Please call me at (800) XXX-XXXX to discuss the status of the past-due balance and the order pending.

Thank you.

Sincerely,

Wayne Smithe
Credit Manager
[creditor company name]

cc: salesperson
    correspondence file

Letter Appealing to Mutual Interest
in Releasing an Order

Clearing On-Account Payments

Comments

1. *Occasionally, a debtor will send a payment without a remittance advice. The creditor has no way to apply the payment; so it is placed on account.*

2. *Since on-account payments do not improve a credit department's accounts receivable aging reports, the credit department is normally anxious to find out quickly how to apply the payment.*

3. *The debtor should be asked to provide written advice on how the payment is to be applied. Experienced credit professionals know it is important that the creditor's records and the debtor's records of outstanding balances match.*

4. *This letter can be sent by mail or by fax to save time.*

5. *If no response is received within five working days to a letter, or within two working days to a fax, the creditor should place a follow-up call to the debtor.*

6. *It is not necessary to copy the salesperson on this type of routine correspondence.*

[date]
[customer name]
[address]

Attention: Tim Betterman

Dear Mr. Betterman:

Thank you for your recent payment on check #2231. When your payment arrived, it did not include information about how the payment was to be applied. Please send me a fax with the remittance advice for this check. My fax number is (800) XXX-XXXX.

Thank you.

Sincerely,

Michelle Nabers
Credit Administrator
[creditor company name]

cc: correspondence file

Letter Clearing On-Account Payments

Old Credit Balance—Suggest Ordering

Comments

1. *First, every attempt should be made to be sure that a credit balance actually exists. An invoice, a debit or credit memo or a payment could have been applied to the wrong account. After two or three months of misapplication, some other account would have had to be out of balance. If this is not the case, then it might be that the credit balance is correct.*

2. *Laws in virtually every state have been written relating to unclaimed property, which would include unclaimed credits or on-account cash balances. These laws state that unclaimed property must be* escheated, *that is, given to the state to hold in trust until the rightful owner can be found.*

3. *This means that credit balances cannot simply be adjusted off and absorbed by the creditor.*

4. *Instead of issuing a credit for the outstanding balance, it is usually a better idea to notify customers of the credit and ask them to place an order to use it.*

5. *Even if the customer buys only once and purchases only enough to clear the credit balance, your company will make a profit on the sale.*

6. *It is not unheard of that a customer who had not bought for some time was prompted to begin buying again because of that creditor's honesty in identifying an open credit balance.*

7. *By copy of the letter, the salesperson is encouraged to contact the customer to make the sale.*

[date]
[customer name]
[address]

Attention: Accounting Manager

Re: Credit balance of $125.45

Dear Sir:

Our records indicate that your firm has a credit balance with us of $125.45. This credit is now over six months old. May I recommend that you place an order with us to take advantage of the credit due you?

I have taken the liberty of asking our salesperson in your area to contact your company to see if we can be of service to you.

Please call me if you have any questions at (800) XXX-XXXX.

Thank you.

Sincerely,

Al Woolcott
Credit Manager

cc: salesperson
    correspondence file

Letter for Old Credit Balance—Suggest Ordering

Approving a Request for a Monthly Statement

Comments

1. *It is not unusual for customers to ask that their accounts be handled in a certain manner. The credit department must do its best to accommodate reasonable requests from customers.*

2. *Occasionally, a creditor will ask that a statement be mailed or faxed by a certain day of the month to a specific person in the debtor company.*

3. *Credit professionals should be wary. In their response, they must emphasize that, while they are happy to provide the statement requested, the terms of sale do not change. For example, if the terms of sale are net 15 days from date of invoice, it does not matter to the due date of outstanding invoices that the customer has asked to receive a statement on the first of each month.*

4. *The customer should also be told that early payment discounts are calculated based on the invoice date, not on the statement date.*

[date]
[customer name]
[address]

Attention: Kathy Kuster

Dear Kathy:

Thank you for your letter and your follow-up telephone call to request that a statement be sent by fax to your Accounts Payable Department in Chicago by the fifth day of each month. While it is not our policy to provide more than one statement a month, we are happy to make an exception for your company. We will generate the requested statement manually each month and as close to the 5th day of the month as possible.

Please keep in mind, however, that the terms of sale on our account are and will remain 2% 15 days, net 20 days from date of invoice. We trust that we will continue to receive periodic payments based on the above referenced terms of sale.

Thank you.

Sincerely,

Robert Ampere
Credit Administrator
[creditor company name]

cc: credit file
    correspondence file

Letter Approving a Request for a Monthly Statement

Denying Request for End-of-Month Terms

Comments

1. *The opening paragraph restates the facts.*

2. *The second paragraph explains why the creditor company is not prepared to change the terms of sale.*

3. *The tone of this letter is matter-of-fact. The customer has made a request. The creditor has considered it and explained why the request cannot be accommodated.*

4. *It is hoped that the account will not take its business elsewhere, but that is a possibility any time customers are told they cannot have something they want.*

5. *The fact that the account making the request is a large dollar volume account is not in itself justification for changing the terms of sale. In reality, the larger the account and the larger the concession requested, the larger is the potential impact on the creditor's cash flows and profits.*

[date]
[customer name]
[address]

Attention: Andrew Reid

Dear Mr. Reid:

Thank you for your recent letter, copy enclosed, in which you indicated a preference for monthly statements rather than invoices. In your letter, you asked to change the terms of sale from net 30 days from date of invoice *to* net 30 days from statement date.

We have reviewed our terms of sale a number of times in the last few years, and have found them to be consistent with industry norms and competitive. If we were to change the terms we offer to your company, we could do no less if another customer requested similar terms. As a result, our cash flow could be adversely impacted. For these reasons, we cannot grant your request.

I note that we do not currently send your company monthly statements. That flag has been changed already and you will receive monthly statements beginning later this month.

We look forward to continuing to serve your company's needs.

Sincerely,

Richard Maher
Credit Manager
[creditor company name]

cc: sales representative
    credit file

Letter Denying Request for End-of-Month Terms

Customer Seeks to Reinterpret the Cash Discount Terms

Comments

1. *Occasionally, customers will respond to a request that an unearned cash discount be repaid with an explanation of why they believe the discount was earned.*

2. *Often, the explanation involves an assertion either that the goods in question arrived late or that the invoice was not received in a timely manner.*

3. *Most companies base the discount on the invoice date rather than on the date the goods were received. This way, creditors avoid having to track each order to see when the goods were received or why shipments were delayed.*

4. *If customers assert that they did not receive the invoice in a timely manner, an appropriate response is to explain that no other customers complained about not receiving invoices on that date, and that debtors always have the option of contacting the creditor for a copy of the invoice during the discount period once they were aware goods were received but the invoice was not.*

5. *The salesperson should be copied on this type of letter because the customer will often call the salesperson rather than the credit department to discuss the contents of the letter.*

[date]
[customer name]
[address]

Attention: Ingrid Jones
          [title]

Dear Ms. Jones:

Thank you for your letter of [date], copy enclosed, regarding a cash discount of $XXX.XX. Your letter makes
reference to the fact that the goods in question were
delivered on [date]. Please note that our terms of sales
are 2% 15 days, net 30 days from date of invoice. These
terms appeared on the credit application signed by your
company, and they appear on each invoice we send. Therefore, the date of receipt of the merchandise is not the
date we use in determining if a discount taken is earned
or late.

Based on these facts, I would ask that you pay the
$XXX.XX open on your account on your next check.

Please call me at (800) XXX-XXXX if you have any questions.

Thank you.

Sincerely,

Lou Ball
Credit Administrator
[creditor company name]

cc: correspondence file
    credit file

**Letter for Customer Seeking to Reinterpret
the Cash Discount Terms**

Letter Recommending Discounting
to Slow Paying Account

Comments

1. *Everyone is looking for ways to trim costs and expenses. The cash discount is more than one could earn at the bank. Further, in most situations, it is cheaper to borrow at the bank and be able to take advantage of discounting.*

2. *Faster turnover of receivables improves a creditor's cash flow. This has a cascade effect. More cash means that the creditor must borrow less, that more cash is available to take advantage of deals from its suppliers, and that the creditor is better able to weather a slow month or an unexpected problem.*

3. *Another advantage is the fact that turning slow paying accounts into discounting accounts results in less credit risk and lower bad debt write-offs.*

4. *When a cash discount is offered, the credit manager should have no ethical concerns about reminding customers that the discount is available to them.*

[date]
[customer name]
[address]

Attention: Accounts Payable Manager

Dear Sir:

Please note that we offer terms of 2% 15 days, net 30 days to your company. I note that your company does not take advantage of the cash discount.

Many of our customers consider these terms advantageous and take advantage of the 2% discount. Doing so builds their reputations as prompt payers, and the 2% discount is a lucrative incentive to expedite payment.

Please consider whether your company would benefit from paying more quickly and taking the discount.

Thank you.

Sincerely,

Kimberly Michelle
Senior Credit Manager
[creditor company name]

Letter Recommending Discounting
to Slow Paying Account

Unearned Discounts Disallowed

Comments

1. *Unearned cash discounts will be around for as long as creditors offer discounts for early payment.*

2. *Debtors continually pay creditors late and take the discount for one simple reason: Sometimes they get away with it.*

3. *Sometimes, debtors assert that the clock starts when they receive the invoice. Other debtors have gone so far as to suggest the clock starts not when they receive the shipment, but when they scan it into their inventory. The trouble is that the creditor does not know exactly when the debtor's clock starts.*

4. *Experience indicates that if a customer is allowed to get away with taking small unearned cash discounts, the discounts taken will become larger.*

5. *If a creditor carefully monitors an account for unearned discounts, chances are that sooner or later the Accounts Payable Department will flag the account as one that does not tolerate late payments with unearned cash discounts taken.*

6. *The letter on the opposite page is an example of how to notify a customer that a cash discount was unearned and was charged back.*

[date]
[customer name]
[address]

Attention: Dan Ho

Dear Mr. Ho:

Thank you for your recent payment on check number 5488. I note that cash discounts were taken on two invoices that were significantly beyond the discount due date.

Here are the specifics:

Invoice #	Discount Due Date	Date Paid	Discount
23356	2/6/XX	2/21/XX	$18.50
23359	2/8/XX	2/21/XX	$ 6.50

Accordingly, the discounts taken have been disallowed and the amounts charged back. Please schedule this $25.00 for repayment with your next payment to us.

Thank you.

Sincerely,

Troy England
Director of Credit
[creditor company name]

cc: correspondence file
    credit file

Letter to Disallow Unearned Discounts

Unjustified Discount Allowed

Comments

1. *See the letter illustrated on page 377 where the discount was not allowed.*

2. *The point of the letter is that while this discount is being allowed, the creditor expects adherence to the terms of the sale.*

3. *Of course, the debtor could have been correct in taking the discount as the shipment date may have been a number of days later than the invoice date. Or, he could have been trying to get an unearned discount.*

4. *Whatever the reason, it is best that the debtor be advised that the creditor has noted that the discount was taken.*

5. *In addition, credit terms should be enforced in the letter.*

6. *The credit file on the account should indicate how many times an apparent unearned discount has been taken. By keeping a track record, one can ascertain how habitual this problem is.*

7. *A certain number of accounts will simply throw the letter on the opposite page away. Even if they do, by writing it, the creditor has (a) put the debtor on notice that the creditor is monitoring the account closely, (b) reminded the customer of the correct terms of sale, and (c) provided a written record of an unearned cash discount problem for the credit file.*

[date]
[customer name]
[address]

Attention: Gail Holland
            [title]

Dear Ms. Holland:

Thank you for your recent check for $845.23 covering our invoice #122990. I note that a cash discount of $18.10 was deducted when this invoice was paid.

Our terms of sale are 2% 15 days, net 30 days. Therefore, this cash discount was unearned according to our records when your payment was received on the 23rd. At that point, the invoice was seven days beyond the discount due date. As a courtesy to your company, the discount has been allowed.

Please remind your Accounts Payable Department of our payment terms for future reference.

Thank you.

Sincerely,

Margaret Spencer
Credit Manager
[creditor company name]

cc: credit file
    correspondence file

Letter to Allow Unjustified Discount

Unearned Cash Discount—Disputed Invoice

Comments

1. *Occasionally, a customer will take a cash discount on an invoice that they claim was in dispute.*

2. *The problem with this excuse is that it can be used for any invoice not paid within the cash discount period.*

3. *The proper way to handle this problem is to allow the cash discount only on that portion of the balance due paid within the discount period.*

4. *The letter on the opposite page makes reference to the fact that the customer is entitled to withhold payment on the portion of the balance due that is legitimately in dispute. However, to earn the cash discount, the debtor must pay whatever portion of the invoice was not in dispute within the discount period.*

5. *Some creditors even allow the debtor to take the cash discount on the remaining balance once the dispute has been resolved, provided the undisputed portion was paid within the discount period by the debtor company.*

[date]
[customer name]
[address]

Attention: James Brand
          [title]

Dear Mr. Brand:

Probably because of your internal accounting procedures, your company deferred payment on our invoice #44188 pending resolution of an alleged pricing error. This presents a problem involving the cash discount taken on this invoice of $XXX.XX. This discount was available only if the invoice was paid within 20 days, since our terms of sale are 2% 20 days, net 30 days from date of invoice. The invoice was paid approximately 45 days after the date of invoice.

In this instance, the disputed item was only a small portion of the invoice amount, and it turned out the price on our invoice was correct. Even if the price was incorrect, we could allow the discount only if your company had paid the undisputed portion of the invoice within the discount period.

Therefore, I must ask that the $XXX.XX be repaid on your next check to us. Please flag our account so that in the future any undisputed balance is paid within the discount period. We normally find that disputes involve only a small portion of the total invoice price.

Thank you.

Sincerely,

Susan Baker
Credit Manager
[creditor company name]

cc: correspondence file
    credit file

Letter for Unearned Cash Discount—Disputed Invoice

Second Letter Regarding Unearned Cash Discounts Taken

Comments

1. *Ignoring an unearned cash discount simply encourages a debtor to continue to take this type of deduction. While individual amounts charged back may be small, they can become large if left to accumulate.*

2. *Normally, one letter is not enough to get a customer to stop taking unearned discounts and to repay unearned discounts already taken.*

3. *The letter on the opposite page is the second letter in a series of notices to a customer about a late discount.*

4. *The amount of detail given is intended to demonstrate that the creditor watches discounts carefully.*

5. *The goal of these letters is not to stop customers from taking discounts. It is to encourage them to pay within the discount period and earn the discount offered.*

6. *If you allow one customer to pay late and take the discount, you have a moral obligation—and may have a legal obligation—to allow other debtors to take unearned discounts.*

7. *Once a credit department allows a customer to take unearned discounts, it is difficult to get them to stop doing so.*

8. *Unless your company requires it or your Sales Department has requested it, copying the salesperson on this type of routine correspondence is not essential.*

[date]
[customer name]
[address]

Attention: John Hanks
            [title]

Dear Mr. Hanks:

On [date], we wrote you about an unearned cash discount of $XXX.XX. A copy of that letter is attached for your review.

I dislike having to continue to bother you about this, but, as I explained in my last letter, your payment was clearly late and therefore the deduction in question was unearned. In fairness to our other customers that pay within the 15-day discount period, I cannot allow our cash discount policy to be subject to interpretation.

Therefore, I must again ask that you include the unearned discount of $XXX.XX with your next payment to us.

Thank you.

Sincerely,

D. Mark Albertson
Credit Manager
[creditor company name]

cc: correspondence file
    credit file

**Second Letter Regarding Unearned
Cash Discounts Taken**

Accepting an Unearned Cash Discount

Comments

1. *Occasionally, a debtor will send a payment with a small unearned cash discount.*

2. *It might not be cost-effective to charge back a small amount, especially when one considers the costs involved in doing so, including (a) generating the debit, (b) printing the debit memo, (c) mailing the debit memo, and (d) following up to collect against the unearned discount.*

3. *On the other hand, simply accepting the payment without comment will encourage the debtor company to continue to take cash discounts that are either unearned or were not offered.*

4. *A letter protesting the unearned discount is a better alternative, if the debtor does not make a habit of taking unearned discounts.*

5. *The letter on the opposite page is intended to make customers aware of the problem and to encourage them not to take unearned discounts in the future.*

6. *Of course, if debtors continue to take unearned discounts, they must be charged back.*

[date]
[customer name]
[address]

Attention: Accounts Payable Manager

Dear Sir:

We recently received your check number 43312 dated April 25th for $843.25 in payment of our invoice #688992. That payment included a deduction of $8.43 representing a 1% cash discount according to your remittance advice.

Our terms of sale are net 30 days. We do not offer a discount for prompt payment or a trade discount of any kind. Therefore, this deduction was an unearned discount.

As a courtesy, we have not charged back this discount. Please make certain our account is flagged so that future payments do not include any cash discounts.

Please call me if you have any questions at (800) XXX-XXXX.

Thank you.

Sincerely,

Carla Shepherd
Zone Credit Manager
[creditor company name]

cc: file

Letter Accepting an Unearned Cash Discount

Requesting an Explanation for a
Decision Not to Discount

Comments

1. *On occasion, a customer that used to take cash discounts suddenly stops doing so. The most likely cause is a (a) cash flow problem or (b) a change in personnel or workflow in the debtor's Accounts Payable Department.*

2. *An observant and inquisitive credit professional will want to know why the debtor is no longer taking cash discounts. It is not idle curiosity. It is important to understand the reason the debtor changed its payment pattern. For example, it could indicate a short-term problem or an impending serious financial crisis.*

3. *A letter to the customer asking about the change in payments is not out-of-line, provided the letter is only an inquiry and makes no accusations about the debtor's financial health.*

4. *The letter should be sent to a Controller or Accounting Manager. By sending it to anyone lower in the chain of command, you risk sending the inquiry to the person who is causing the problem rather than to the person who can solve it.*

5. *A response is not necessary if the letter prompts the debtor company to take the cash discount once again.*

6. *One of the goals of sending the letter on the opposite page is to indicate that the credit department is paying attention, and is interested and concerned about the change in payments.*

[date]
[customer name]
[address]

Attention: Kelsey Bracken
            [title]

Dear Ms. Bracken:

I note that, beginning last month, your company is no longer paying invoices within our discount terms and taking advantage of our cash discount. This could indicate some sort of minor difficulty.

If there is something I can do to assist you, please feel free to call me at (800) XXX-XXXX.

Sincerely,

Jane Tran
Credit Manager
[creditor company name]

cc: credit file

Letter Requesting an Explanation
for a Decision Not to Discount

Extended Terms Rescinded

Comments

1. *Occasionally, a debtor will have a compelling need, and a creditor will allow extended dating terms. Such extensions should be for a specific reason and for a specified time period.*

2. *At the end of that time period, the credit department must remind the customer that it is time to go back to the regular terms of sale.*

3. *Like a child at an amusement park, the debtor may be content where they are and not happy about the idea of going back. Credit professionals know that they must control the terms of sale they offer, and not allow customers to dictate payment terms and conditions.*

4. *It can become embarrassing if the creditor does not enforce the move back to standard terms and other customer/debtors find out what kind of deal their competitor is getting. At best, you can expect other customers to demand equal treatment— meaning the same extended terms.*

[date]
[customer name]
[address]

Attention: Robert Parker

Dear Bob:

As you may recall, three months ago you requested (and I agreed to offer) extended terms on your account of net 60 days. The agreement we made called for this extension to last 90 days to allow your company to get back on its feet after the flood at your Alabama warehouse.

The 90-day term of the agreement has expired. Based on our discussion and agreement, all invoices shipped beginning tomorrow will revert to our standard terms of sale of 2% 20 days, net 30 days from date of invoice. I hope that you can take advantage of our cash discount by paying in 20 days.

I trust the extended dating arrangement helped. We look forward to a long and mutually beneficial business relationship.

Sincerely,

Samuel Thomas Adair
Corporate Credit Director
[creditor company name]

cc: salesperson
    credit file

Letter for Extended Terms Rescinded

Order Received Prior to Receipt of Credit Application

Comments

1. *From time to time, a salesperson may jump the gun by submitting an order before the customer submits a credit application.*

2. *Completing a credit application actually speeds up the process of reviewing and approving an applicant for open account terms. It also normally results in a larger credit limit since, in the absence of complete information, the proper course of action is to set a conservative credit limit.*

3. *Most companies require a completed and signed credit application from every new account.*

4. *Temporary exceptions can be made, especially when the applicant is a large, well-known or publicly traded company.*

5. *When a rush order is pending, the credit manager might be asked to release the order and assign a temporary credit limit. When this happens, the diligent credit professional will make certain the customer promptly completes and returns the application.*

[date]
[customer name]
[address]

Attention: Frances Kelly

Dear Ms. Kelly:

Thank you for your opening order submitted under PO number 877416. The order was shipped today by Clark Overnight Transport.

Unfortunately, I have not been able to complete my credit review and assign a permanent credit limit to your account because I have not yet received a completed credit application. For your convenience, I have enclosed another copy of our standard credit application form.

Please call me if you have any questions at (800) XXX-XXXX.

Thank you.

Sincerely,

Tim Cronmiller
Corporate Credit Manager
[creditor company name]

enc.

cc: sales representative
    credit file
    correspondence file

Letter for Order Received Prior to
Receipt of Credit Application

Unacceptable Purchase Order Terms

Comments

1. *Sales personnel are happy to accept most purchase orders. However, if some of the terms and/or conditions listed on the customer's PO are unacceptable to the seller, the shipment should be held until a correction in writing is received from the customer. To save time, the customer can be asked to fax the correction to the creditor company.*

2. There is always the chance that business will be lost. *However, the purpose of credit policies is to protect profits. If one has to give away part of the profits to obtain business, it may be a matter for senior management. Generally, credit terms are the policies of higher management.*

3. *This letter makes it as easy as possible for the customer to understand and accept the seller's terms and conditions of sale.*

4. *A copy of the letter should be sent to the salesperson for quick follow-up with the customer to try to explain the seller's policies.*

5. *The letter itself could be sent by fax to save time.*

[date]
[customer name]
[address]

Attention: Erna Pearson
           Senior Buyer

Dear Ms. Pearson:

Thank you for your recent order on purchase order number
8841. Unfortunately, we have found two discrepancies
that must be addressed before the order can be released.

First, the purchase order lists terms of 2% 30, net 31
days. Our invoice terms are 2% 15, net 30 days. Second,
the PO lists the terms as being FOB Destination. Our
shipping terms are FOB origin, meaning that risk of loss
or damage to the shipment passes to you upon consignment
of your order to a common carrier.

To facilitate processing this purchase order, please
sign a copy of this letter acknowledging these two
changes and return it to my attention as soon as possible or issue a new PO. To expedite your order, please
fax this signed document or your PO to (800) XXX-XXXX.

Thank you.

Sincerely,

Tom Ackley
Credit Manager

Acknowledged and agreed by: _____

Title: _____

cc: correspondence file

Letter for Unacceptable Purchase Order Terms

New Order Approved for Marginal Account

Comments

1. *If a decision is made to reopen a marginal account, the credit department needs to exercise appropriate care.*

2. *This letter informs the customer that the past has not been forgotten, and any indication that the account is "picking up where it left off" will result in open account credit terms being withdrawn.*

3. *The specific payment terms are listed for the debtor's review.*

4. *The salesperson and the sales manager should be copied on the letter. They should be informed that any repeat of past delinquencies will result in COD cash terms.*

5. *This customer account should be flagged (or in some other way noted) as a high risk so that it can be monitored closely.*

[date]
[customer name]
[address]

Attention: Tim Pomen
            Purchasing Manager

Dear Mr. Pomen:

Thank you for your recent order and for your confidence in our ability to serve you. The requested product will be shipped tomorrow.

Our records indicate that payments in the past have not always been received within our terms of sale. For us to provide the best possible service, please remind your Accounts Payable Department that our terms of sale are net 30 days from date of invoice.

Our ability to continue to ship to you on open account terms will be influenced in large part on your Accounts Payable Department's continuing observance of our credit terms.

Thank you for your assistance in this matter.

Sincerely,

Jim Blatt
Assistant Credit Manager
[creditor company name]

cc: sales representative
    credit file

Letter to Approve New Order for Marginal Account

Written Warning to an Irregular Paying Account

Comments

1. *This account may adhere to the squeaky wheel principle. That is, the creditor who makes the most noise will get the grease. Whoever is silent, will wait.*

2. *Some accounts must be constantly reminded to pay invoices. Follow-up on commitments is often necessary. In these situations, make certain the collection call or the dunning notice is sent as soon after the account becomes past due as possible.*

3. *If a debtor is paying others on time and your company slowly, the debtor is in effect using your money to pay other creditors.*

4. *Debtors will always act in their own best interest. If they can find a competitor that can ship similar quality products at competitive prices that does not require strict adherence to payment terms, then the debtor would be acting irrationally if it did not take advantage of the other opportunity.*

5. *The credit manager and the sales manager have the difficult chore of getting the account on a current basis and getting business away from the competition.*

[date]
[customer name]
[address]

Re: $843.24 past-due balance

Dear Mr. White:

According to a credit report we recently reviewed, your firm pays a number of its suppliers within terms. Yet your account with this company has been paid an average of 31 days late over the last six months.

As a businessperson, you can surely appreciate that as a creditor we want to get paid on time or at least as promptly as you pay other creditors in our industry. Accordingly, I must ask that our account be flagged for more prompt payment.

Please call me to discuss this issue. My telephone number is (800) XXX-XXXX.

Thank you.

Sincerely,

Wayne Smithe
Corporate Credit Director
[creditor company name]

cc: sales representative
    credit file

Letter to Warn an Irregular Paying Account

Order Shipped Despite Arrears

Comments

1. *Holding orders any time an account is past due is impractical. However, it is a good idea to remind customers from time to time that you have continued to ship despite a delinquent balance due.*

2. *Sometimes it is appropriate to hold a delinquent account. That is a difficult decision to make, and normally a senior member of the credit department should make the decision.*

3. *Often, creditors are willing to ship against a "reasonable commitment" for payment. There is no single definition of the term "reasonable commitment." Each creditor must determine its own tolerance for delays in payment.*

4. *Admittedly, it may be easier to ship on a COD basis, but would that gain the goodwill that has been desired or would such a step diminish the existing goodwill with the account?*

5. *See the letter illustrated on page 401 where an order is held pending payment.*

6. *This message and the accompanying documents could be sent by fax to speed up the payment cycle.*

[date]
[customer name]
[address]

Attention: Sandra Eagers
             Controller

Dear Ms. Eagers:

Thank you for your recent order, referencing your purchase order #8838A. This order was shipped despite the fact that there was a past-due balance of $834.25 open at the time. This was done because your company is a valued customer.

For your convenience, I have enclosed a copy of the outstanding invoice(s) for your review. Please arrange for payment to be issued this week to clear the past due balance.

Thank you.

Sincerely,

Arthur Moter
Area Credit Manager
[creditor company name]

enc.

cc: credit file
     correspondence file

Letter for Order Shipped Despite Arrears

Order Held Pending Settlement

Comments

1. *This letter is intended to notify a customer when an order is put on credit hold. The hope is that the recipient will not close its account and take its business elsewhere.*

2. *Customers occasionally overreact to a credit hold. However, most debtors understand the collection process and recognize that they have to pay the penalty from time to time for delaying payments to creditors.*

3. *This letter is intended to make it as easy as possible for debtors to remit.*

4. *Note that no specific commitment has been made to the debtor that, if the past-due balance is paid, the order pending will be released on open account terms. It would be a mistake to make such a commitment. Suppose an offer to release on receipt of payment was made in writing. In theory, the customer could remit payment 120 days later, just prior to being placed for collection, and then demand that the order be released.*

5. *If any account becomes significantly past due, credit professionals should determine whether the account is still creditworthy before resuming shipments.*

6. *Salespersons normally have a vested interest in seeing that an order is released from credit hold. Therefore, they may be willing to participate actively in helping collect the delinquent balance.*

7. *This letter could be sent by fax to save time.*

[date]
[customer name]
[address]

Attention: Oliver Olsen
Accounts Payable Manager

Re: Purchase order #10188

Dear Mr. Oliver:

We received a new order yesterday referencing your PO #10188. Our records indicate that your account has an unpaid balance of $834.25. That balance is well over 60 days past due.

Please remit payment as soon as possible to clear the above referenced delinquent balance so that I can re-lease the order pending and currently on credit hold.

Thank you.

Sincerely,

Mary Whiter
Credit Manager
[creditor company name]

cc: sales representative
    credit file

Letter for Order Held Pending Settlement

No Commitment Received—Involuntary Bankruptcy Filing Contemplated

Comments

1. *Many credit professionals consider an involuntary bankruptcy filing to be the ultimate threat in dealing with an uncooperative debtor. An involuntary bankruptcy filing will enable creditors to gain more control over the actions and the affairs of the delinquent debtor.*

2. *An attorney best answers the question about whether a debtor qualifies for an involuntary bankruptcy petition. The goal of the filing is to preserve the debtor's assets for the benefit of creditors.*

3. *An attorney can also advise a creditor considering an involuntary filing about how to discuss the possibility of an involuntary bankruptcy filing with other creditors.*

4. *The outcome of a bankruptcy from an unsecured creditor's perspective is always a matter of speculation. There is no way of knowing the debtor's intentions, or if and when you might have been paid. Therefore, an involuntary filing should be considered only as a last resort.*

5. *If a bankruptcy filing has been made in bad faith, the bankruptcy court may invalidate the petition. At that point, the petitioning creditors who filed the petition may be subject to civil penalties for damage to the firm or loss of business.*

6. *If the creditors falsified the involuntary petition, they may be subject to more serious and more severe consequences.*

7. *Once an involuntary bankruptcy filing has been completed, a trustee will be appointed to oversee the case. That trustee has extraordinary powers under the bankruptcy code to recover preferential transfers as well as payments made to insiders.*

8. *Occasionally, the mere threat of an involuntary bankruptcy filing will cause the debtor to address the delinquent balance.*

[date]
[customer name]
[address]

Attention: Wayne Miller
            Chief Financial Officer

Dear Mr. Miller:

Unfortunately, I have had no response to the messages I have left for you regarding the outstanding balance of $8,750.23. This balance is over 90 days past due.

If I do not hear from you by [date], I will assume that you do not plan to pay this past-due balance voluntarily. At that point, I will have no alternative but to consider trying to place your account into involuntary bankruptcy. I hope this does not become necessary.

The next step is up to you. Please call me at (800) XXX-XXXX to discuss this serious problem.

Thank you.

Sincerely,

Dennis Stevens
Area Credit Manager

cc: Fred Murray
    President—[debtor company]
    salesperson
    sales manager
    credit file

Letter for No Commitment Received—Involuntary Bankruptcy Filing Contemplated

Questions to Ask before Hiring a Professional to Represent the Unsecured Creditor's Committee

Comments

1. *Members of the official unsecured creditor's committee in a Chapter 11 bankruptcy are permitted to have legal counsel to protect the rights of all unsecured creditors.*

2. *Creditors should attempt to hire an attorney (and other professionals when required) that have the experience necessary to advise the committee during the crucial first few weeks or months after the bankruptcy has been filed.*

3. *Legal counsel is chosen through an interview process conducted by the members of the committee.*

4. *The key questions to ask an attorney who wants to represent the committee are: (a) Does the attorney have any prior experience with the debtor, the counsel for the debtor or the judge in the case? (b) What are the hourly rates of the attorney and other professionals he/she plans to use? (c) What experience qualifies the attorney for this position?*

5. *When inviting professionals to address the committee, inform the professionals in advance about the questions you expect answers to.*

[date]
[law firm name]
[address]

Attention: [name of attorney]

Dear Mr. [name]:

The official unsecured creditor's committee in the [name of bankruptcy] case plan to interview qualified candidates for the position of counsel to the committee on [date] in [city] and [state]. You have been recommended to us by [name].

If you would like to be considered for this position, we would like to meet with you. In preparation for that meeting, we would ask you to address the following issues during your presentation:

- Your experience as counsel to other committees.
- Any specific experience with a bankrupt debtor in this industry.
- Your hourly billing rates and other charges.
- Your specific knowledge of this case, along with a brief outline of what action you would take immediately if you were selected to represent the committee.
- Your experience before the judge handling this case.
- The status of your license to practice law in [state] and before this bankruptcy court.

If you are interested in meeting with the committee, please call me at (800) XXX-XXXX to arrange a mutually convenient time.

Thank you.

Claudia Coughran
Credit Manager
Canwell Ice Company
(Committee Chairman)

cc: creditor committee members

Letter for Questions to Ask before Hiring a Professional to Represent the Unsecured Creditor's Committee

Confirmation of Verbal Commitment

Comments

1. *Some debtors may say anything in order to get a creditor off the telephone—even a promise to pay. "Yes, I will put a check in the mail by the first of the month."*

2. *If a promise gets the creditor off the phone, the debtor can postpone dealing with a financial or cash flow crisis.*

3. *Sometimes, a confirmation of the debtor's commitment should be sent, particularly when the debtor has a history of making and then breaking payment commitments.*

4. *Putting a commitment in writing makes the debt and the commitment more concrete. This increases the chances that the commitment will be kept.*

5. *Unfortunately, every promise that the check is in the mail should be viewed with suspicion.*

6. *See the letter illustrated on page 409 for a reminder after the target date.*

[date]
[customer name]
[address]

Attention: John Kim
         Accounts Payable Manager

Dear Mr. Kim:

This letter is to confirm the commitment you made in our telephone conversation this morning. You stated that a check would be mailed by Friday for $15,000 of the $21,321.00 past-due balance.

Enclosed is a self-addressed business envelope for your convenience is remitting payment.

Thank you for your cooperation and assistance.

Sincerely,

Ann Major
Director of Credit
[creditor company name]

enc.

cc: correspondence file
    credit file

Letter to Confirm Verbal Commitment

Reminder of Promise Possibly Broken

Comments

1. *The customer promised the collector that a check would be mailed the same day they spoke. Even allowing for mail delays, the check should have been received at least two days ago.*

2. *Unforeseen events could have caused a delay in payment. The written reminder letter is one way of addressing the problem.*

3. *The letter does not accuse, and it does not call the customer a liar. It merely states the facts.*

4. *This letter should be faxed to save time.*

5. *The salesperson should be copied on the letter to bring some pressure to bear on the debtor to get this problem resolved quickly.*

[date]
[customer name]
[address]

RE: $885.24 past due

Dear Mr. Stone:

In our telephone conversation last Thursday, you promised a payment would be mailed that day for $885.24.

We have not received your payment and at this point we are concerned. Please call me with an update on this payment at (800) XXX-XXXX.

Thank you.

Sincerely,

Roberta Frost
Collection Specialist
[creditor company name]

cc: correspondence file
    credit file

Letter for Reminder of Promise Possibly Broken

Prior Problem Account Seeks Open Account Terms

Comments

1. *An old customer wants to start buying again on open account terms. The trouble is that this was a problem account.*

2. *However, if sales can be made safely, why let a competitor have the business? Credit professionals must look for ways to make a sale safely, not for excuses to hold customer orders.*

3. *The letter on the opposite page is not intended to be vindictive or critical, but it contains some interesting language. For example, the phrase "close cooperation" can in reality only mean paying promptly.*

4. *This account will have to be carefully monitored. Any repeat of the old paying habits should be addressed immediately.*

5. *Any failure to return to the straight and narrow path after this reminder should result in a withdrawal of the open account privilege.*

6. *It would not be unusual for the creditor to establish a low credit limit. Many creditors want to see such accounts walk before they are allowed to run, especially when the debtor is running while holding the creditor's money.*

[date]
[customer name]
[address]

Attention: Olive Stone
            Controller

Dear Ms. Stone:

After careful consideration, we have reestablished an open account term for your company. We want to "wipe the slate clean" and try to establish a new and better working relationship with your company this time.

It is expected that shipments will be paid within our terms of sale of net 30 days from date of invoice without any reminders from us.

Your credit limit has been set at $X,XXX. We will continue to extend this amount based on a continuing record of close cooperation between this company and your Accounts Payable Department.

Thank you for your continued interest in our company and its products.

Sincerely,

Sidney Saferr
District Credit Manager
[creditor company name]

cc: sales representative
    credit file

Letter for Prior Problem Account
Seeks Open Account Terms

New Account Opened—Some Restrictions Applied

Comments

1. *Creditors should look for a reason to ship, not for an excuse to hold orders.*

2. *The debtor is made aware that orders will be shipped on an order-to-order basis, with one order being released only after the prior one has been paid.*

3. *The size of each order must also be regulated to properly manage credit risk.*

4. *If the account continually pays promptly over a period of time, the credit limit or order size could be increased on a temporary or test basis.*

5. *If the payment pattern is poor or deteriorates, then other terms, including COD, will have to be considered.*

[date]
[customer name]
[address]

Attention: Mrs. Wiley

Dear Mrs. Wiley:

Thank you for submitting a credit application to us. After a careful review, we are prepared to offer your company an open account under the following terms and conditions:

For the time being, we will extend credit on an order-by-order basis for up to $1,000. Under this program, the net terms will be 30 days. However, if you require additional products we will require a payment sufficient to bring the total dollar exposure to $1,000 or less.

In the future, as conditions change and as our experience with you grows, we will be happy to consider making our credit terms more liberal.

We look forward to being of service to you.

Sincerely,

Chris Cromwell
Area Credit Administrator
[creditor company name]

cc: sales manager
    credit file

Letter for New Account Opened—
Some Restrictions Applied

Poor History Account—Try COD Terms

Comments

1. *COD is not risk-free. If a shipment is refused, the creditor will have to pay freight costs in both directions.*

2. *Companies with a history of slow payment with other trade creditors on open account terms are likely to treat your company no better.*

3. *The first paragraph reminds the customer of past problems with your firm.*

4. *Occasionally, COD customers become better risks and may eventually become strong and solid accounts—another reason not to alienate any customer.*

[date]
[customer name]
[address]

Attention: Barry Frank

Dear Mr. Frank:

A review of our records indicates that due to certain circumstances our company had to stop shipping to your firm on open account terms last year. Fortunately, we were able to resolve the matter short of legal action.

With these facts in mind, we believe it would be appropriate if we were to ship the order pending on COD terms.

By copy of this letter, I am asking that our salesperson contact you to discuss this option.

Thank you for your interest in this company and its products.

Sincerely,

Jeff Sams
Credit Administrator
[creditor company name]

cc: sales representative
    credit file

Letter for Poor History Account—Try COD Terms

Foreign Account Needs Open Account Terms

Comments

1. *Selling overseas on open account terms is normally fairly high risk for a U.S. company. Most foreign buyers prefer to buy on open account terms.*

2. *The credit department is expected to find a way to sell without requiring the buyer to provide a letter of credit. Being able to sell without requiring a letter of credit can be a significant competitive advantage. L/Cs are inconvenient to work with and add cost to the sale.*

3. *One mechanism to sell overseas without requiring a letter of credit is export credit insurance. Similar to the type of policy that can be obtained domestically, an export credit insurance policy can be written to cover a single risk, selected multiple accounts or all foreign credit sales.*

4. *Being able to offer open account terms helps to build customer loyalty and to increase the amount of business you do overseas, which results in increased sales and profits.*

[date]
[foreign customer name]
[address]

Attention: Fernando Alfonso
            Purchasing Manager

Dear Mr. Alfonso:

Thank you for your confidence in our company and our products. We are pleased to be doing business with you.

The opening order has been released on net 60-day terms as you had requested. Please ask your Accounting Department to remit payment (in U.S. dollars) to my attention at the address shown below.

We look forward to a long and mutually beneficial relationship.

Sincerely,

Christine May
Credit Director
[creditor company name]

cc: sales representative
    credit file

Remit to: XYZ Corporation
           123 Anywhere St.
           City, State, USA 90001

Letter for Foreign Account Needs Open Account Terms

Request to Reopen an Account—
Old Item Must Be Settled First

Comments

1. *This letter is to be sent to an account that the creditor cut off after the debtor refused to clear a delinquent balance, disputing the balance due. The size of the disputed balance did not justify placing the account for collection.*

2. *The subtext of this letter is this: "Let's forgive and forget — after you pay the past-due balance."*

3. *The message is clear: If the customer is unwilling to pay the balance due, there is no point in considering an open account.*

4. *Salespersons are copied on this letter to help them to understand why open account terms are not being offered immediately.*

[date]
[customer name]
[address]

Attention: Steven Stark

Dear Mr. Stark:

Thank you for your recent order. We would like to do business again with your company, but our records indicate there is a balance of $834.25, which remains open and unpaid.

We are prepared to offer your company open account terms again, once this past-due balance has been cleared. I have enclosed a copy of our account statement and copies of previous correspondence for your review.

Please call me if you have any questions. My telephone number is (800) XXX-XXXX.

Thank you.

Sincerely,

Winston Abeles
District Credit Manager
[creditor company name]

enc.

cc: sales manager
    credit file

**Letter Requesting to Reopen an Account—
Old Item Must Be Settled First**

Inactive Account Seeks to Reestablish Open Account

Comments

1. *Most computer systems inactivate accounts after a specified period without any business. The purpose is to make certain that orders do not get released on a formerly active account based on an out-of-date credit line.*

2. *Inactive accounts might want to begin buying again for many reasons. One possible reason is that the company might be having trouble getting shipments from other creditors.*

3. *In certain industries, updating credit files every 12 months is sufficient. In more volatile industries, having information that was obtained within the last 6 months is more appropriate.*

4. *This letter welcomes the possibility of new shipments, but it makes no specific commitments. Reestablishing an open account depends on the outcome of a credit investigation.*

5. *In many ways, reestablishing credit terms with an inactive account is identical to evaluating a new account. The difference is that the creditor has the benefit of experience with the customer.*

[date]
[customer name]
[address]

Attention: Harvey Hilton

Dear Mr. Hilton:

Thank you for your interest in doing business with this company. It is always a pleasure to hear from an old and valued customer.

We would like to extend credit to you as we did in the past. Unfortunately, our credit file on your company is out-of-date. Please fax or mail a copy of your company's current bank and trade references, along with your firm's most current financial statements.

Thank you for your cooperation.

Sincerely,

Cyril Corrigan
Western Regional Credit Manager
[creditor company name]

cc: sales representative
    credit file

Letter for Inactive Account Seeks
to Reestablish Open Account

Poor History Account—Alternative Suggested

Comments

1. *No one wants to reject an order or a customer. Sometimes, if a sale cannot be made safely, the right decision involves walking away from the order—at least on open account terms.*

2. *However, if the creditor can recommend an alternative, the business might be saved.*

3. *One alternative is to recommend that the customer buy through a local distributor. The advantage is that a local distributor might be able to provide the customer with small enough quantities that the credit risk would be acceptable to that company.*

4. *Another alternative is for the debtor to contact a flooring company with which the creditor has a business relationship. The flooring company assumes the risk of loss in return for a commission (or fee) on each sale on which it assumes the risk.*

5. *By copy of the letter, the salesperson is made aware of the situation. The salesperson may even be able to create some goodwill with a local distributor by providing the name of the applicant as a sales lead.*

[date]
[customer name]
[address]

Attention: Sam Sheraton

Dear Mr. Sheraton:

Thank you for your interest in our company and for your request that we reestablish an open account for your company. After careful review and consideration, we are unable to honor your request at this time. However, we can suggest these two options:

1) You may wish to contact Fast Pace Distributors at (800) XXX-XXXX. Fast Pace Distributors is a distributor of our products in your area. Of course, the decision to extend credit to your company is entirely up to them.

2) If your company has a business relationship with a flooring company, please call me with the particulars and I will contact the flooring company and establish an account for you as quickly as possible.

Thank you for your interest in doing business with us.

Sincerely,

Steve Worth
Credit Administrator
[creditor company name]

cc: salesperson
    credit file

Letter for Poor History Account—Alternative Suggested

Poor Risk Account—Alternative Sought to Minimize Credit Risk

Comments

1. *A creative credit professional can lower the risk of selling on open account terms, even to a substandard credit risk, by selecting the appropriate risk management tool.*

2. *The credit professional might consider a number of options, including requiring a personal guarantee or an intercorporate guarantee before offering open account terms.*

3. *Another option is to require security in the form of a pledge of collateral or to grant a purchase money security interest.*

4. *Creditors can require a standby letter of credit from a marginal risk account; however, both documentary and standby letters of credit tend to be cumbersome and expensive.*

5. *Another tool involves shortening the terms of sale. By shortening the credit terms, the creditor can also reduce the credit line. For example, if a customer had a $10,000 line and 30-day terms, the customer in theory could be fine with net 15-day terms and a $5,000 limit.*

6. *A creditor should also investigate credit insurance or flooring if the risk of extending open account terms is too high.*

7. *These are only some of the ways risk can be managed. Creditor professionals are expected to take whatever steps necessary to reduce credit risk to an acceptable level.*

[date]
[customer name]
[address]

Attention: Lou Meyer

Dear Mr. Meyer:

Thank you for your recent request for open account credit terms. I have carefully reviewed the credit information available and have determined that an open account
cannot be granted at this time for the amount requested
unless a standby letter of credit is issued for $XX,XXX
with this company as the beneficiary.

If you want to discuss this proposal, please feel free
to call me at (800) XXX-XXXX.

Thank you.

Sincerely,

Margie Spencer
Credit Manager
[creditor company name]

cc: credit file
    sales representative
    sales manager

Letter for Poor Risk Account—Alternative
Sought to Minimize Credit Risk

COD Customer Switched to Open Account Terms

Comments

1. *One of the credit manager's more pleasant duties is to grant open account credit to a previous COD basis account.*

2. *Normally, a history of paying for orders on a COD basis does not in itself qualify a customer for open account terms.*

3. *Changing terms from COD to open account requires a comprehensive credit review.*

4. *In this letter, the customer is told that the change to open account terms is being made on a trial basis and that the account will be monitored carefully.*

5. *If the customer is not able to honor the credit terms, the account should be put back on COD terms quickly.*

6. *One way to limit credit risk is to set the credit limit low enough so that the customer can buy only "hand to mouth" quantities of your product.*

[date]
[customer name]
[address]

Attention: Wally Wilson

Dear Mr. Wilson:

Our Sales Department has asked that your account be switched from COD terms to open account, net 30-day terms.

I have made this change on a trial basis. Please remind your Accounts Payable Department that our invoices must be paid within 30 days from the date of invoice.

We will offer an opening credit limit of $X,XXX.

Thank you for your continuing confidence in this company and our products.

Sincerely,

Florence Titlebaum
Credit Manager
[creditor company name]

cc: salesperson
    credit file

**Letter for COD Customer Switched
to Open Account Terms**

Marginal Account Requests Terms Be Reestablished

Comments

1. *From time to time, marginal accounts that have lost their open account ask that they be reevaluated for open account terms.*

2. *The letter on the opposite page grants open account credit terms, but cautions the customer that the account will be monitored carefully. If the customer fails to pay as agreed—again—the open account terms must be withdrawn.*

3. *If the customer is a corporation, the creditor may request or require a personal guaranty as additional assurance of payment.*

4. *The size of the orders could be kept down to* hand-to-mouth quantities *which reduces possible bad debt exposure.*

5. *Some credit managers examine the marginal account's potential for turnaround or a possible trend toward improvement. The account could be recovering from a bad slump in business covering even several bad years.*

6. *The salesperson can assist by making certain the customer flags your account for prompt payment. It is in their best interest to do so.*

[date]
[customer name]
[address]

Attention: Wendy Wolfson

Dear Ms. Wolfson:

Thank you for your recent request to reestablish open account credit terms with this company.

After careful consideration, I am pleased to inform you that we are going to extend credit to your firm. The credit limit will be $X,XXX.

As you know, our past history with your account was not without problems. As a result, we will need to monitor your account closely.

I trust you have flagged our account so that payments are made within our standard terms of sale of net 15 days from date of invoice.

Please call me if you have any questions.

Thank you.

Sincerely,

Dale Gonzalez
Credit Administrator
[creditor company name]

cc: salesperson
    credit file

Letter for Marginal Account Requests
Terms Be Reestablished

Denying a Request for Larger Credit Limit

Comments

1. *Every business wants to buy goods and services on open account terms from its suppliers. Sometimes, customers want a larger credit limit. Unfortunately, offering a larger line is not always appropriate.*

2. *The goal of the credit department is to deny the increase without damaging goodwill with the customer—often a difficult task.*

3. *Both the customer and the salesperson will be pushing for a larger credit line, but, to manage credit risk, it is sometimes necessary to say "no!"*

4. *After thorough and careful investigation and study, a credit manager should give the maximum credit line that can be extended with safety.*

5. *In denying the request, the credit department should always leave the door open for reconsideration of the decision in the future.*

[date]
[customer name]
[address]

Attention: Paul Smith

Dear Mr. Smith:

Our salesperson has forwarded your request for a $10,000 increase in your credit limit. We have updated our credit file and reviewed our history with your company.

At this time, and based on the information we have on file, I cannot offer this larger credit limit. I will be happy to reevaluate this decision from time to time as conditions change.

Thank you for your confidence in our ability to be of service to you.

Sincerely,

Dan Whitfield
Assistant Credit Manager
[creditor company name]

cc: salesperson
    credit file

Letter Denying a Request for Larger Credit Limit

Collection Letters for Credit Cards

Comments

1. *Almost everyone is familiar with how credit cards work.*

2. *Businesses often obtain credit cards for their key executives as a convenience, specifically for entertaining and for business travel. Credit cards for business travel often have significantly higher credit limits than credit cards for consumers.*

3. *The credit card company always has the right to cancel the credit card if necessary.*

4. *Credit card companies typically charge high interest rates on balances they carry from month to month on the credit card account. As a result, credit card companies can afford to take more risk and are often reluctant to cancel a credit card, especially to a business account.*

5. *Like other creditors, credit card companies typically use a series of calls and written reminders to obtain payment against delinquent balances.*

6. *On the opposite page is a typical friendly reminder of a past-due credit card debt to be sent to a corporate cardholder.*

[date]
[customer name]
[address]

Attention: Alex Crable
            [title]

Dear Mr. Crable:

Perhaps you have been busy ... and that is why you have overlooked paying your most recent monthly credit card bill. For your convenience, a summary of that bill is attached. Please issue payment immediately.

Of course, if your check and this letter have crossed in the mail, please disregard this reminder.

Thank you.

Sincerely,

Martina Morley
Credit Manager
[creditor company name]

cc: file

Collection Letter for Credit Cards

Delinquent Corporate Credit Card Accounts

Comments

1. *Bills for corporate credit cards sometimes remain unpaid despite the best efforts of the credit card company's Collection Department to resolve the matter amicably.*

2. *When this happens, credit card companies will incur additional credit risk if they continue to allow the debtor to use the cards they hold.*

3. *Although they dislike doing so, credit card companies have the ability to electronically cancel outstanding credit cards. For a corporate client, this might result in an executive being stranded at a hotel or an airport trying to use a canceled credit card.*

4. *For this reason, credit card companies try to give corporate clients fair warning if they are considering canceling outstanding cards.*

5. *On the opposite page is a strongly worded warning letter to the corporate debtor company.*

6. *This letter may be sent by fax to save time.*

[date]
[customer name]
[address]

Attention: Jackie Grossi
          [title]

Dear Ms. Grossi:

On several occasions, we have called to your attention the delinquent balance on your account of $8,433.25. We have had no response to our calls and correspondence, and as of this morning we have not received your payment.

Usually, we cancel outstanding credit cards when an account is this far past due, but we dislike doing so since it often creates a tremendous inconvenience for our cardholders (your employees), some of whom may be traveling with our credit card on business.

Some response from you is needed immediately in order to prevent the cancellation of the outstanding credit cards.

Please call me today to discuss payment status. My telephone number is (800) XXX-XXXX.

Thank you.

Sincerely,

Shirley McCloskey
Credit Manager
[creditor company name]

cc: file

Letter for Delinquent Corporate Credit Card Accounts

Reviewing a Request for Larger Credit Limit

Comments

1. *Every business wants to buy goods and services from its suppliers on open account terms. Not all accounts are creditworthy enough to be given the credit line they want.*

2. *A goal of the credit department is to make sound and prudent credit decisions. Without the right information, this can be a difficult task.*

3. *Both the customer and the salesperson might be pushing for an immediate decision on a larger credit line. It takes courage and conviction to ignore the pressure and to ask for more information to make a better informed credit decision.*

4. *Among the best sources of information about a customer's creditworthiness are audited financial statements. A request for financial statements would not be unexpected when the customer is requesting an increase in the credit limit.*

[date]
[customer name]
[address]

Attention: Paul Jones

Dear Mr. Jones:

Our salesperson has forwarded your request for a $10,000 increase in your credit limit. We have updated our credit file and reviewed our history with your company.

Unfortunately, based on the information we have on file, I cannot offer this larger credit limit at this time. If you can, please forward me a copy of your company's most current financial statements. I will be happy to evaluate your company for the larger limit based on this new information.

Thank you for your confidence in our ability to be of service to you.

Sincerely,

Dean Lopez
Area Credit Manager
[creditor company name]

Letter Reviewing a Request for Larger Credit Limit

Negative Credit Decision Communicated—
Customer Misunderstood

Comments

1. *It has been said that people hear what they want to hear. This is true of debtor companies when a creditor rejects a request for open account terms, a larger line of credit, or extended dating.*

2. *No matter how candid and clear the credit manager might have been, the debtor may choose to misinterpret or misrepresent the creditor's comments.*

3. *A letter might be the best way to address this "misunderstanding."*

4. *The tone of the letter should be patient, without anger and without sarcasm. The creditor's comments and decision should be restated.*

5. *The salesperson should certainly be copied on this type of letter.*

[date]
[customer name]
[address]

Attention: Steven Z. Gardiner
          [title]

Dear Mr. Gardiner:

After speaking with our salesperson, I think there is some misunderstanding about our conversation late last week regarding your account. As you recall, you requested a $XXX,XXX credit line. I regret that I did not make our position clear in our conversation.

To reiterate, we cannot grant this large a credit line to your company on an open and unsecured credit basis. We are prepared to increase your company's credit limit to $XX,XXX. You might recall that I suggested as an alternative that your company take the 1% cash discount available if invoices are paid within 15 days of the invoice date. Your company currently pays us in an average of 38 days and does not take the discount.

I regret any misunderstanding. Please call me at (800) XXX-XXXX if you have any questions.

Thank you.

Sincerely,

Sandy Nichols
Credit Manager
[creditor company name]

cc: salesperson
    credit file

**Letter for Negative Credit Decision Communicated—
Customer Misunderstood**

How to Respond to a "We Have Cash Flow Problems" Letter

Comments

1. *Occasionally, a debtor will send all its creditors a form letter claiming cash flow problems. Typically, the reason given is that one of the debtor's customers filed for bankruptcy protection.*

2. *The first step is to acknowledge receipt of the letter. The next step is to explain that the creditor company also has debts to pay, and that the debtor cannot simply assume its creditors will carry this burden. The debtor company is trying to turn its problems into its creditors' problem.*

3. *The creditor should suggest that the debtor look to more "regular" sources of working capital, including banks, factors and finance companies.*

4. *The creditor should ask the debtor to either issue an immediate payment in full or call to discuss the situation.*

[date]
[customer name]
[address]

Attention: Kerry McDonald
          [title]

Dear Ms. McDonald:

In response to my calls and letters regarding a past-due balance of $843.25, I received today your letter of [date] in which you explained that your cash flow problems were caused by the bankruptcy of one of your customers. Unfortunately, your letter did not indicate when we would be paid.

It is our policy to cooperate with our customers by granting extensions when asked and if it is reasonable to do so. In this case, we were not asked for assistance. Your company simply stopped paying, and ignored our calls and letters. As a result, your account is now almost 60 days past due.

We also have obligations to our creditors, and this situation does not warrant additional extensions of credit. We suggest that you look to your bank for additional working capital, and ask that you schedule the entire past-due balance for immediate payment.

Thank you.

Sincerely,

Kent Payne
Credit Manager
[creditor company name]

cc: salesperson
    sales manager
    credit file
    correspondence file

**How to Respond to a "We Have
Cash Flow Problems" Letter**

Chapter 7

Managing Slow Paying Accounts

To some credit professionals, collection letters are more or less a last resort. They devote time and effort to more direct and immediate collection techniques, such as collection telephone calls. Most credit professionals do not limit themselves to one method of collection. Instead, they use collection calls, customer visits, collection letters and dunning notices in combination to speed up collections.

Volume Considerations

Clearly, one of the criteria that dictate how often customers will be either called or sent collection or dunning notices is the volume of accounts, as well as the average dollar value of invoices. For example, if there are thousands of delinquent accounts, unless the credit department has a large staff of collectors, making telephone calls to each delinquent account will not be practical or even possible. In such circumstances, only seriously delinquent accounts or customers with large balances can expect to receive special attention, For the less serious accounts, less-labor intensive collection techniques, such as the use of dunning notices, must be used.

The Role of Correspondence

No credit professional would suggest that collection letters can or should be eliminated. A series of collection letters and dunning notices can be established. The fax machine can also be used to expedite delivery of these messages—and possibly to increase their perceived importance.

Telephone Collections

The telephone is an important collection tool. Although it is labor-intensive, a call is more direct and typically more effective than a collection letter. A letter can be ignored or even thrown away, but a collection call normally requires an immediate answer.

Late Payment Interest Charges

Many companies threaten to charge delinquent customers interest on past-due balances. To enforce this program, the customer has to agree in advance to pay interest charges. That can best be accomplished by listing interest charges as one of the terms and conditions contained in the credit application, a document that all customers should be required to sign. In addition, a statement about interest charges on past-due balances should be included on every invoice mailed to customers.

While receiving interest income is fine, the real purpose of threatening to charge interest on late payments is to encourage customers to pay invoices as they come due.

Caution: Laws vary from state to state regarding the legality of charging interest. It is important to know the laws in the states in which you do business. An attorney should be able to give you the advice and information necessary to avoid problems.

Personal Visits

One useful collecting technique is the personal visit by the credit manager. Visits of this type are controversial, but they do not need to be. Collection visits are not intended to be confrontational. Visits are a legitimate business tool that should be used when necessary to discuss and resolve past-due balances. In fact, occasionally disputes between debtor and creditor are so complex that a personal visit is the best and only practical way to resolve them.

Most credit departments are centralized. Therefore, customer visits by the credit manager are normally expensive. Some companies try to use their sales personnel as collectors. This is not an ideal situation for the following reasons:

- Salespersons have a vested interest in keeping the relationship with the debtor as stress-free as possible and will not relish having to demand money of the debtor.

- Even if salespersons are willing to do so, they lack expertise in this area.

- Salespersons may correctly convey the message they were asked to deliver by the credit department, but fail to convey a sense of urgency about the unpaid balance. As a result, the debtor might be lulled into a false sense of security.

Personal visits also provide the credit manager with a unique perspective on the business world in which their company competes. This first-hand view of the world simply cannot be obtained sitting behind a desk at the corporate office.

Personal visits also provide the opportunity for credit professionals to build rapport with the debtors they visit. As a result of this rapport, creditors will enjoy a number of benefits, including:

- Getting paid faster.
- Having calls returned more promptly.
- Receiving updated financial statements more easily and more frequently from the debtor.

Changing Collection Techniques

Constantly using one collection technique can—over time—have a lessened effect. For example, over time the same series of dunning notices become less impactful. Similarly, having the same collector call the same debtor every month might not produce the desired results in the long run.

One successful technique is to switch territories for collectors from time to time. Some might argue that, because the collector gets to know the accounts, switching collectors is not efficient. In reality, the efficiency that may be lost can be more than offset by the fact that a new collector brings with them different collection techniques and a new perspective.

Other advantages of this technique are:

- The problems one collector might be trying to bury or hide will come to the surface when the new collector takes over the territory.
- When collectors switch territories, they can create a new baseline for collections. For example, the old collector might have

allowed a ten-day grace period before calling about past-due balances. The new collector might be told to allow only five days. Similarly, the old collector might have allowed a five-day grace period on unearned cash discounts while the new collector can cut that back to three days.

Suggestion to Establish a Different Type of Business Relationship

Comments

1. *The reference section pinpoints the past-due amount.*

2. *The opening paragraph recites the history of the current problem.*

3. *The letter raises the possibility that the customer might not be paying the bill for the service agreement because the firm no longer wishes to participate in the service agreement program.*

4. *If the customer wishes to avoid what would be a more costly billing arrangement, a check must be sent within ten days.*

5. *The last paragraph provides the debtor with the opportunity to pay the bill and to continue with "business as usual" under the service agreement. However, the debtor is informed that, if payment is not received within ten days, the service contract will be terminated.*

[date]
[debtor company name]
[address]

Account Number: 4369371
Total Amount Due: $73.61
Type of Billing: S/A

Dear Mr. [name]:

We have not received a remittance for your Mainframe
Service Agreement invoice number 8XLH488 and 9740960,
dated August 29, 19XX and July 24, 19XX, or a reply to
our previous requests for payment. Therefore, we must
assume that you are uncertain about continuing your service agreement.

This letter affords you the opportunity to confirm con-
tinuance of your service agreement. However, we will assume you do not wish to continue if your remittance is
not received within ten days.

If you should decide not to continue your service agreement, we look forward to furnishing the same high-quali-
ty service on your photocopier and fax equipment at our
current hourly rates of $XXX.XX per unit, plus applica-
ble parts and travel expense.

If payment has been made or if there are any questions
in regard to your account, please contact Alisa Summers
at the above telephone number, extension XXX.

Sincerely,

Walter Nauheim
CE Branch Manager

XXX:xx

**Collection Letter with Suggestion to Establish
a Different Type of Business Relationship**

Automated Notice of Partial Payment

Comments

1. *A computer can quickly and easily apply a partial payment against an outstanding balance.*

2. *Even moderately sophisticated computer systems should also be able to generate a notice when a short payment is received.*

3. *That notice should contain a request for either payment in full or an explanation of the reason for the partial payment.*

4. *A phone number (ideally, toll-free) should be provided to allow the debtor to call to discuss the debt.*

SHERTZ SYSTEM, INC.

P. O. BOX 254 · OKLAHOMA CITY, OKLAHOMA 73125

TELEPHONE
(405) 721-6440

PLEASE SHOW THIS NUMBER ON CHECK
AND ON ALL CORRESPONDENCE

XXXXXXXXXXX
XXXXXXXXXXXXXXXXXXX
XXXXXXXXXXXXXXXXXXX
XXXXXXXXXX   XXXX

1 3017

DATE	ACCOUNT NUMBER		CUSTOMER REPRESENTATIVE
01/09/	1724-1 -0000-2		J. WILSON

STATEMENT DATE	STATEMENT BALANCE	PAYMENTS RECEIVED	BALANCE DUE
12/27/	998.22	43.22	955.00

CASH & ADJUSTMENTS POSTED TO: 01/05/

Dear Customer:

Your monthly statement for car rentals shows the above past due charges. If this does not agree with your records, please contact your Customer Representative; otherwise, we shall appreciate your prompt remittance. Thank you for your cooperation.

Very Truly Yours,
SHERTZ SYSTEM, INC.

**PLEASE MAKE CHECK PAYABLE TO: SHERTZ SYSTEM, INC. P.O. BOX 254
OKLAHOMA CITY, OKLAHOMA 73125, AND RETURN YOUR STATEMENT COPY OR THIS CARD WITH YOUR REMITTANCE.**

Automated Notice of Partial Payment

Past-Due Notice Card Inserts

Comments

1. *This is a series of three past-due notices. They graduate from 60, to 90, to 120 days delinquent.*

2. *Note that the statement date is December 27th, but cash and other adjustments are posted to January 5th.*

3. *The card notice is mailed along with the monthly statement. In a sense, the card and the statement contain the same information. That is exactly the point. This card is a simple and inexpensive second reminder that the balance is seriously past due. If nothing else, it prompts the debtor to investigate the matter of the past-due balance.*

4. *The tone of the message is relatively mild. This can be effective when the past-due item is a small, skipped invoice or an unpaid unearned cash discount that has been charged back.*

THE EXACTO
132 Main Street, City, State 00000

This is just a friendly reminder to let you know that at the end of 60 days this balance remains open.

Very truly yours,

C. S. Hull   **[blue]**

THE EXACTO
132 Main Street, City, State 00000

This matter, now having exceeded 90 days past due, has been brought to my attention. Since we have always maintained a favorable business relationship with your firm, it is assumed this delay in payment is only of a temporary nature.

I trust you to share our concern in this matter, and that every attempt will be made to bring these delinquent charges to a current status.

Very truly yours,

C. S. Hull   **[white]**

THE EXACTO
132 Main Street, City, State 00000

Approximately 30 days ago, a statement concerning this outstanding balance was sent to your firm. As this balance presently remains open, and exceeds 120 days past due, prompt payment would be greatly appreciated.

If there are any questions concerning this matter, please contact me.

Very truly yours,

C. S. Hull   **[pink]**

Past-Due Notice Card Inserts

Past-Due Account—Alternative Card Method

Comments

1. *See the card series illustrated on page 453 and the related comments.*

2. *The notice is printed on card stock cut to fit in a number 10 envelope. It is included with the monthly statement.*

3. *The greeting and the first paragraph indicate that the creditor wants to be of service to the customer.*

4. *The last sentence of this brief reminder gives the customer the options of either paying promptly or calling to explain why the balance due is not being paid.*

5. *While the card device is not expensive, it may be wasteful. The statement is a collection tool on its very own—if it is not, its format and content can be improved. A statement can have the very same computer-generated message that appears on the card. Such a message has to go along with the statement wherever it goes; however, the card does not.*

Mega System Inc.
P.O. BOX XXXXX
OKLAHOMA CITY, OK 73125

Dear Customer:

Your business, as reflected on the enclosed statement, is most appreciated. We sincerely hope that you have found our service to be entirely satisfactory.

You will note from the enclosed statement that your account shows a balance which is past due. If this does not agree with your records, please inform this office; otherwise, we shall appreciate your prompt remittance.

Past-Due Account—Alternative Card Method

Form Collection Letters

Comments

1. *Form letters save time and money. Collection form letters that look like form letters are not particularly effective.*

2. *From the debtor's perspective, receiving a collection notice that is obviously a form letter might indicate that the creditor is not concerned enough about the past-due balance to either call or send a personalized collection letter. The "Dear Sir" is one indication that the letter was computer-generated.*

3. *The tone of the letter is strong. It cites previous notices. The fact that previous notices were sent makes it unlikely that the balance due is in dispute. If it were, the debtor would have already notified the creditor of the problem.*

4. *A specific demand is made for remittance. The benefit of a prompt payment is the fact that the credit record will remain clear—incentive enough for most debtors.*

5. *A copy of this letter is also being sent to the local sales office with the expectation that, if there is a problem, the salespeople will know about it. If there is not a problem, the office might be able to bring pressure to bear on the debtor.*

MEGA

[date]
[customer name]
[address]

THE MEGA SYSTEM INC.
Post Office Box XXXXX
Oklahoma City, OK 73125
Telephone: XXX-XXX-XXXX

August 14, 19XX

A/C#   —171-0000-2
RE: —$44.79

Dear Sir:

Our records do not indicate a response to our previous notices concerning your past-due account.

We have been hesitant to proceed with any stronger action because we value our relationship with your organization. However, we must now insist that you immediately forward your remittance in the enclosed envelope.

Your prompt attention to this matter will maintain your excellent credit record with us.

Sincerely,

[name]
Commercial Credit Supervisor

XX/xx

enc.

cc: Sales Office 19XX

Form Collection Letter

Past-Due Account Statement Labels

Comments

1. *Statement labels are stickers attached to statements to draw attention to the past-due status of the account.*

2. *Many credit professionals consider statement labels to be a gimmick. They are intended to get your statement noticed. Hard core slow paying accounts are likely to ignore both statements and stickers.*

3. *An alternative to the past-due label is a printed message on the statement requesting immediate payment of the past-due balance.*

Past-Due Account Statement Labels

Humorous Past-Due Account Statement Labels

Comments

1. *Those who propose the use of humorous labels for account statements argue that humorous notices are more likely to be acted on than statements without them.*

2. *Such labels are effective only when the customer is occasionally late in paying. Chronic delinquent accounts will ignore statements with and without stickers and labels.*

3. *Never use a humorous label that might be deemed offensive.*

4. *Opponents of humorous labels believe that collecting a past-due balance is a serious matter and that humor does not and will not compel customers to pay more quickly.*

5. *Opponents also maintain that using humor trivializes the message.*

Humorous Past-Due Account Statement Labels

Application for Commercial Credit

Comments

1. *Letters of credit (L/C) are not used frequently in domestic sales transactions for one simple reason: A customer can usually find a less expensive and less complicated alternative to arranging for a letter of credit to be issued.*

2. *The buyer must request that the L/C be issued by its bank. The seller cannot initiate this process. However, the creditor should provide the debtor with a list of requirements for the L/C if it is agreed that one is to be issued.*

3. *Once the letter of credit is issued, the creditor need not be concerned about the creditworthiness of the debtor company. By issuing the L/C, the creditor/seller relies on the creditworthiness of the debtor's bank rather than on the creditworthiness of the debtor company.*

4. *The creditor must carefully review the terms and conditions contained in the letter of credit. If any of the terms and conditions listed are unacceptable, the creditor must withhold shipment until an amended L/C is delivered.*

5. *The creditor should never rely on the promise either of the debtor or of the issuing bank that the L/C will be amended.*

6. *This application calls for payment to be made "at sight." The L/C can be paid immediately (at sight), or the tenure can be from 30 days to one year or more.*

APPLICATION FOR COMMERCIAL CREDIT

DATE March 23rd, 19XX

To: JUPITER NATIONAL BANK, N.A.

International Department

PLEASE ISSUE AND EITHER

a) NOTIFY THROUGH YOUR CORRESPONDENT BY ☐ MAIL/AIR MAIL ☐ WIRE IN FULL ☒ WIRE BRIEFLY, DETAILS BY AIRMAIL

OR b) ☐ RETURN TO US FOR TRANSMISSION TO BENEFICIARY: OR c) ☐ MAIL DIRECTLY TO BENEFICIARY

YOUR IRREVOCABLE CREDIT (THE "CREDIT") AS FOLLOWS:

IN FAVOR OF Canadian Cycle Corp., 999 Industrial Drive, Montreal, Canada

(NAME)　　　　　　　　　　　　　　　　(COMPLETE ADDRESS)

UP TO THE AGGREGATE AMOUNT OF Five hundred thousand U.S. dollars ($500,000.00)

BY ORDER OF AND
FOR ACCOUNT OF J.H. Importing Corp., 111 LaSalle Ave., Chicago, Illinois

(NAME)　　　　　　　　　　　　　(COMPLETE ADDRESS)

AVAILABLE BY DRAFTS AT sight

(INDICATE TENOR)　　　　　　　　DRAWN AT YOUR OPTION ON YOU OR ANY OF YOUR

CORRESPONDENTS FOR 100 % OF THE INVOICE VALUE WHEN ACCOMPANIED BY THE FOLLOWING DOCUMENTS
(YOU MAY, HOWEVER, AT YOUR OPTION, WAIVE PRESENTATION OF DRAFTS):

DOCUMENTS REQUIRED AS INDICATED BY CHECK (X)

☒ COMMERCIAL INVOICES

☒ SPECIAL CUSTOMS INVOICE, IN DUPLICATE

☐ MARINE/WAR INSURANCE POLICY OR CERTIFICATE **OR** ☐ MARINE/WAR INSURANCE COVERED BY US

☒ OTHER DOCUMENTS Statement of Country of Origin

(IF SPECIAL DOCUMENTS ARE REQUIRED, PLEASE SPECIFY NAME OF ISSUER)

☒ FULL SET OF "ON BOARD" OCEAN BILLS OF LADING RELATING TO SHIPMENT

FROM Canada TO Chicago, Illinois

(IN EACH CASE PLEASE SPECIFY PORT OR COUNTRY ONLY)

DRAWN TO ORDER OF JUPITER NATIONAL BANK, N.A. MARKED NOTIFY ABOVE ACCOUNT PARTY

RELATING TO Motorcycles

(please specify commodity only, omitting details as to grade, quality, price, etc.)

Invoices must include substantially the above description, but only general description of the commodity in the remaining documents will be required. You will not be responsible for descriptive matter included in any document additional to the description so required for such document.

DRAFTS MUST BE DRAWN AND NEGOTIATED NOT LATER THAN April 30th, 19XX

UNLESS OTHERWISE STATED HEREIN, YOU MAY AUTHORIZE THE NEGOTIATING/PAYING BANK TO SEND ALL DOCUMENTS TO YOU IN ONE AIRMAIL.

SPECIAL INSTRUCTIONS

A/C# 113 18 7948

The Security Agreement on the reverse hereof is hereby accepted and made applicable to this Application and the Credit.

We warrant that no shipment involved in this Application is in violation of U.S. Treasury Foreign Assets Control or Cuban Assets Control Regulations.

J.H. Importing Corp.

(APPLICANT)

111 LaSalle Ave., Chicago, Ill.

(ADDRESS)

We further warrant that the Agreement below has been duly and validly executed by or on behalf of the Account Party.

J. Horn Treas.

(AUTHORIZED SIGNATURE)　　　　　(TITLE)

Application for Commercial Credit

Automated Past-Due Statements

Comments

1. *Most creditors send debtors monthly statements. These statements typically list all open invoices, as well as stating the current and past-due balances by aging "bucket."*

2. *The statement should include a telephone number and a message asking debtors to call if their records differ from the information on the statement.*

3. *When an account is past due, the statement should contain a clear message such as, "PAST DUE NOTICE" or "PLEASE ISSUE PAYMENT IMMEDIATELY" or "THANK YOU FOR YOUR PROMPT REMITTANCE."*

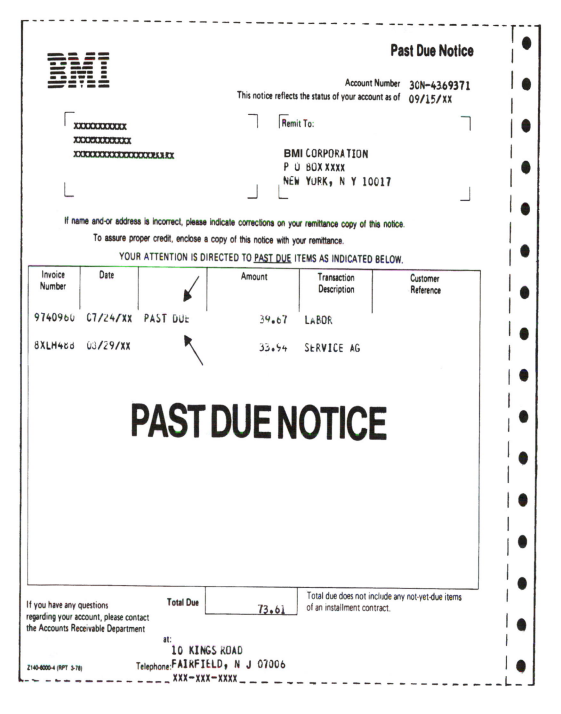

Automated Past-Due Statements

Automated Second Past-Due Notice

Comments

1. *The accounts receivable statement run is probably accomplished with a number of on-line printers, each having a different preprinted statement format.*

2. *On the statement on the opposite page, both items are past due and the statement has a bolded notice: "SECOND PAST-DUE NOTICE."*

3. *A telephone number should be provided if the customer wishes to discuss the status of the account or the information in the statement.*

4. *Problem accounts are unlikely to pay based on receipt of a statement, a second notice or even a collection letter. Monthly statements and second notices are useful with accounts that pay fairly well but that occasionally skip invoices or run into cash flow problems.*

5. *Statements are a supplement to collection calls and other more direct collection techniques, such as personal visits.*

IBM

Second Past Due Notice

Account Number   30N-4369371
This notice reflects the status of your account as of   10/15/XX

XXXXXXXXXXXXXX
XXXXXXXXXX
XXXXXXXXXXXXXXXXXXXXX

Remit To:

IBM CORPORATION
P O BOX XXXX
NEW YORK, N Y 10017

We have not received payment for the past due items indicated in your account. If you have any questions, please contact our Accounts Receivable Department at the address or telephone number shown below. If not contacted, we will expect immediate payment.

To assure proper credit, enclose a copy of this notice with your remittance.

Invoice Number	Date		Amount	Transaction Description	Customer Reference
8XLH488	08/29/XX	PAST DUE	33.94	SERVICE AG	
9740960	07/24/XX	PAST DUE	39.67	LABOR	

SECOND PAST DUE NOTICE

If name and-or address is incorrect, please indicate corrections on your remittance copy of this notice.

Total Due   73.61

Total due does not include any not-yet-due items of an installment contract.

Z140-2027-2 (RPT

Inquire At: 10 KINGS ROAD
FAIRFIELD, N J 07006
Telephone: XXX-XXX-XXXX

Automated Second Past-Due Notice

Computer-Generated Statement with Aging Analysis

Comments

1. *The statement on the opposite page acts as a collection tool because the past-due balances are listed by aging "bucket."*

2. *The chronic slow payer will ignore the statement and the aging buckets. Other customers are likely to be concerned if they see a large dollar amount past due.*

3. *Statements are typically generated once a month, on the first day of the month.*

4. *Statements can be used as collection tools. To do so, creditors usually program the computer to generate messages at the bottom of the statement in a large, bold type font.*

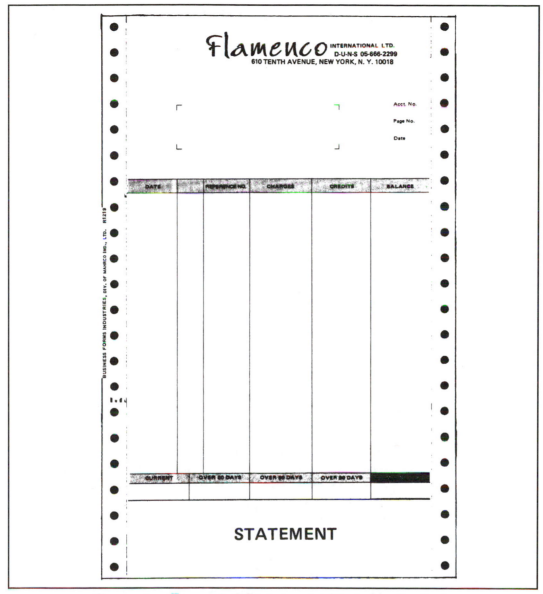

Computer-Generated Statement with Aging Analysis

Computerized Past-Due Notices

Comments

1. *Computers can be programmed to generate one or a series of simple past-due notices.*

2. *If a series of notices is used, they are normally progressively more strident in demanding payment or resolution of the past-due balance.*

3. *Computer-generated notices are a fairly blunt instrument for collections.*

4. *Typically, credit department personnel can specify which customers will and which will not receive these notices.*

5. *Other variables under the control of the credit department include how often the notices will be sent and what message each notice will contain.*

6. *Past-due notices (often referred to as dunning notices) are simply one tool in a collection "toolbox." Past-due dunning notices should never be relied on to do the entire job of collecting or clearing a past-due balance.*

7. *At some point, the creditor must call or meet the debtor to discuss the status of a past-due balance.*

8. *Some past-due notices are generated to fit into window box envelopes and to look like a check from the outside of the envelope. The intention is that this technique will interest the recipient enough to open the envelope.*

302 NORTH STREET • FARGO, NORTH DAKOTA 58102 • PHONE (701) 555-3300

MUTUAL
LIFE INSURANCE CO

```
AVOID POLICY FORFEITURE
YOUR PREMIUM OF    109.10 IS PAST DUE




MR POLICY HOLDER
123 HOME ST
ORANGE, N.D. 58100
```

FORM 009 UNIVERSAL

PRINTED BY THE STANDARD REGISTER COMPANY U.S.A.

IMPORTANT
This is a multi-purpose form used by the Company to notify policyowners of policy information including premiums due or past due, policy loan interest due, and dividend credits. Premiums due should be paid to the Company before the end of the grace period of 31 days after the due date; otherwise the policy and all payments thereon will be forfeited, except as provided in the policy. If there is interest due on a policy loan, it is payable in accordance with the loan provisions of your policy. Checks and drafts constitute payment only if honored when presented for payment. Your check is your receipt.

Notice: The Insured is a voting member of the Mutual Life Insurance Company, and the annual meetings of such Company are held at its Home Office in Fargo, North Dakota, on the first Wednesday in March in each year at 10:00 a.m.

NAME _____

NEW
ADDRESS _____

CITY
STATE _____

POLICY
NUMBERS _____

PLEASE LIST ANY ADDRESS CHANGE ALONG WITH CURRENT POLICY NUMBERS IN SPACE ABOVE, THEN RETURN TO MUTUAL LIFE INSURANCE COMPANY.

Computerized Past-Due Notices

Automated Past-Due Notice with Built-In Envelope

Comments

1. *This form includes a mailing envelope as part of its construction. This is considered an unusual request.*

2. *The account name, address and other details are computer printed on the past due notice. By use of a spot carbon, the name and address are also printed on the mailing envelope.*

3. *Another copy of the notice is also spot carboned for return with the remittance.*

4. *Compare this past-due notice with the one illustrated on page 471 which is also computer generated.*

Automated Past-Due Notice with Built-In Envelope

Debtor–Creditor Life Insurance

Comments

1. *Occasionally, a creditor might request protection in the form of life insurance in the event the owner of a debtor company dies. This is considered an unusual request.*

2. *As unusual as this may seem, requiring a life insurance policy listing the creditor as the beneficiary is actually sound risk management.*

3. *In the event of the death of the debtor, this type of life insurance policy protects the creditor as well as the family of the deceased. With this type of policy in place, the creditor does not have to wait until probate to collect the balance due.*

4. *Typically, the policy is written so that the creditor receives only the amount owed at the time of death. No creditor wants to be seen as profiting from the death of a customer.*

NORTH AMERICAN LIFE INSURANCE COMPANY

EXECUTIVE & ADMINISTRATIVE OFFICES   XXXX MAIN AVENUE   BOX XXXX   MORRISTOWN, N.J. 07960

(Herein called the Company)

I hereby apply for and accept a Single Premium Decreasing Term Life Insurance Policy with Total and Permanent Disability Benefits as follows:

NAME AND ADDRESS OF INSURED DEBTOR		Account No.
xxxxxxxxxxx xxxxxxxxxxxx xxxxxxxxxxxxx		6901OA5AA
		Policy No. 605384
		Amount of Monthly Installments $ 239.76

Initial Amount of Insured Indebtedness	Term (Months)	Effective Date of Insurance Mo. Da. Yr.	Age of Insured	Insurance Charge	
				Life	Disability
5754.24	24	9/29/xx	50	47.76	none

Beneficiary **G.M.A.C.**

Maximum Amount of Life Insurance $15,000
Maximum Daily Benefit $10.00
Maximum Monthly Benefit $300.00
Maximum Age 65

I represent that I am now in good health as far as I know and believe and I have not attained my 65th birthday. I declare that I have read this application and all statements herein are correct and that my request for the purchase of this insurance is entirely voluntary.

X _____
(Signature of Applicant - Insured Debtor)

The above premium is deemed to have been collected from the Insured Debtor. The amount so collected shall not exceed the premium charged by the Company.

MAXIMUM AGE: This Policy shall not cover any Debtor who has attained his 65th birthday on or before the Effective Date of Insurance stated above. If the Insured Debtor misstates his age and he has attained his 65th birthday on or before the Effective Date of Insurance stated above, the Company's liability shall be limited to a refund of the entire premium.

EFFECTIVE DATE OF INSURANCE: The insurance shall become effective on the date the Insured Debtor becomes obligated to the Creditor as stated above.

LIFE

In consideration of the application herefor, a copy of which appears above and is hereby made a part of this Policy, and in consideration of premium received, the Company hereby insures the life of the above named Insured Debtor. Upon receipt at its Administrative Office of due proof of death of the said Insured Debtor, provided such death occurs within the above specified term, beginning with the effective date hereof, which is the date of inception of debt, the Company agrees to pay to the Beneficiary (hereinafter called the Creditor) the amount for which the life of the Insured Debtor is insured to reduce or extinguish the indebtedness indicated in the Application. The initial amount of life insurance shall not exceed the total amount payable under the contract of indebtedness and in no event and under no condition shall the aggregate amount of life insurance exceed the Maximum Amount of Life Insurance shown above.

Debtor–Creditor Life Insurance

Debtor–Creditor Life Insurance

Comments

1. *See page 475 for the illustration of the top half of this form.*

2. *State laws regarding life insurance on the life of the debtor vary from state to state. In addition, consumer credit laws as regards installment contracts and life insurance premiums as a part of the cost of credit have requirements on disclosure.*

3. *Generally, such life insurance is voidable by the insurance carrier under certain conditions. One of the more usual conditions is that if the insured debtor died of an ailment for which he had been treated within a certain time prior to the effective date of the insurance, the insurance carrier is only obligated to return the paid-in premium. The creditor would then have to present a claim to the decedent's estate for the amount owed.*

4. *In many states such insurance has to be voluntary on the part of the debtor and cannot be a condition for the granting of credit. In such states, if there is proof of the precondition, the insurance contract may be voidable.*

Immediately upon receipt of due proof of said Insured Debtor's death the Company will pay to the Creditor an amount of insurance equal to the amount of insurance in force on the date of said Insured Debtor's death. The amount of insurance in force during the first month of coverage shall be an amount equal to the Initial Amount of Insured Indebtedness or the Maximum Amount of Insurance stated above, whichever is less, which amount shall hereafter be referred to as the Initial Amount of Insurance. Coverage shall commence on the Effective Date of Insurance stated above which shall be the effective date of the Insured Debtor's indebtedness to the Creditor. Thereafter, the amount of insurance in force shall be determined by progressively decreasing the Initial Amount of Insurance by an equal reduction at the end of each month after the Effective Date of coverage. The amount of such monthly reduction shall be determined by dividing the Initial Amount of Insurance by the number of months of the term in the Application. In no event and under no condition shall the amount of insurance on the life of any one Insured Debtor exceed the Maximum Amount of Life Insurance stated above. Any amount of insurance remaining after payment of the Insured Debtor's indebtedness to the Creditor shall be paid to a beneficiary, other than the Creditor, named by the Insured Debtor or to his estate.

EXCEPTIONS: The Company's liability shall be limited to a refund of the entire premium if death results from any illness or disease for which the Insured Debtor received treatment within ninety days prior to the effective date of insurance stated above if the Insured Debtor's death occurs within ninety days of said Effective Date of Insurance.

TOTAL AND PERMANENT DISABILITY BENEFITS

The Insured Debtor is also covered for Total and Permanent Disability benefits if a charge for such insurance is shown above. If the Insured Debtor becomes wholly and continuously disabled as a result of bodily injury or sickness and is prevented therefore from performing each and every duty pertaining to his occupation, he shall be deemed to be Totally Disabled. If such Total Disability continues uninterrupted for a period of __14__ days during which time the Insured Debtor is under the care of a legally qualified physician other than himself, he shall be deemed to be Permanently Totally Disabled.

The provisions on the reverse side hereof are hereby referred to and made a part hereof.

Witness the signatures of the proper officials of said Company.

May R. Berwin

MARY R. BERWIN
Secretary

R. Gleeli

R. DONALD GLEELI
President

Countersigned _____
Licensed Resident Agent (Where Required by Law)

DEBTOR-CREDITOR INSURANCE

Single Premium Decreasing Term Insurance with Total and Permanent Disability Benefits
Non-Participating

Debtor–Creditor Life Insurance

Collection Agency Services

Comments

1. All collection agencies are not created equal. Each agency offers a different menu of services and features. Some typical services include:

A free demand service. *Most collection agencies offer their customers a free preliminary collection letter that can be sent directly to the debtor. If this letter produces payment within a specified time, usually ten days, the creditor owes nothing to the collection agency.*

Access to the agency database. *More and more agencies are allowing their customers the opportunity to find out if a debtor is in the agency's database of accounts that have been placed for collection in the past. Some agencies even allow their clients to learn the outcome of their previous collection efforts.*

Letter writing service. *For a fee, some collection agencies will generate a series of collection letters to the debtor company.*

Collection service. *Many collection agencies use telephone collectors to call debtors placed for collection by their clients. The collectors are trained to speak with decision makers and to be persistent but professional in their collection efforts.*

Personal service. *Some agencies will send a collector to the debtor's place of business if the debt owed is large enough to justify the visit.*

Forwarding service. *Recognizing that certain accounts will not respond to their collection efforts, no matter how persistent or professional, most collection agencies have an affiliate network of attorneys who specialize in filing lawsuits to collect outstanding debts.*

Reporting services. *Most collection agencies provide their customers with periodic progress reports on the status of their collection efforts, even when those efforts have not resulted in any agreement being reached or any payment being made.*

Collection Agency Benefits

1. *Psychological.* An independent agent can create an emotional impact on the debtor. Tactful but more aggressive tones can be used without impairing the buyer-seller relationship.

2. *Wider implications.* Without specifically being able to identify the risk or threat, debtors are aware that other parties have been alerted to the debtor's financial problems. Debtors may pay because they are concerned that an unfavorable credit history may prevent them from getting open account credit terms from other creditors in the future.

3. *Profitability.* Most agencies are paid on a contingency basis; if there is no recovery, the creditor owes nothing. Collection fees or commissions are significant, but the fees are far less than having to write off the entire balance due to bad debt.

4. *Expertise.* Most collection agencies employ a calm, reasonable and matter-of-fact approach to their collection efforts. They have no emotional involvement in the collection process, while their client (the creditor) may be less objective and more emotional.

5. *Targeting.* By having an alternative collection system, the credit manager can concentrate on more fertile or beneficial areas of collection activity. In addition, greater effort can be allocated to other areas of credit activity such as closer monitoring of credit granting.

6. *Goodwill.* Use of an agency minimizes opportunities for any damage to goodwill with particular accounts or with an entire industry. The potential for future business with an account that has been turned over may be possible.

7. *Staffing.* The careful use of experienced agency personnel reduces the requirements for higher-salaried collection personnel in-house.

8. *Debtor data.* A collection agency may be more informed about a particular account through the handling of other creditors' problems with that account.

Choosing a Collection Agency

Comments

1. *Agency collection fees vary widely, even if their services and results do not.*

2. *Collection agencies use a wide array of collection techniques.*

3. *Whatever agency you use, it must be professionally managed, and the collectors be experienced. Under civil law, a creditor may be held liable for any inappropriate actions taken by their collection agency.*

4. *The honesty and integrity of an agency should somehow be verified. Remember, the agency will be collecting money on behalf of the creditor.*

Checklist for Qualifying a Collection Agency

1. The agency should be licensed and bonded.
2. Collection rates should be competitive, and the agency should be willing to negotiate rates when a client is considering placing a large claim.
3. The agency should arrange for the proceeds of any collection effort to be placed into a separate escrow or trust account.
4. The agency should provide periodic updates on collection activities.
5. No negotiated settlements or protracted payout arrangements should be made without the express, written approval of the client's credit manager.
6. The agency should subscribe to a strict code of ethics. One such code of ethics is observed by members of the Collection Agency Section of the Commercial Law League of America.
7. The agency should have been in business for at least three years, and the senior managers of the company should be collection professionals with many years of collection experience.

Chapter 8

Legal Matters and Bankruptcy

There is no substitute for competent legal advice, and this book is no such substitute. However, the credit manager should know enough about commercial and bankruptcy law in order to determine when expert legal advice should be sought out. A credit manager should also know about specific laws relating to the extension of credit and collection activities.

Creditor Versus Debtor

Many credit professionals feel that the law currently favors debtors over creditors to a very significant extent. For example, it is often not sufficient to prove that the debtor received the product and has not paid for the goods. The creditor must also be able to prove that the merchandise was not subsequently returned and/or that the merchandise in question was not defective.

Bankruptcy Law

The stated purpose of the U.S. Bankruptcy Code is to help the debtor to rehabilitate. As a result of changes in the Bankruptcy Code relating to business bankruptcy filings, business bankruptcies are at or near an all-time high.

As a result, the Bankruptcy Courts are overloaded. The U.S. Trustee's office (which helps to administer bankruptcy cases) is similarly burdened with a large caseload. As a result, trustees have less and less time to devote to individual cases. Thus bankrupt debtors are given more and more latitude in operating their businesses as debtors-in-possession.

Seller's Remedies upon Discovery of a Buyer's Insolvency

A portion of the Uniform Commercial Code provides that under certain conditions where a seller has shipped merchandise to a buyer that is insolvent, the creditor may reclaim the merchandise. If the merchandise in question has not been delivered, the creditor may contact the carrier and stop delivery. The goods in question can be reconsigned to another consignee or returned to the seller. Of course, the creditor/consignor is responsible for additional freight costs, but that might be a small price to pay for the return of the goods in question.

Also according to the Uniform Commercial Code, the creditor has a right, under the UCC, under certain circumstances, to demand that an insolvent debtor return goods delivered, typically within ten days of receiving the notice. Reclamation works this way: Once the creditor is convinced the debtor is insolvent (as defined in the UCC), the debtor must be given formal, written notice of the creditor's intent to reclaim the goods. If the debtor has misrepresented the insolvency, the reclamation period may be extended under various state laws.

The reclamation rights of creditors under the Uniform Commercial Code are complex. Prior to making any reclamation demand, consulting an attorney might be appropriate.

What happens to reclamation rights if the debtor files for bankruptcy protection? The U.S. Bankruptcy Code provides for the reclamation rights of a creditor against the bankrupt debtor company. The Bankruptcy Code establishes specific limitations on an unsecured creditor's right to reclaim goods shipped prior to the bankruptcy filing date.

This is a very technical provision of the U.S. Bankruptcy Code, and creditors should seek legal advice as to whether and how a reclamation claim may be properly filed with the debtor and/or the Bankruptcy Court.

Creditor's Correspondence and Mail Fraud

If an applicant for credit or an existing customer uses the U.S. mail in misrepresenting the company's creditworthiness, that entity and the individual who mailed the document may be guilty of mail fraud. Similarly, a company that uses a fax machine in misrepresenting the company in an attempt to defraud creditors may be guilty of wire fraud.

Federal law has a very broad description or these two crimes. For example, the federal mail fraud statute states, in part:

> *Whoever, having devised or intended to devise any scheme or artifice to defraud, or for obtaining money or property by means of fraud or fraudulent pretenses, representations or promises, shall, for purpose of executing such scheme or artifice or attempting to do so, place or cause to be placed in any depository of the mails, any letter, shall be fined not more than $1,000 or imprisoned for not more than five years or both.*

Each letter or fax is a separate violation of the law. As many debtor–creditor communications are handled via the mail or fax, the federal mail and wire fraud laws and their enforcement are a way to guaranty honest business communications. This is of particular importance to credit professionals since one of the offenses covered by the mail and wire fraud laws is fraudulently obtaining open account credit shipments from a creditor. Even if the mails are not used, state laws cover criminal fraud and deliberate misrepresentation.

Statute of Limitations

Iron rule: The law is usually on the side of the diligent creditor. The law cannot be used to collect a debt after an unusually long wait. Each state has laws defining the period during which a creditor may file a lawsuit to collect a delinquent balance from a debtor. Your attorney will be able to tell you about the statutes of limitations in the states in which your company does business.

Libel Considerations in Credit Correspondence

Comments

1. *Most of the time, libel suits do not end in a decision determined by a judge or jury. Usually they are settled out of court, and only the lawyers for both parties win. Who loses? Certainly, the defendant will be unhappy about being sued regardless of what was actually said or meant.*

2. *Libel is to be avoided in any credit correspondence. Some credit departments have taken the extra step of not sending any correspondence that is in any way derogatory.*

3. *Other credit organizations have an iron-clad policy of sticking to the facts. The truth (provided it is the absolute truth) is a good defense against libel.*

4. *It is especially important to avoid libel in responding to credit inquiries from other trade creditors. This can be a problem area because the task of responding to this type of correspondence is often delegated to a clerk, who must be carefully taught how to respond to credit inquiries.*

Libel Considerations in Credit Correspondence

1. *Libel*. Defaming the reputation of an individual or company in writing.
2. *Libelous per se*. Proving libel is virtually unnecessary for the plaintiff if any of the following statements were written:
   - "This customer is a thief and a swindler."
   - "Watch out. This company is trouble and the company president is a con artist."
   - "They are insolvent but they just aren't telling anyone."
   - "This account is simply not creditworthy. They are incapable of paying creditors on time, no matter what they might tell you."
3. *Publication*. An essential element of the tort of libel is that the statement must be communicated (published) to a third party. In other words, it may not be if I tell a customer that has broken commitments that he is a liar. But it can be libelous if I write on a credit inquiry, "This customer is a liar, and breaks every promise he makes."
4. *Defense*. The best defense against slander is that the statements made were the truth. But let's examine the statement made above more closely to see if we could use the truth as a defense: The truth is that the debtor broke three payment commitments to me. The statement I published was that he "breaks every promise he makes." That statement is almost certainly untrue.
5. *Repetition*. This is not a defense against libel. For example, one cannot defend against libel by writing, "I was told by the credit manager at EFG Plumbing that the owner of this company was convicted of fraud in Texas and cannot be trusted."

How to Respond to Credit Inquiries

Comments

1. *There is no legal obligation to respond to any request for a credit reference. Creditors respond to credit inquiries as a business courtesy to other creditors.*

2. *It is a good idea to establish a policy that credit reference requests must be put in writing. (A fax is normally considered acceptable.) By requiring the requester to put the reference request in writing, the company responding has a written record of what was said to whom.*

3. *Whoever is assigned to respond to credit reference requests must be taught to stick to the facts. If any facts are unclear, the response should be "not available." For example, if the computer system does not list the date the account was opened, the response to this question must be "not available" rather than someone's best guess.*

4. *The only questions that should be answered on a reference check are:*

   - *Date opened.*
   - *Date of last sale.*
   - *Balance owing.*
   - *Amount past due.*
   - *Payment terms.*
   - *Normal manner of payment.*
   - *Security held by the creditor.*

5. *Creditors should never "rate" an account. Ratings are totally subjective.*

6. *Creditors should not respond when asked for "comments" about the debtor company for the same reason; they are subjective.*

7. *Credit department personnel must be aware of the laws pertaining to libel. Libel involves written correspondence in which an individual or company is defamed.*

How to Respond to Credit Inquiries

1. Require reference requests in writing (a fax is acceptable).
2. Stick to the facts. If the facts are unclear, the response is "not available."
3. Provide only factual responses regarding dates for opening the account and the last sale, balance due (if any), amount past due (if any), payment terms and manner of payment, security (if any).
4. Never "rate" the account.
5. Do not supply "comments."
6. Be aware of libel law.

Debt Recovery by Lawsuit

Comments

1. *Collection litigation must be handled by attorneys, unless the amount owed is small and can be handled in small claims court.*

2. *A dispute should result in a lawsuit being filed only after all intermediate remedies have been tried and have failed.*

3. *The exact course of the lawsuit depends on a number of variables. Probably the most important variable is the action taken by the debtor in response to the filing of the lawsuit.*

4. *Creditors hope that the debtor will not answer the complaint. This normally results in a default judgment being entered in favor of the plaintiff and against the defendant/debtor.*

5. *Defendants have a number of options. They may seek to have the complaint dismissed. They may seek a negotiated settlement in response to the filing of the complaint. They may file an answer (a Responsive Pleading) to the complaint or a counterclaim.*

6. *The creditor must be certain its attorney has the expertise necessary to deal with all the contingencies possible in a lawsuit of this type. The credit professional also has an obligation before and during the case to watch and manage the costs associated with recovering the balance owed by the debtor.*

7. *The creditor should be prepared to recommend at any point that the case be dropped if the costs of pursuing it outweigh the benefits.*

Debt Recovery by Lawsuit—General Civil Procedures

1. A Complaint is filed in a court with appropriate jurisdiction. (The debtor/defendant can contest the jurisdiction of the court to hear the case.)

2. The debtor is served with the complaint that sets forth the facts of the case.

3. Unless a Preliminary Motion to Dismiss is approved, the debtor must file an answer with the court, typically within 30 days of receiving the Complaint.

4. If the debtor fails to file within the statutory deadline, the creditor/plaintiff may ask the court to enter a default judgment against the debtor.

5. Assuming the defendant answers the complaint, the matter is placed on the court calendar.

6. Prior to the trial, the legal process called *discovery* takes place. During discovery, either party may submit written questions for information to the other party. Requests for the production of documents are not uncommon. Witnesses who can testify to the facts of the case are interviewed under oath in a deposition.

7. At the trial, the creditor may present evidence of the debt owed. The debtor may either challenge the evidence or present facts in support of its counterclaim.

8. At any time prior to the rendering of a decision by the court, the parties can stipulate—or agree to—a judgment or settlement that will be entered into the records.

9. If the matter is settled in favor of the creditor, the court will enter a judgment in the plaintiff's favor.

10. After the judgment has been entered, in theory the debtor pays the creditor and the matter is resolved. Unfortunately, the debtor does not always have the money to pay the creditor. Legal remedies are available if this occurs.

Motion for Summary Judgment

Comments

1. *At any time after the filing of the complaint by the plaintiff and the response by the debtor/defendant, either party may petition the court in a Motion for Summary Judgment.*

2. *A Motion for Summary Judgment is filed when one party feels there are no material issues of fact to be tried and the party entering the motion is entitled to payment as a matter of law.*

3. *A Motion for Summary Judgment is filed in an effort to find a legal shortcut to the civil litigation process. This motion is filed when one party believes the matter under review is so clear-cut that additional delays are unnecessary.*

4. *If the Court denies the Motion for Summary Judgment, the process that will ultimately result in a civil trial continues.*

Example of a Scenario in Which a Motion
for Summary Judgment May Be Filed

1. A creditor files a complaint that the debtor bounced a check for $50,000 and has never made the check good.

2. The debtor responds that goods were not received in good condition and that the creditor has refused to pick up the merchandise in question and issue a credit.

3. During the discovery process, the defendant's warehouse manager is asked during a deposition where the goods in question are at this time. He responds: "They were sold." The attorney for the creditor asks if there were any problems with the merchandise in question and is told: "No, no problems at all. That's why we sold them."

4. At this point, the plaintiff enters a Motion for Summary Judgment. The plaintiff asserts that the debtor received the goods, inspected them, inventoried them, sold them and now has raised the defense that the goods were not merchantable simply to avoid paying the $50,000 owed to the creditor.

5. The decision to grant this Motion is up to the judge. The defendant will have an opportunity to respond to the motion. If this ploy to delay payment is as transparent as it seems, the judge will likely grant the motion and require the debtor to pay the creditor immediately.

Request for Preliminary Default Judgment

Comments

1. *After a certain number of days, the debtor/defendant is required to answer the complaint made against the company. In many jurisdictions, this time limit is 20 days for service within the jurisdiction—otherwise, it is 30 days.*

2. *After a reasonable time has elapsed for the filing of an answer, the attorney for the creditor can file a motion with the court requesting a preliminary default judgment.*

3. *In some jurisdictions, filing appropriate documents with the court is sufficient to request a Motion for a Default Judgment be entered. Other jurisdictions require live testimony in which the creditor's attorney presents proof that the complaint was served on the debtor, along with evidence of the indebtedness. The court might require witnesses and interview those witnesses under oath.*

4. *If the judge is satisfied that all of the procedural steps have been complied with and that there is prima facie proof of the indebtedness, he or she may grant a preliminary default judgment.*

5. *After a period of time, the preliminary default judgment becomes final. Usually, only in unusual circumstances can the preliminary default judgment be set aside or vacated.*

MOTION FOR PRELIMINARY DEFAULT

On motion of _____William Williams_____, Attorney for the Plaintiff, and

on suggesting to the court, that a (X) personal or (   ) domicilliary citation

was served on the _____23rd_____ day of _____March_____, 19XX_, upon

_____Mr. John Doe DBA Variety Wholesalers_____

_____444 Main Street_____

_____Appleton, La._____

defendants herein, and the said defendants having failed to appear or to file

an answer hereto, and the legal delays for so answering having elapsed, it

is ordered by the Court that a PRELIMINARY DEFAULT be entered herein.

Granted and signed this _____30th_____ day

of _____April_____, 19XX_

_____J. Johns_____

Judge, 24th Judicial District Court

Index # XX/1234

William Williams
Attorney at Law
555 Canal Street
Metarie, La.

Request for Preliminary Default Judgment

Final Judgment Upon the Default of the Debtor

Comments

1. *See the form illustrated on page 497 in regards to the granting of a preliminary default judgment upon motion of the attorney for the plaintiff creditor.*

2. *After a period of time, during which the debtor has not attempted or succeeded in setting aside the preliminary default judgment, the attorney for the creditor may apply to the court to make the judgment final.*

3. *Even after a judgment has been rendered by the court, it is still possible for an attorney for the debtor to be successful in having that same court set aside or vacate the judgment. Grounds for such a motion to vacate include, for instance, an error on the part of the court, improper service of the summons and complaint or fraud.*

4. *The granting of the judgment is only one step in the process of eventually obtaining payment from the debtor in satisfaction of the judgment. Execution of the judgment upon the assets of the debtor must take place if the debtor cannot satisfy the judgment voluntarily and immediately. If the debtor has no assets or has filed for bankruptcy protection, then the task of collecting the bad debt is far from over.*

STATE OF LOUISIANA

24th Judicial District Court for the Parish of Jefferson

No. XX/1234   DIVISION " C "

```
Charlie Dog Corp., Plaintiff )
555 Factory Drive              )
Orange, Louisiana             )
        VS                     )      CIVIL ACTION
                               )
Mr. John Doe, Defendent        )
DBA Variety Wholesalers        )
444 Main Street                )
Appleton, La.                  )
```

JUDGMENT

On motion of _____ William Williams, Esq _____ , attorney for

plaintiff, and on producing to the Court due proof in support of the plaintiff's demands, the Court

considering the law and the evidence to be in favor of the plaintiff, for the reasons orally assigned.

IT IS ORDERED, ADJUDGED AND DECREED, that the default herein entered on

_____ April 30th, 19XX _____ , be now confirmed and made final and,

accordingly, let there be judgment herein in favor of the plaintiff.

JUDGMENT read, rendered and signed in open Court on this _____ Tenth _____

day of the month of _____ June _____ , 19 XX .

_____
         J.B. JOHNS
            JUDGE

Final Judgment Upon the Default of the Debtor

Judgment Against Debtor

Comments

1. *The illustrations on pages 497 and 499 relate to instances where the creditor was granted a judgment by default (*failure to answer the summons and complaint*).*

2. *The debtor, Mr. John Doe, received and responded to the Complaint filed, answered the discovery requests for information, attended the mandatory arbitration meeting, attended the pretrial conference and testified at trial.*

3. *After hearing both sides, the court ruled in favor of the creditor, Able Baker Company. A judgment was granted in the amount of $1,000.*

4. *Even though the matter seems resolved, Mr. Doe has the option of filing an appeal. Assuming he does not do so, the judgment by the court does not settle the matter. The debtor might not pay despite the judgment in favor of the creditor by the court.*

5. *In these circumstances, the creditor's attorney has to seek satisfaction by having the judgment executed. This requires a court order to seize and sell certain assets of the debtor identified to the court by the creditor.*

STATE OF LOUISIANA
Civil District Court for the Parish of Orleans

No.   475   DIVISION " L "   DOCKET # XX/1234

Able Baker Company, Plaintiff)
999 Industrial Drive   )
Orange, Louisiana   )
)
          Vs   )   CIVIL ACTION
)
Mr. John Doe, Defendent   )
123 Home Street   )
Orange, Louisiana   )

JUDGMENT

This cause came on this day for trial.

Present: Mr. Gordon Gordons, representing the plaintiff and
Mr. John Doe, Per Se

When, after hearing the pleadings, evidence and argument of counsel, the Court considering the law and the evidence to be in favor of the plaintiff for the reasons orally assigned;

IT IS ORDERED, ADJUDGED AND DECREED that there be judgment herein in favor of the plaintiff, Able Baker Company in the amount of One Thousand Dollars ($1,000.00)

JUDGMENT read, rendered and signed in open Court___December 2nd, 19XX_____

*R. Roberts*_____
JUDGE

Judgment Against Debtor

Citation to Garnishee

Comments

1. *On the preceding page is an illustration of a judgment granted in favor of the creditor. Unfortunately, a judgment does not guarantee payment. All too frequently, it is just the start of the legal entanglements involved in trying to get the debtor to satisfy the judgment and retire the past-due balance.*

2. *While the debtor might be evasive about the location of assets, third parties also pose a problem to creditors. For instance, banks frequently do not want to reveal information about their clients to creditors, especially if the bank is also a creditor of the client.*

3. *Frequently, records and even oral testimony are required in order to have judgments properly executed.*

4. *In the illustration, a bank is ordered by a court to provide information regarding Mr. John Doe to the court. If the bank complies with the court order, information may be available which can result in a garnishee of the debtor's bank account.*

5. *If the bank does not comply with the court order, it may be liable for the amount of the judgment or subject to other sanctions imposed by the court.*

Form 51—3M—Sou.

STATE OF LOUISIANA

Civil District Court for the Parish of Orleans

No. XX/1234   LAW DIVISION A   DOCKET

Able Baker Company)
999 Industrial Drive)
Orange, Louisiana)
)
      Vs   )   CIVIL ACTION
)
Mr. John Doe)
123 Home Street)
Orange, Louisiana)

Louisiana Bank Corporation   **GARNISHEE:**

YOU ARE HEREBY CITED, to declare on oath, what property belonging to the Defendant in this case you have in your possession, or in what sum you are indebted to said Defendant, and also, to answer in writing, under oath, the interrogatories annexed to the

petition of which a copy accompanies this citation, and deliver your answer to the same, in the office of the Clerk of the Civil District Court for the Parish of Orleans, within fifteen days after the service hereof, otherwise judgment will be entered against you for the amount claimed by the plaintiff with interest and costs.

WITNESS, the Honorable   Robert L. Lee   Judge of the said Court,

    27th day of   October   in the year of our Lord, 19 XX

                    _____ *J. Davis* _____Deputy Clerk.

Citation to Garnishee

Interrogatories for Garnishee

Comments

1. *An Interrogatory is a court order. It requires the recipient to provide information to the court about assets of the defendant debtor.*

2. *An Interrogatory could be delivered by court order to a bank, a stockbroker, an employer, life insurance companies, trust and estates, and almost any third party with which the debtor did business.*

3. *The failure of the recipient of the order to promptly and properly respond to such an order can result in the recipient being responsible for the amount of the judgment or other recourse of the court.*

4. *Laws vary from state to state as to the limitations on garnishment of the salary of a defendant debtor.*

5. *Attorneys who specialize in commercial collections are experienced in seeking out the location of assets the debtor has attempted to hide and converting those assets into cash for the creditor.*

6. *Collection litigation may seem lengthy and complex, but one of the basic laws of the land involves the protection of personal property rights. The law must be certain a debt is owed before a court will compel a debtor to pay a creditor.*

STATE OF LOUISIANA
Civil District Court for the Parish of Orleans
INTERROGATORIES
To Be Answered Categorically Under Oath, in Writing, Fifteen Days From Service.

1st. Had you in your hands, or under your control, directly or indirectly, at the time of service of these interrogatories, or at any time since, any money, rights, credits, or other property whatsoever, belonging or due to the said defendant in_____or in which_____ha or had any interest for the whole or for a part; and if yea, what is the nature, description and amount thereof, and is the same sufficient to pay or satisfy the full amount of said_____or if less, to what amount?—you being asked and required to make a full disclosure in relation to the same.

2nd. Interrogatory:—Were you not, at the time of service upon you of these interrogatories, or since, directly or indirectly, indebted or obligated unto the said defendant _____, in _____ for anything or for any sum whatever, whether for yourself alone or together with others, in consequence of any sale or exchange or transaction of any kind whatever, whether the same be due or to become due, and whether the interests of said defendant in _____ be direct or indirect, or be for the whole or a part only or whether it be by bill, note or otherwise; and if yea, what is the nature, description and amount thereof, and is the same sufficient to pay or satisfy the full amount of said _____ and costs, or if less, what amount?—you being asked and required to make a full and detailed disclosure in relation to the same.

3rd. Interrogatory:—Have you, at any time since the service of notice of seizure in your hands herein made, directly or indirectly, unto or with the said defendant in _____ any payment or innovation or compromise, or arrangement or given _____ any note or written obligation, or received from _____ directly or indirectly any receipt or acquittance?—and if yea, state the nature, description and amount thereof, and the time, place and circumstances of the same.

4th. Is the defendant in the suit employed by you, and if so what is his rate of compensation, in what manner is it paid, and are there or not other judgments or garnishments affecting such wage, salary or compensation? You being asked and required to make a full disclosure in relation to the same as provided by R.S. 13:3924.

5th. If the defendant is indebted unto you as his employer, you shall make a full and complete disclosure of the status of such account, showing the time that the debt was incurred, the exact amount of such debt, the credits applicable thereto, the manner in which said debt is being liquidated, and all other facts in connection therewith and pertinent thereto, in accordance with R.S. 13:3925.

6th. If the defendant works on a commission basis, you as his employer, shall make a full disclosure of the terms of employment, the amount of the commission, and the method of payment of such commission and the dates on which settlements are made with the employee; all in accordance with R.S. 13:3926.

Let this supplemental petition be filed, and let Mr._____

_____

_____

be made garnishee herein, and ordered to answer the accompanying interrogatories, under oath, in writing, within 15 days from service, and as the law directs, as herein prayed for, and let the sum of $5.00 be deposited with the Clerk of Court, as per R.S. 13:3927.

New Orleans, La.,_____19_____. _____ Judge

Interrogatories for Garnishee

The Federal Equal Credit Opportunity Act Notice

Comments

1. *Federal law prohibits businesses from discriminating in granting credit on the basis of several factors unrelated to the creditworthiness of the applicant.*

2. *For example, credit cannot be denied on the basis of sex, marital status, race, age, national origin, or religion. Creditors are also prohibited from discouraging applicants from applying for open account terms on the basis of any of these factors.*

3. *The Equal Credit Opportunity Act (ECOA) provides that, if an application for business credit is denied, the rejected party may request in writing an explanation for the denial.*

4. *Creditors involved in consumer credit may not discount the income of an applicant because of the sex, age or marital status of the applicant. For example, a creditor may not discount the income of a woman of childbearing age on the assumption that she might at some point stop working and start a family.*

5. *The ECOA, which is administered by the Federal Trade Commission, does not guarantee that all applicants for open account credit terms will be granted credit terms, but anyone in a position to review credit applications must be familiar with ECOA regulations.*

**NOTICE
CREDIT HISTORY FOR
MARRIED PERSONS**

The Federal Equal Credit Opportunity Act prohibits credit discrimination on the basis of race, color, religion, national origin, sex, marital status, age (provided that a person has the capacity to enter into a binding contract); because all or part of a person's income derives from any public assistance program; or because a person in good faith has exercised any right under the Federal Consumer Credit Protection Act. Regulations under the Act give married persons the right to have credit information included in credit reports in the name of both the wife and the husband if both use or are responsible for the account. This right was created, in part, to insure that credit histories will be available to women who become divorced or widowed.

If your account with us is one that both husband and wife signed for or is an account that is being used by one of you who did not sign, then you are entitled to have us report credit information relating to the account in both your names. If you choose to have credit information concerning your account with us reported in both your names, please complete and sign the statement on the attached panel and return it to us.

Federal regulations provide that signing your name will not change you or your spouse's legal liability on the account. Your signature will only request that credit information be reported in both your names.

If you do not complete and return the attached form, we will continue to report your credit history in the same way that we do now.

When you furnish credit information on this account, please report all information concerning the account in both our names.

_____
Account Number

Send to: XXXXX Company
P.O. Box 80
Tulsa, OK 74102

_____
Print or Type Name

_____
Print or Type Name

_____
Signature of Either Spouse

Federal Equal Credit Opportunity Act Notice

Truth in Lending Act

Comments

1. *The Truth in Lending Act is designed to give potential borrowers information about the cost of their loans so that they may compare these costs with those of other potential lenders.*

2. *The Act requires lenders to disclose the true cost of credit or a loan expressed as an annual interest rate (APR). The APR is a complex calculation involving a combination of the note interest rate, along with any points or origination costs, underwriting fees and other processing fees on the loan.*

Contents of a Typical Truth in Lending Disclosure Form

1. Creditor name and address.
2. Debtor name and address.
3. Property address.
4. Loan number and preparation date.
5. Annual percentage rate (APR).
6. Finance charge and amount financed.
7. Total of payments to be made, along with a payment schedule.
8. Information about any required deposit.
9. If the loan has a variable interest rate, a description of that feature.
10. Filing or recording fees.
11. Requirements for property insurance coverage to be purchased by the buyer.
12. Description of late charges.
13. Provisions relating to prepayment of the loan.

Guide for Creditors' Committee Meetings in Bankruptcy

Comments

1. *Creditors' meetings should be businesslike. Otherwise, participants will be wasting each other's time.*

2. *The meeting should remain focused on maximizing recovery to the unsecured creditors and on getting the plan or reorganization prepared, presented, and confirmed as soon as possible. This will result in payments to prepetition creditors being received as soon as possible.*

4. *Meetings will be shorter and more productive if a chairperson is appointed from among the committee members to keep the meeting on track.*

5. *The attorney for the creditor's committee can offer valuable advice. However, committee members must remember that professionals hired by the committee work for them. Committee members are not required to accept the advice offered by these professionals.*

5. *In fact, if the committee is unhappy with the performance of the professional(s) hired to advise them, they terminate the professionals and hire a suitable replacement.*

Guide for Creditors' Committee Meetings in Bankruptcy

1. The first meeting to form an Official Unsecured Creditor's Committee is called by the Office of the United States Trustee.

2. The Office of the United States Trustee is charged with helping the U.S. Bankruptcy Courts administer bankruptcy cases.

3. The first meeting of the creditors should direct itself to the organization of the committee.

4. Creditors on the committee should refrain from individual discussions with the debtor. Doing so can create confusion since the debtor might not know if the creditors are speaking for themselves or as representatives of the committee.

5. Detailed minutes should be kept of all committee meetings.

6. The initial focus of the committee should be to determine if it should recommend the immediate liquidation of the debtor company. Creditors have a right to request that the debtor be liquidated if they can demonstrate that the recovery would be larger than if the debtor were allowed to continue in business and eventually present a plan of reorganization.

7. There is always a temptation to share information from committee meetings with other creditors who are not on the committee. However, all discussions of the committee should be held in strictest confidence.

Claim Against an Estate—Front

Comments

1. *If a creditor sells to a proprietorship, there is a risk that the owner will die and the company will not have a contingency plan in place. If this occurs, collection problems can ensue.*

2. *In some jurisdictions, a creditor is required to file a claim and an affidavit of the indebtedness in the estate of the deceased.*

3. *Documents such as correspondence, purchase orders, invoices, delivery receipts, etc. should be included with the claim and the affidavit.*

4. *An attorney for the executor or administrator of the estate will normally handle the decedent's affairs. Correspondence regarding the debt should be addressed to that individual.*

5. *The claim can be more easily prepared and expedited if the creditor's attorney handles the claim.*

6. *Collection problems resulting from the death of a debtor can be minimized if life insurance exists on the debtor for the benefit of the creditor.*

Surrogate's Court, County of   SALEM

In the Matter

of

The Estate of **Mr. Joseph Roe
   DBA Roe Machine Shop
   999 Purdue Street
   Glendale, N.Y.**

Deceased

File No.   **XX/789**

CLAIM AGAINST ESTATE

TO: **Mr. John Doe with offices at 123 Office Drive, Glendale, N.Y.**

as *   **Executor**   *of the estate of* **Mr. Joseph Roe**   *deceased,*

The undersigned claimant does hereby present the following claim against the estate of the above named decedent.
Amount of Claim $ **18,650.00**   *with interest from*   **May 10th**   *19* **XX** .

   The facts upon which the claim is based are as follows:

1. On March 23rd, 19XX, Mr. Joseph Roe signed a purchase order for one Whitney Drill Press and attachments thereto.

2. On April 10th, 19XX, the press and attachments were delivered to Mr. Joseph Roe.

3. An invoice was mailed on April 7th, 19XX for the drill press and attachments with a total amount of $18,650.00

4. The terms of the sale were payment within ten days after the month of delivery. Payment being due on May 10th, 19XX.

5. No discounts or other deductions were allowable.

6. The invoice amount nor any part thereof has been paid to date.

7. Interest at the legal rate accrues from May 10th, 19XX.

8. None of the interest has yet been paid.

9. Photocopies of the purchase order and invoice are attached hereto.

Dated: **July 14th, 19XX**

Drill Press Corporation
Claimant

Firm or Corporate Claimant By *Robert Congars*   **Treasurer**
**1000 Industrial Drive
Bartonville, New York**
Address of Claimant

*Insert the male or female, singular or plural form
of either executor or administrator.

Claim Against an Estate—Front

Claim Against an Estate—Back

Comments

1. *In many instances, an affidavit in support of the claim is required.* The assistance of an attorney should be sought.

2. *Typically, the credit manager can execute the claim and affidavit since he or she is familiar with the creditor's books and records and can attest to the facts related to the indebtedness.*

3. *A claim can be amended if additional facts concerning the balance due or other matters come to light. However, it is best to be in complete possession of the facts before execution of the claim and affidavit. Files and records can be fully researched before making the claim. Severe penalties may ensue regarding a false claim.*

4. *Usually, a simple telephone call can determine who the executor or administrator is. A call to that party by the credit manager will reveal which attorney is handling the estate.*

5. *From time to time, a call can be made to the estate's attorney for information on progress toward settling the outstanding amount.*

CLAIM AGAINST DECEDENT ESTATE

AFFIDAVIT IN SUPPORT OF CLAIM

STATE OF NEW YORK
COUNTY OF BARTON   } *ss.:*

being duly sworn, deposes and says:

That *he resides at*

(a) *INDIVIDUAL*
That *he is the claimant named in the attached claim (or as appears below)*

(b) *CO-PARTNERSHIP*
That *he is a member of*
a co-partnership, the claimant named in the attached claim, composed of the undersigned and
of

and carrying on business at No.
County of   *State of*   *(or as appears below)*

(c) *CORPORATION*
That *he is the* Treasurer *of* Drill Press Corporation
a corporation organized and existing under the laws of the State of New York *and carrying on business*
at No. 1000 Industrial Drive *in* Bartonville
County of Barton *State of* New York *and is duly authorized to make this*
affidavit of claim on its behalf. Said corporation is the claimant named in the attached claim.

That *the said claim against* Mr. Joseph Roe *deceased*
is just and true; that the amount of the claim is justly due; that all payments thereon, if any, have been credited; that
he knows of no offsets and no evidence of indebtedness and that the claimant holds no security (except)

Sworn to before me
this 14th *day of* July   19 XX.

Robert Congars
Print or type name beneath signature
Robert Congars

Claim Against an Estate—Back

Notice to Creditors Under Uniform Commercial Code—Bulk Transfers

Comments

1. *Article 6 of the Uniform Commercial Code provides for the disclosure to creditors when a debtor sells a significant portion of the assets of the company other than in the ordinary course of business.*

2. *An example of an ordinary course of business sale is a retail store's selling inventory to customers. An example of a sale not in the ordinary course of business is the same retailer's selling the inventory along with the shelves, the display cases, the cash registers and other fixtures.*

3. *A written notice must be sent to creditors notifying them of the debtor's intention to enter into an agreement for a sale that may constitute a* bulk sale *under the laws of that state.*

4. *The notice must contain the date the assets will be transferred, the name of the seller, the name and address of the buyer and a listing of the assets to be sold.*

5. *Sometimes, when a business is sold the buyer assumes the liabilities of the seller. This is not always the case. In a situation in which the buyer is not assuming the debts of the seller in a bulk sale or transfer of assets, a trade creditor should be concerned about payment.*

6. *This is why the bulk transfer notice law was passed. It is intended to give creditors fair warning that a significant event is going to occur involving the debtor company.*

7. *The fact that the buyer is not going to assume the liabilities of the company does not mean that the debtor will not be paid. The seller/debtor might be able to retire all the outstanding obligations out of the proceeds of the sale of the assets of the company.*

8. *Regardless of who is responsible for the debt, collection can be complicated by the bulk sale of assets. The seller/debtor might have every intention of retiring debts from the proceeds of the sale only to find out that the proceeds are not sufficient to cover all the outstanding obligations. Or the buyer might assume the liabilities of the company and then experience cash flow problems, which presents the payment of debts as intended.*

9. *At times, a portion of the proceeds of the bulk sale may be placed into an escrow account for the settlements of existing obligations. In this situation, the creditor may be required to contact the person in charge of the escrow account to demand payment.*

10. *If you are unsure if, when, how, or by whom you will be paid when you receive a Notice of Bulk Transfer, you might want to consult with your attorney and discuss your rights and options under the law.*

11. *Typically, a notice to creditors of a bulk sale must be sent in writing at least ten days prior to the sale. If that notice is not sent, creditors may have recourse against both the transferor and the transferee.*

To the creditors of [debtor name], transferor:
_____

You are hereby notified that the Transferor is about to make a bulk transfer of property to the undersigned Transferee.

That the business address of the Transferee is: _____ , and the business address of the Transferor is: _____

That the location of the property to be trans-ferred is: _____

That the property to be transferred consists of: _____

To the best knowledge of the transferee, the transferor has not used a business name other the one that is stated above during the last three years, *or*
The transferee is aware that the transferor has also used the following business names in the last three years: _____

The transfer is / is not for new consideration.

The proceeds of the transfer are / are not ex-pected to be used to pay all of the antecedent debts of the Transferor.

The bulk transfer is to be made on order after *date*, at *City and State*, in the office of

Dated: _____   _____
                                              Transferor

Typical Notice of Bulk Sale

General Assignments

Comments

1. *On rare occasions, a creditor may receive from the debtor an assignment of an amount due from one of its debtor/customer's customers. An assignment of this type will benefit the creditor only if the debtor's customer is more creditworthy than the debtor company itself.*

2. *Typically, a General Assignment is made as an inducement to a creditor to extend open account terms. The assignment may involve one or all of the debtor/customer's receivables.*

3. *Once the General Assignment has been executed, in theory the creditor can present the contract to its debtor's customer(s) and demand payment.*

4. *Although General Assignments are relatively simple contracts, they are rarely used for several reasons. First, to be of value the creditor must know the creditworthiness of the debtor's customer. Second, to collect, the debtor's customer must be willing to pay the assignee upon presentation of the contract. Frequently, the debtor's customer will not want to become involved in a three-way transaction of this type.*

Know all Men by these Presents,

THAT   JOHN DOE, DBA SLOWLY WHOLESALERS

of   999 MAIN AVENUE, ORANGE CITY, UTAH

assignor(s),

in consideration of $ 1.00   , *the receipt whereof is hereby acknowledged, has sold and by these presents does grant, assign and convey unto*

      GLASS LUGGAGE CORPORATION

of   123 OFFICE DRIVE, OCEAN BEACH, NEVADA   *assignee(s)*

the following:

     Accounts receivable due from Roe Retail Corporation of
     777 Elm Street, North Orange City, Utah in the amount
     of $9,000.00 (Nine thousand dollars) which is evidenced
     by Slowly Wholesalers invoice number 1234 in like amount.

TO HAVE AND TO HOLD *the same unto the said assignee(s) executors, administrators and assigns forever, to and for the use of the assignee(s), hereby constituting and appointing said assignee(s) true and lawful attorney(s) irrevocable, in assignor's name, place and stead, for the purposes aforesaid, to ask, demand, sue for, attach, levy, recover and receive all such sum and sums of money which now are, or may hereafter become due, owing and payable for, or on account of all or any of the accounts, dues, debts, and demands above assigned, and giving and granting unto the said attorney(s) full power and authority to do and perform all and every act and thing whatsoever requisite and necessary, as fully, to all intents and purposes, as assignor's might or could do, if personally present, with full power of substitution and revocation, hereby ratifying and confirming all that the said attorney(s) or attorney's substitute shall lawfully do, or cause to be done by virtue hereof.*

     IN WITNESS WHEREOF, *the undersigned has hereunto set* HIS *hand(s) and seal(s) the* 23rd

day of   MARCH   *19*

SIGNED, SEALED AND DELIVERED
IN THE PRESENCE OF

          JOHN DOE   L.S.

                                 L.S.

General Assignments

Bankruptcy—General Procedures

Comments

1. *The U.S. Bankruptcy Code is a complex group of laws. Often, the assistance and advice of an attorney is required to protect the rights of creditors of a bankrupt company.*

2. *Upon notification of a bankruptcy filing, the creditor should immediately print a statement of the account. It is also a good idea to reprint all open invoices and to request proofs of delivery for all outstanding invoices.*

3. *If the debtor contemplates selling to the debtor while in bankruptcy, a new account number should be established to distinguish prepetition from postpetition debits or credits.*

4. *The creditor should determine what sort of bankruptcy was filed, when the first meeting of creditors is scheduled, as well as whether a Bar Date for filing a Proof of Claim has been established.*

5. *Creditors should also review their books and records to determine if they received any payments within the 90 days prior to the bankruptcy filing date, which might be considered a Preferential Transfer. An attorney can assist you in evaluating this risk in detail and discussing your options.*

6. *Creditors should review their records and determine if any shipments are in transit. If so, the creditor must decide if the shipper should be asked to reconsign the goods or make the delivery.*

7. *Creditors should review their records with their attorney and determine if a reclamation claim should be filed on merch-andise delivered prior to the bankruptcy filing.*

8. *Creditors should also review their records to determine if anyone in the debtor corporation signed a personal guaranty. If so, the guarantor should be contacted immediately and a demand made for payment in full. It may be appropriate to ask your attorney to review the guaranty and to draft the demand letter.*

Chapter 11 Bankruptcy General Procedures

1. A petition is filed by the creditors (involuntary) or by the debtor (voluntary). An involuntary petition may be contested by the debtor in court.

2. Once a customer has filed for bankruptcy protection, an automatic stay is issued. Prepetition creditors are barred from certain actions to collect prepetition debts including filing civil suits in state court.

3. A representative of the Office of the United States Trustee calls a meeting of creditors.

4. An Official Committee of Unsecured Creditors is formed, normally consisting of seven members. Membership is voluntary. The trustee normally asks for volunteers from among the top 20 creditors.

5. The creditors schedule additional meetings to review the progress of the debtor company and to evaluate the debtor company's plan of reorganization.

6. The creditor's committee recommends for or against the plan or reorganization. That plan is sent to all unsecured creditors for a vote.

7. Upon acceptance of the plan or reorganization, the debtor will be discharged from bankruptcy.

Bankruptcy First Meeting Notice

Comments

1. *See the general procedure outlined on page 521 and the related comments.*

2. *After receiving notice of the bankruptcy, the creditors are notified of the first meeting.*

3. *The first meeting is an opportunity for creditors to interrogate the bankrupt debtor and to elect a creditor's committee. During the first meeting, creditors may interview and possibly hire professional advisors, such as an attorney, to the committee.*

4. *Creditors are prevented from initiating any court actions against the debtor. Other collection efforts are pointless.*

5. *Secured and unsecured creditors have varying rights at a creditors' meeting. Some creditors may be partially secured and the balance of the indebtedness unsecured.*

6. *The meetings are continued from time to time as necessary.*

7. *Bankrupts with complex financial structures may take many years before there is a discharge.*

B.O.F. 12   APPENDIX "A"

United States District Court

For the _____ District of _____

In re

                                  Bankruptcy No. _____

Bankrupt *

ORDER FOR FIRST MEETING OF CREDITORS AND FIXING TIMES FOR FILING OBJECTIONS TO DISCHARGE AND FOR FILING COMPLAINT TO DETERMINE DISCHARGEABILITY OF CERTAIN DEBTS, COMBINED WITH NOTICE THEREOF AND OF AUTOMATIC STAY

To the bankrupt, his creditors, and other parties in interest:

of **   ,

having been adjudged a bankrupt on a petition filed by [*or against*] him on
it is ordered, and notice is hereby given, that:

     1.   The first meeting of creditors shall be held at

on   , at   o'clock   .m.

     2.   The bankrupt shall appear in person [*or, if the bankrupt is a partnership,* by a general partner, *or, if the bankrupt is a corporation,* by its president *or other executive officer*] before the court at that time and place for the purpose of being examined.

     3.   is fixed as the last day for the filing of objections to the discharge of the bankrupt.

     4.   is fixed as the last day for the filing of a complaint to determine the dischargeability of any debt pursuant to § 17c (2) of the Bankruptcy Act.

You are further notified that:

The meeting may be continued or adjourned from time to time by order made in open court, without further written notice to creditors.

At the meeting the creditors may file their claims, elect a trustee, elect a committee of creditors, examine the bankrupt as permitted by the court, and transact such other business as may properly come before the meeting.

As a result of this bankruptcy, certain acts and proceedings against the bankrupt and his property are stayed as provided in Bankruptcy Rules 401 and 601.

If no objection to the discharge of the bankrupt is filed on or before the last day fixed therefor as stated in subparagraph 3 above, the bankrupt will be granted his discharge. If no complaint to determine the dischargeability of a debt under clause (2), (4), or (8) of § 17a of the Bankruptcy Act is filed within the time fixed therefor as stated in subparagraph 4 above, the debt may be discharged.

In order to have his claim allowed so that he may share in any distribution from the estate, a creditor must file a claim, whether or not he is included in the list of creditors filed by the bankrupt. Claims which are not filed within 6 months after the above date set for the first meeting of creditors will not be allowed, except as otherwise provided by law. A claim may be filed in the office of the undersigned bankruptcy judge on an official form prescribed for a proof of claim.

Unless the court extends the time, any objection to the report of exempt property must be filed within 15 days after the report has been filed.

     Dated:

                                            _____

                                              Bankruptcy Judge

* *Include all names used by bankrupt within last 6 years.*
** *State post office address.*

Bankruptcy First Meeting Notice

Bankruptcy Proof of Claim

Comments

1. *An important document to the creditor is a Proof of Claim. Before the claim is submitted, the credit manager should review the company's books and records to obtain accurate information to complete the Proof of Claim form.*

2. *Documents that support the claim must be attached to it. Do not send originals. Required documents include account statements, invoices, credits, proofs of delivery, security agreements and proof of perfection of such agreements.*

3. *As there is a vast distinction between secured and unsecured debt, an attorney is recommended to review the supporting documentation.*

Bankruptcy Proof of Claim

1. The U.S. Bankruptcy Code is complex. It may be appropriate to employ an attorney that specializes in this area of the law.
2. It would not be unusual for several creditors to obtain the services of the same lawyer in a bankruptcy.

Bankruptcy Notice of Hearing

Comments

1. *It is not unusual when a significant asset or portion of the business of the debtor is to be sold, that the bankruptcy court will have a hearing on the matter.*

2. *At the hearing, the court will review other offers for purchase of the asset(s) of the debtor. If a better offer is made at the hearing, the court will almost certainly require the debtor to accept it.*

3. *On occasion, these hearings turn into a kind of slow motion auction, with the judge acting as auctioneer.*

4. *If there are no better offers, the court will allow the transaction to be consummated—unless there is an objection. An objection might be made by a creditor with specific knowledge of the value of the asset(s) to be sold.*

5. *The objecting party might inform the court that the price being proposed is well below market value. The objecting party might ask the judge to delay a decision on the sale until other potential buyers have been contacted and given an opportunity to make an offer.*

6. *In fact, a hearing of this type is designed to prevent a situation in which assets are sold at less than their fair market value since such a sale would be to the detriment of the prepetition creditors.*

UNITED STATES DISTRICT COURT
NORTHERN DISTRICT OF GEORGIA
ATLANTA DIVISION

IN THE MATTER OF:	)
	)
GREAT AMERICAN MANAGEMENT	) IN PROCEEDINGS FOR AN
AND INVESTMENT (formerly	) ARRANGEMENT UNDER CHAPTER XI
GREAT AMERICAN MORTGAGE	) OF THE BANKRUPTCY ACT
INVESTORS),	)
	) CASE NUMBER B77-760A
DEBTOR.	)

<u>NOTICE TO CREDITORS</u>

CREDITORS AND OTHER PARTIES AT INTEREST:

YOU ARE HEREBY NOTIFIED that the Debtor-in-Possession in the above-styled proceeding has made application to this Court to sell partially improved property located on the ocean front south of Pompano Beach in Broward County, Florida. Conveyance will be made to Florida Communities Oceanside, a joint venture being represented by Zaremba Pompano Co., an Ohio corporation. Details of the proposed transaction, as contained in the Application, are available in the records of this Court for examination.

Creditors are advised that the Court will hold a hearing on the 5th day of _October_ , 19 , at _10:00_ A.M. in Room 312, United States Courthouse, 56 Forsyth Street, N.W., Atlanta, Georgia, to consider the application to sell and to entertain other offers.

This _20_ day of _Sept_ , 19 .

_____
A. D. KAHN
U.S. BANKRUPTCY JUDGE

Bankruptcy Notice of Hearing

Index